Fairness and validation in language assessment:
Selected papers from the
19th Language Testing Research Colloquium,
Orlando, Florida

STUDIES IN LANGUAGE TESTING...9
Series editor: Michael Milanovic

Also in this series:

Fairness and validation in language assessment: Selected papers from the 19th Language Testing Research Colloquium, Orlando, Florida

Antony John Kunnan

California State University, Los Angeles

Published by the Press Syndicate of the University of Cambridge
The Pitt Building, Trumpington Street, Cambridge CB2 1RP, UK
40 West 20th Street, New York, NY 10011–4211, USA
10 Stamford Road, Oakleigh, Melbourne 3166, Australia

First published 2000

Printed in Great Britain at the University Press, Cambridge, UK

British Library cataloguing in publication data

University of Cambridge, Local Examinations Syndicate

Fairness and validation in language assessment: Selected papers from the 19th
Language Testing Research Colloquium, Orlando, Florida.

Antony John Kunnan

1. Education. Assessment 2. Education. Tests. Setting

ISBN   0 521–651034   hardback
        0 521–658748   paperback

Contents

Series Editor's note

This volume is included in the Studies in Language Testing series because it represents an important statement in the on-going discussion on fairness in language testing. Fairness and its natural relationship with language test validation has been a key feature of debate in the field for the last decade. We have seen a broadening of views away from a relatively narrow focus on reliability and validity, to one, which recognises a complex set of relationships. Concern about this rich interaction has long been a tradition in many European language examinations. Indeed, I remember, at the time of the Cambridge-TOEFL comparability study, which took place in the late eighties, John Reddaway, secretary of the University of Cambridge Local Examinations Syndicate (UCLES) at the time, used the term 'felt fair' about Cambridge examinations in general and EFL ones in particular. Many of us did not realise how important this concept was until much later. Feeling something is fair may not be the same as it being fair but it is, perhaps, a necessary prerequisite.

Throughout the nineties, UCLES has continued the process of making its EFL examinations and tests as fair as possible. Much care and attention has gone into the materials that appear in tests. Language and topics are scrutinised, item writers and examiners carefully trained and extensive systems for monitoring quality have been enhanced. Test materials are fully pretested and examinations constructed which balance testing focus and content in accordance with published specifications. Extensive support materials are provided for candidates and training programmes for teachers. Much effort goes into developing customised test papers and procedures for candidates who are not able to deal with the conventional papers. Special circumstances, which may have disadvantaged candidates, are reported and investigated. The examination centre network is being extended continuously with about 3,000 centres where candidates can take a Cambridge EFL examination now operating throughout the world. Principles underlying performance have been investigated and instruments developed to try and understand the relationships. Much work has gone into developing and validating user-oriented scales to improve test users' understanding of language levels and what examination scores mean in terms of performance. Many dimensions of the direct assessment of speaking and writing have been investigated and documented. Investigations into the impact of examinations have been carried out and instrumentation developed which is being shared with researchers around the world.

Given the importance of fairness and validation to the field, UCLES is pleased to add this title, edited with great care and commitment by Antony Kunnan, to the series.

Michael Milanovic
Cambridge
December 1999

Preface

Fairness of language tests and testing practices has always been a concern among test developers, test users and test researchers and the traditional manner of ensuring fairness has been through investigations of the tests' reliability and validity. However, in the past decade educational and language assessment researchers have begun to focus directly on fairness and related matters such as test standards, test bias, equity and ethics for testing professionals.

The 19th annual Language Testing Research Colloquium which was held on March 6–9 1997 in Orlando, Florida, USA, brought this overall concern to sharp focus by having 'Fairness in Language Testing' as its theme. The conference presentations and discussions attempted to understand the concept of fairness, define the scope of the concept and connect it with the concept of validation of test score interpretation. The different presentation formats provided ample opportunities for the participants to meet and discuss these and other relevant matters.

The plenary address entitled 'A "post-modern" view of the problem of assessment or Why do I get such a headache thinking about test design?' was given by Henry Braun, Vice President for Research Management, Educational Testing Service, Princeton. This was followed by a panel discussion on the theme of the conference by Lyle Bachman, Liz Hamp-Lyons, Bonny Norton, Elana Shohamy and Antony John Kunnan, who together laid out some of the critical issues that are relevant to the concept.

Two invited speakers, William Grabe from Northern Arizona University and John Swales from the University of Michigan, also gave addresses. Grabe spoke on 'Reading research, the development of reading abilities and reading assessment' and Swales on 'English triumphant, ESL leadership and issues of fairness'.

There were two pre-colloquium workshops featuring Lyle Bachman and Adrian Palmer on 'An approach to the design and development of language test tasks' and Fred Davidson on 'Statistical data handling: A principled process'. The two colloquia during the LTRC were 'Computers and language testing: Evaluating access and equity' organized by Carol Taylor and 'Examining test taker characteristics and second language test performance using a structural equation modeling approach' organized by James Purpura.

In addition, over the three days, over 40 presentations in the form of papers, works in progress, and posters were made and approximately 140 people attended the Colloquium. A closing panel discussion by Mary Spaan, Caroline Clapham, Brian Lynch and Randy Thrasher on the themes of the papers concluded the presentations. A listing of all invited addresses, colloquia and presentations is given after this preface.

This volume presents selected papers from the Colloquium. It is organized in four sections: Section One presents short articles by six language assessment specialists who were invited to discuss the notion of fairness in language assessment. The articles by Antony John Kunnan, Elana Shohamy, Bonny Norton, Liz Hamp-Lyons, Mary Spaan and Lyle Bachman help develop the concept of fairness and outline its context and limitations through argument, illustrations, examples and personal reflection.

Section Two focuses on three concerns of fairness: test standards, criteria and test bias. The four papers by Peter Lowenberg, Dan Douglas and Ron Myers, Catherine Elder, and Yong-Won Lee examine the assumptions regarding test standards and criteria and examine ways by which test bias can be investigated and understood.

Section Three focuses on validation matters as a way of ensuring fairness. The four papers by Alfred Appiah Sakyi, Beryl Meiron and Laurie Schick, Charles Stansfield *et al.*, and Ebrahim Khodadady and Michael Herriman deal with ways in which validation of test score interpretation can be enhanced by examining ratings and rater background and test development theory and practice.

In the final section, Section Four, William Grabe presents a current view of reading comprehension and the implications and dilemmas for second language reading assessment. This volume concludes with Henry Braun's futuristic vision of an ecological approach to test design in which consultations among various constituencies such as clients, customers, academe and industry will help build a better model for test design, development and delivery.

I hope the papers in this volume collectively offer a fine first introduction to fairness and validation in the field of language assessment. I hope these papers will lead to presentations, discussions and debates in the field so that a full understanding of what constitutes fairness, and how it can be enhanced and ensured in tests and testing practice emerges soon.

In editing this volume I have acquired a few debts. Some of these I would like to acknowledge here. I am indebted to the authors of the papers who were all patient with changes and adjustments I suggested, and to Alister Cumming and Glen Fulcher for providing valuable reviews of all the papers. I also want to thank my graduate assistant Yutaka Kawamoto at CSULA and Paulo Pinto da Cunha at UCLES for editorial assistance in the preparation of the final manuscript. I am also grateful to my language testing colleagues Lyle

Bachman and Mary Spaan, (co-chair) who helped me organize the Colloquium that gave birth to this volume and to Mike Milanovic for accepting my proposal for this volume. Without the goodwill of all these good people I would never have been able to bring this volume to you.

Antony John Kunnan
San Gabriel, California
March, 1999

List of all 19th LTRC invited addresses, colloquia and panel discussions, papers, works in progress and posters

Pre-Colloquium Workshops
1. Lyle Bachman and Adrian Palmer, *An Approach to the Design and Development of Language Test Tasks*
2. Fred Davidson, *Statistical Data Handling: A Principled Process*

Plenary Address:
Henry Braun, *A 'Post-modern' View of the Problem of Assessment or Why Do I Get Such a Headache Thinking About Test Design?*

Invited Speakers
1. William Grabe, *Reading Research, the Development of Reading Abilities, and Reading Assessment*
2. John Swales, *English Triumphant, ESL Leadership and Issues of Fairness*

Colloquia
1. Carol Taylor (Organizer), Irwin Kirsch, Joan Jamieson, Dan Eignor (Presenters), Charles Alderson, William Grabe (Discussants), *Computers and Language Testing: Evaluating Access and Equity*
2. James Purpura (Organizer), Antony John Kunnan, Geoff Brindley and Steve Ross (Presenters), *Examining Test Taker Characteristics and Second Language Test Performance using a Structural Equation Modeling Approach*

Panel Discussions
1. **Opening Panel:** Antony John Kunnan (Organizer), Lyle Bachman, Liz Hamp-Lyons, Bonny Norton, Elana Shohamy (Discussants), *Fairness in Language Testing*
2. **Closing Panel:** Mary Spaan (Organizer), Caroline Clapham, Brian Lynch, Randy Thrasher (Discussants), *Summary of Conference Themes*

Papers

1. Rosemary Baker, *Assessment of language impairment across cultures*
2. Gary Buck, Kumi Tatsuoka, C. Tatsuoka, Irene Kostin, *The effect of first language background on the cognitive and linguistic attributes underlying performance on the TOEIC*
3. Jeff Connor-Linton, Elana Shohamy, *Multidimensional analysis and oral proficiency sampling: Performance effects of task and elicitation context*
4. Alan Davies, Kathryn Hill, *Questioning an early start – the transition from primary to secondary foreign language learning*
5. John de Jong, Fellyanka Stoyanova, *The relation between reliability and validity: An issue of fairness*
6. Hui-Chun (Angie) Liu, *Constructing and validating parallel forms of performance-based writing prompts in academic settings*
7. Catherine Elder, *Is it fair to assess both NS and NNS on school 'foreign' language examinations?*
8. H. Gary Cook, *Investigating bias over time*
9. Daniel Reed, Gene Halleck, *The relationship between interviewer style and OPI ratings at three levels of proficiency*
10. Constant Leung, Alex Teasdale, *Raters' understanding of oral scales as abstracted concept and as instruments of decision making: A phenomenographic study*
11. Swee-Heng Chan, *Methods of assessing and displaying salient features of coherence in ESL writing*
12. Jared Bernstein, *Computer-based oral proficiency assessment: Field results*
13. Noriko Iwashita, *The validity of the paired interview of format in oral performance testing*
14. Carol Moder, Gene Halleck, *Balancing fairness and authenticity in performance test: An alternative rating approach for ITAs*
15. Dan Douglas, Ron Myers, *Assessing the communication skills of veterinary students: Whose criteria?*
16. Peter Lowenberg, *Non-native varieties and issues of fairness in testing English as a world language*

Works in progress

1. Amma Kazuo, *A multidimensional approach to learners' grammatical proficiency*
2. Jayanti Banerjee, *Establishing predictive validity: Methodological considerations*
3. Samia Belyazid, *Task-based language test specifications designed for an adult TEFL context in Morocco*
4. Alejandro Brice, *The bilingual classroom protocol: Its development and use*

Section One
Fairness: Concept and Context

Based on the opening and closing panels at the Colloquium, six language assessment specialists were invited to discuss the notion of fairness in language assessment. These short articles are slightly expanded versions of the oral presentations and discussions. Antony John Kunnan opens the discussion with the notion of fairness as social justice. Elana Shohamy examines fairness in the broader context of 'test use' by discussing three research studies based on test use in Israel. Bonny Norton examines the marking or scoring guidelines in three writing assessment contexts in South Africa, the US and Canada. Liz Hamp-Lyons focuses through personal reflection on fairness for test takers, which she argues is only one of the many kinds of fairness. Mary Spaan focuses on how test developers can enhance fairness through cooperation among test developers, test users and test takers. Lyle Bachman concludes this discussion by raising questions about the nature and extent of our responsibility for fairness.

1 Fairness and justice for all

Antony John Kunnan
California State University, Los Angeles

Introduction

Although it has been argued that language test developers and researchers are concerned with the concept of fairness when they investigate tests for technical qualities like validity and reliability, the primacy of fairness has not been considered or acknowledged. Furthermore, fairness as a concept within a framework of social justice has not been developed and debated. I hope to make a beginning on these matters in this short chapter by discussing a possible definition of fairness and connections between fairness and four critical areas in language testing or assessment: research, test development, legal challenges and test developers. As a concept, fairness is seemingly clear but quite complex and thus often lends itself to dangerous misunderstandings. Moreover, often it is said that fairness is in the eye of the beholder and such discussions of fairness are obviously interminable. So, a clarifying definition seems to be difficult and elusive. One document that provides direction on this matter is the *Code of Fair Testing Practices in Education* (*Code* from now on) prepared by the Joint Committee on Testing Practices (1988). It presents standards for educational test developers and users in four areas: developing and selecting tests, interpreting scores, striving for fairness and informing test takers.

Here is the excerpt from Section C, Striving for Fairness, of the *Code*:

Test developers should strive to make tests that are as fair as possible for test takers of different races, gender, ethnic backgrounds, or handicapping conditions.

Test developers should:

---

14 Review and revise test questions and related materials to avoid potentially insensitive content or language.

15 Investigate the performance of test takers of different races, gender, and ethnic backgrounds when samples of sufficient size are available. Enact procedures that help to ensure that differences in performance are related primarily to the skills under the assessment rather than to irrelevant factors.

16 When feasible, make appropriately modified forms of tests or administration procedures available for test takers with handicapping conditions. Warn test users of potential problems in using standard norms with modified tests or administration procedures that result in non-comparable scores.

Test users should select tests that have been developed in ways that attempt to make them as fair as possible for test takers of different races, gender, ethnic backgrounds, or handicapping conditions.

Test users should:

---

14 Evaluate the procedures used by test developers to avoid potentially insensitive content or language.

15 Review the performance of test takers of different races, gender, and ethnic backgrounds when samples of sufficient size are available. Evaluate the extent to which performance differences may have been caused by inappropriate characteristics of the test.

16 When necessary and feasible, use appropriately modified forms of tests or administration procedures for test takers with handicapping conditions. Interpret standard norms with care in the light of the modifications that were made.

(Code 1988, p.2-3)

Towards a definition

Using the *Code* as a set of guiding principles, a definition of fairness for language assessment can be attempted. In general, the *Code* urges both test developers and test users to strive for fair tests and testing practices as far as possible for all test takers. Specifically, in the three points the *Code* urges test developers and test users to review and revise insensitive test content or language, investigate differential test performances and ensure construct irrelevant factors are not being assessed, and provide accommodations for test takers with disability. In addition to these three points, two other main concerns such as access to tests and impact of testing practice have been of considerable recent interest and therefore need to be added to the list. Table 1.1 summarizes the main concerns of fairness and their specific focuses.

Table 1.1

Main concerns of fairness

Main concern	*Specific focus*
Validity	construct validity content and format bias Differential Item/Test Functioning insensitive language stereotyping of test taker groups
Access	financial: affordability geographical: location and distance personal: accommodations for disabled persons educational: opportunity to learn equipment and test conditions
Justice	societal equity legal challenges

Validity

The focus of this concern is on whether test-score interpretations have *equal construct validity* (and reliability) for different test-taker groups as defined by salient test-taker characteristics such as gender, race/ethnicity, field of specialization and native language and culture. Construct-irrelevant factors in terms of content bias that might cause unfairness among groups include topical knowledge and technical terminology, specific cultural content and dialect variations. Format bias could include multiple-choice, constructed response, computer-based responses and multi-media materials. The *Code* calls for investigations of test performance of *different test-taker groups* so that test developers and test users are confident that the differences in performances are related primarily to the abilities that are being assessed and not to construct-irrelevant factors. Other key construct-irrelevant factors include *insensitive* or *offensive test materials* and materials that *stereotype* and show certain test-taker groups in unfavourable light.

Access

The focus of this concern is on whether tests are accessible to test takers from various aspects such as financial, geographical, personal, and educational access and familiarity of test conditions and equipment. *Financial* access in terms of affordability is a key concern as the consequences of unaffordable tests in all regions should be known to test developers and test users. Similarly, *geographical* access to test sites is critical too and this also varies from context to context. Once again, what is considered accessible in one region may not be so in another. Another focus is *personal access*. The focus here is on providing where feasible appropriate accommodations in test administration procedures for test-takers with disability or impairment. *The Code* calls for this modification in order that test takers who are disabled are not denied access to tests that can be offered without compromising the construct being measured. *The Code* also indicates that test users should be warned of the type of accommodations provided so that test-score interpretations can be made in the light of the accommodations. In terms of educational access, the focus is on opportunity to learn. There is no doubt that opportunity to learn plays a major role in test-takers' success on tests when test-takers have had the opportunity to learn the material on which they are assessed. Further, if test-taker groups have differential opportunities to learn, then group performance on a test will most certainly differ significantly. In large-scale assessment programs, in many cases differential opportunities to learn among test takers is common, and therefore, unequal advancement may result. Yet another focus is on whether test takers have had prior *access to test-taking equipment and test-taking conditions* so that they are familiar with these conditions. Relevant examples here are the use of computers in computer-based tests and the use of multi-media in web-based testing.

Justice

The focus of this concern is on justice in terms of *societal equity* and *legal challenges*. Specifically, the notion of societal equity goes beyond equal validity and access and focuses on the social consequences of testing in terms of whether testing programs contribute to social equity or not and in general, whether there are any pernicious effects due to them. For example, if a test taker group (defined by political ideology, native language, race/ethnicity, gender, national origin or socioeconomic status) as a result of a testing program does not gain equal access to college or promotion on the job in the same proportion when compared to other test-taker groups, there could be legitimate concern that the testing program is causing the inequity rather than that the inequity among the groups actually exists. The focus of this concern would be to devise a mechanism that can investigate the burden on the testing program to show that the societal inequity is not an artifact of the testing program.

Related to societal equity and assessment is the issue of standards in assessment practices which have not been clearly formulated and this has led to *legal challenges* particularly in the US and UK. In the US, Title VII of the Civil Rights Act of 1964 (and subsequent related legislation) provides remedies for persons who feel they are discriminated against due to their gender, race/ethnicity, native language, national origin and so on. This Act has been used broadly; for example, to challenge the use of test scores, the curricular validity and predictive validity of tests in school and in employment contexts.

In summary, the way the different concerns of validity, access and justice contribute to the multi-faceted definition of fairness indicates that the concept is an interdisciplinary one; not only based on the psychometric view of tests and testing practice but also on social, ethical, legal and philosophical views. A definition of fairness along these lines is stated by Jensen, an unlikely scholar on the subject, who writes that fairness refers

> *'to the ways in which test scores (whether of biased or unbiased tests) are used in any selection situation. The concepts of fairness, social justice, and equal protection of the laws are moral, legal, and philosophical ideas and therefore must be evaluated in these terms.*
>
> (Jensen 1980: 376)

Fairness and research studies

The research studies that have focused on fairness in language assessment over the last 15 years (taken from Kunnan 1998a) are not many in number nor part of a coherent research program either. Table 1.2 presents some of the best examples of such placed within the fairness framework listed in Table 1.1.

Table 1.2
Studies with fairness concerns in language
assessment (1985–1999)

Fairness concerns	*Studies*	*Specific focus*
Validity:		
construct validity	Alderson and Urquhart 1985a, b	academic major and reading
	Hale 1988	major field and test content
	Clapham 1996 1998	ESP testing
	Norton and Stein 1998	test taker feedback
	Kunnan 1995	+/- Indo-European languages
	Ginther and Stevens 1998	native language groups
	Kunnan, 1992	standard setting and placement
	Wall and Alderson 1993	washback
	Alderson and Hamp-Lyons 1996	test preparation
DIF	Alderman and Holland 1981	native language
	Chen and Henning 1985	native language
	Zeidner 1986,1987	sex, age and minority bias
	Kunnan 1990	native language and gender
	Ryan and Bachman 1992	gender
content	Lowenberg 1989	different Englishes
format	Shohamy 1984	test method and reading
	Shohamy and Inbar 1991	question type and listening
Access:		
test conditions	Brown 1993	tape-mediated test
	Taylor *et al.* 1998	computer familiarity
Justice	none	

Although these studies may seem like many examples of research focused on fairness, there is clearly a great need for more studies in this area. Also, most of these studies listed are generally post-hoc analyses and independent studies that are not part of a coherent fairness research program that is part of test development, maintenance and research program. Quite obviously more needs to be done. Perhaps, examples of research studies and general articles from the field of general assessment that are relevant to the fairness program could help propel language assessment researchers. For example, many fairness issues in the US have been brought to the forefront in recent years. Among the issues discussed include gender differences in education (Sadker and Sadker 1994), gender differences scores on the SAT-Math section (Wainer and Steinberg 1992), bias in the assessment of bilingual students (Hamayan and Damico 1991), testing African American students (Hilliard, 1991), and bias in reading tests for Black language students (Hoover, Politzer and Taylor 1991). In addition, articles on test sensitivity review (Ramsey 1993), assessment and diversity (Garcia and Pearson 1994), equity issues and American testing policy (Madaus 1994), educational equity and performance assessment (Darling-Hammond 1994) and equitable assessment policies for

English language learners (Lacelle-Peterson and Rivera 1994) can provide an understanding of how fairness concerns are discussed outside the language assessment arena.

Fairness and test development

A framework to focus on the fairness concerns articulated during all stages of the test development, maintenance, and research needs to be developed. Table 1.3 presents the stages and the fairness concerns that need to be focused on for optimum administration of the fairness agenda.

Table 1.3

Fairness concerns and stages of test development

Stages	Fairness concerns	
Thinking	Validity:	construct content and format scoring and reporting
	Access:	financial: affordability geographical: location and distance personal: accommodations educational: opportunity to learn equipment and test conditions
	Justice:	societal equity
Writing	Validity:	tasks, topics, canon language standards insensitive language review stereotyping of societal groups
Piloting	Validity:	norming samples
Analyzing	Validity:	item/task analysis internal structure scoring, raters differential item/test functioning speededness
	Justice:	societal equity
Maintenance and Research	Validity: Access: Justice:	all areas all areas all areas

As Table 1.3 shows, fairness concerns need to begin with the *thinking* stage which involves thinking about the construct(s), thinking about the content and possible tasks and task methods, and thinking about scoring and reporting issues. In addition, it is critical that issues of access are discussed at this stage and not left until a later stage. In terms of justice, test developers should check to see if the test under development will generally bring about societal equity rather than disharmony. In other words, the question that should be discussed is whether the test will generally do good to society.

Fairness concerns at the *writing stage*, which include decisions about operationalization of constructs into actual written tasks, include discussions regarding the canon from which topics and tasks may be chosen. In other words, the discussion should centre round whether the canon is something that all potential test takers share and learn. In addition, decisions regarding the language standard(s) (or dialects) that are to be adopted for the test need to be made by the developers and writers. Finally, after tasks are written, reviews of tasks for insensitive language and stereotyping of societal groups needs to be conducted.

The third place for fairness concerns is the *piloting* stage in which a test is typically piloted or pre-tested with a norming sample from the intended test-taking population. The sample should be a truly representative sample and not a sample of convenience. This choice is very critical at this stage because how the sample's performance on the tasks is used in making decisions about the tasks.

The fourth place for fairness concerns is the *analyzing* stage in which data collected from test-takers is analyzed. Traditional item analysis, internal structure analysis, rating reliability and rater conduct should be conducted. In addition, investigations of differential item/task or testlet functioning should be conducted in order to be able to state confidently that score differences in performance on the test from different test taker groups are due to relevant construct variance. Further, the issue of speededness needs to be investigated so that the speed of the test is not felt differently by the various test-taker groups (for example, non-native speakers as opposed to native speakers). The analyses should also include how the test might contribute to societal equity.

In the *maintenance and research* stage, all fairness concerns itemized in Table 1.3 should be routinely investigated.

Collectively then, these different fairness concerns at the different developmental stages should uncover any invalidities or unfairness a test might carry, and when follow-up corrective action is taken, it might be clearly possible to minimize or eliminate any invalidites or unfairness.

Fairness and legal challenges

The notion of fairness may be sufficient grounds for challenging a test wherever *equal protection* legislation has been provided by a state constitution or through separate legislation. In addition, whenever a test is in clear violation of a code of standards, if such a code exists, there may be sufficient grounds for a challenge.

A few examples of US Court rulings will be briefly presented in order to provide a flavour of how US courts have viewed legal challenges in the general educational and employment arena. A fuller discussion of relevant court cases is discussed by Bersoff (1981, 1984), McDonough and Wolf (1988), Hood and Parker (1991), Pullin (1994), Fulcher and Bamford (1996) and Lippi-Green (1997). A selected list of cases with sources from all these discussions is presented in Appendix A.

As an example, one ground for legal challenge has been based on the perception that there is lack of societal equity due to tests that track and classify students in schools. Examples of litigation in the US in this area were *Hobson v. Hansen* (1967), *Larry P. v. Riles* (1971, 1984) and *PASE v. Hannon* (1980). In all three cases, the plaintiffs charged that African American children were being discriminated against as disproportionate numbers of such children were placed based on test scores into a lower-track program (in the first listed case), into a mildly mentally retarded program (in the second case) and into an educable mentally handicapped program (in the last case). The courts found for the plaintiffs in all three cases. In *Debra P. v Turlington* (1981), the ground for legal challenge was curricular after African American students who took a minimum competency test had initially approximately ten times the failure rate of White students. The Court found for the plaintiff stating that 'if the test covers material not taught the students, it is unfair and violates the Equal Protection and Due Process clauses of the US Constitution' (Debra P., at 402).

In *Griggs v. Duke Power Co.* (1971), the ground for challenge was the requirement of a passing test score in addition to a high school diploma for promotion on the job after African Americans working at the company were denied promotion. The Court found for the plaintiff stating that employment tests should be job related: 'What Congress has commanded is that any tests used must measure the person for the job and not the person in the abstract' (Griggs, at 436). In *Albermarle Paper Co. v. Moody* (1975), a test was found invalid as it was not designed to the standards laid down by the American Educational Research Association, particularly referring to the technical quality of employers' validity and reliability studies. In *Golden Rule Insurance Co. v. Mathias* (1984), an out-of-court settlement was agreed upon between the Golden Rule Insurance Company on the one hand and the Illinois Department of Insurance and Educational Testing Service (ETS, the test developer) on the other. All the parties agreed that 'a raw difference, favouring White applicants over Black applicants, of .15 or more in an item's p-values was to be taken as evidence that the item is to be considered biased in the social sense, that is, unfair to the lower-performing group, and identified as an item not normally to be included in the test' (Angoff 1993: 14).

It should be noted here that US Courts have intervened in some contexts but ignored others and have made a few controversial rulings. As Garcia and Pearson (1994) state, '(US courts) have intervened to offset the adverse impact of using test scores to place students of colour in remedial programs' they have not actively constrained the use of the same or similar tests to keep minority students from being placed in gifted programs or college-bound high-school tracks' (p. 353). Moreover, in employment related cases, they have ruled that 'separate prediction equations and/or lower cut scores must be used to counteract employment discrimination' (ibid: 353). The Golden Rule out-of-court settlement is also an example of court-directed modification in ETS' test development practice for the Illinois insurance licensing examinations.

In summary, challenging a test is possible but until appropriate legislation and a code of standards exists, test takers may have difficulty seeking and obtaining remedies. And, from the test developers' perspective, a test can be challenged because standards and legislation do not exist or are somewhat poorly defined. These issues need to be addressed in every state/province or country where tests are developed and administered so that fair tests are available.

Fairness and test developers

One of the best ways to attain fairness in a test is when test developers (such as thinkers, writers, raters, and researchers) are from a diverse group (in terms of gender, race/ethnicity, native language, etc.) and trained to examine all aspects of a test for its fairness. This would help first, in obtaining different viewpoints concerning the canon, topics, tasks, format, and second, in examining tasks for the specific fairness concerns and third, in setting a research agenda that can enhance fairness.

Conclusion

In conclusion, this paper attempts to present an argument that fairness in language assessment consists of validity, access and justice. The paper also demonstrates that fairness is critically connected to research, test development, legal challenges and test developers. Newer methodologies such as item level exploratory and confirmatory factor analysis (see Bachman and Eignor 1997), structural equation modeling (see Kunnan 1998b), Multidimensional Item Response Theory for DIF (Ackerman 1998), Rule Space (Buck and Tatsuoka, 1998) and verbal protocol analysis (Greene 1997) may provide new avenues for research investigations in these areas. Furthermore, the paper implicitly argues that fairness is a critical central component not just connecting traditional components like validity and reliability (see Kunnan 1997). This conceptualization gives primacy to fairness and in my view if a test is not fair there is little or no value in it being valid and reliable or even authentic and interactive. As Rawls (1971) states, one of the principles of fairness is that institutions or practices must be *just*. Echoing Rawls then, there is no other way to develop tests but to make them such that primarily there is fairness and justice for all.

References

Ackerman, T. (1998) A discussion of measurement direction in a multidimensional latent space and the role it plays in bias detection. In D. Laveault, B. Zumbo, M. Gessaroli, and M. Boss (Eds.) *Modern Theories of Measurement: Problems and Issues:* 105-140).Ottawa, Canada: Edumetrics Research Group, University of Ottawa.

Alderman, D. and P. Holland (1981) Item performance across native language groups on the TOEFL. *TOEFL Research report 9*. Princeton, NJ: Educational Testing Service.

Alderson, J. C. and L. Hamp-Lyons, (1996) TOEFL preparation courses: A study of washback. *Language Testing* 13: 280–297.

Alderson, J. C. and A. H. Urquhart (1985a) The effect of students' academic discipline on their performance on ESP reading tests. *Language Testing* 2: 192–204.

Alderson, J. C. and A. H. Urquhart (1985b) This test is unfair: I'm not an economist. In P. C. Hauptman, R. LeBlanc and M. B. Wesche (Eds.) *Second Language Performance Testing*. Ottawa: University of Ottawa Press.

Angoff, W. (1993). Perspectives on Differential Item Functioning Methodology. In Holland and Wainer, pp. 3–23.

Bachman, L. F. (1990) *Fundamental Considerations in Language Testing*. Oxford: Oxford University Press.

Bachman, L. F. and D. Eignor (1998) Recent advances in quantitative test analysis. In D. Corson and C. Clapham (Eds.) *Encyclopedia of language and Education*. (Volume 7. Language and assessment). Dordrecht: Kluwer Academic Publishers.

Bersoff, D. (1981) Testing and the law. *American Psychologist* 36: 1047–1056.

Bersoff, D. (1984) Social and legal influences on test development and usage. In B. Plake (Ed.) *Social and Technical Issues in Testing*: 87–109. Hillsdale, NJ: Lawrence Erlbaum Associates, Publishers.

Brown, A. (1993) The role of test taker feedback in the test development process: Test takers' reactions to a tape-mediated test of proficiency in spoken Japanese. *Language Testing* 10: 277–304.

Buck, G. and K. Tatsuoka (1998) Application of Rule-space methodology to listening test data. *Language Testing* 15: 118–142.

Camilli, G. (1993) The case against item bias detection techniques based on internal criteria: Do item bias procedures obscure test fairness issues? In (*Holland and Wainer*) 397–413.

Chen, Z. and G. Henning (1985) Linguistic and cultural bias in language proficiency tests. *Language Testing* 2: 155–163.

Clapham, C. (1996) *The Development of IELTS*. Cambridge: Cambridge University Press.

Clapham, C. (1998) The effect of language proficiency and background knowledge on EAP students' reading comprehension. In Kunnan (1988a) 141–168.

Code of Fair Testing Practices in Education. (1988) Washington, DC: Joint Committee on Testing Practices.

Darling-Hammond, L. (1994) Performance-based assessment and educational equity. *Harvard Educational Review* 64: 5–30.

Fulcher, G. and R. Bamford (1996). I didn't get the grade I need. Where's my solicitor? *System* 24: 437–448.

Garcia, G. and D. Pearson (1994) Assessment and diversity. *Review of Research in Education* 20: 337–391.

Ginther, A. and J. Stevens (1998) Language background, ethnicity, and the internal construct validity of the Advanced Placement Spanish language examination. In Kunnan (1988a) 169–194.

Green, A. (1997) *Verbal Protocol Analysis in Language Testing Research*. Cambridge: Cambridge University Press.

Hale, G. (1988) Student major field and text content: Interactive effects on reading comprehension in the TOEFL. *Language Testing*, 5: 49–61.

Hamayan, E. and J. Damico (Ed.) (1991) *Limiting Bias in the Assessment of Bilingual Students*. Austin, TX: Pro-Ed.

Hilliard, A. G. (Ed.) (1991) *Testing African American Students*. Morristown, NJ: Aaron Press.

Holland, P. and H. Wainer (Eds.) (1993) *Differential Item Functioning*. Hilsdale, NJ: Lawrence Erlbaum Associates, Publishers.

Hood, S. and L. Parker (1991) Minorities, teacher testing, and recent US Supreme Court holdings: A regressive step. *Teachers College Record* 92: 603–618.

Hoover, M., R. Politzer and O. Taylor (1991) Bias in reading tests for Black language speakers. In Hilliard, 81–98.

Jenson, H. R. (1980). Bias in mental testing. New York, N.Y: FreePress

Kunnan, A. J. (1990) DIF in native language and gender groups in an ESL placement test. *TESOL Quarterly* 24: 741–746.

Kunnan, A. J. (1992) An investigation of a criterion-referenced test using G-theory, and factor and cluster analysis. *Language Testing* 9: 30–49.

Kunnan, A. J. (1995) *Test-taker characteristics and Test Performance: A Structural Modeling Approach*. Cambridge: Cambridge University Press.

Kunnan, A. J. (1997) Connecting fairness and validation. In A. Huhta, V. Kohonen, L. Kurki-Suomo and S. Luoma, *Current Developments and Alternatives in Language Assessment:* 85–105. Jyvaskyla, Finland: University of Jyvaskyla.

Kunnan, A. J. (Ed.) (1998a) *Validation in Language Assessment*. Mahwah, NJ: Lawrence Erlbaum Associates, Publishers.

Kunnan, A. J. (1998b) An introduction to structural equation modeling for language assessment research. *Language Testing* 15: 295–332.

Lacelle-Peterson, M. and C. Rivera (1994) Is it real for kids? A framework for equitable assessment policies for English language learners. *Harvard Educational Review* 64: 55–75.

Lippi-Green, R. (1997) *English with an Accent.* London: Routledge.

Lowenberg, P. (1989) Testing English as a world language: Issues in assessing nonnative proficiency. In J. Alatis (Ed.) *GURT* 1989: 216–227. Washington, DC: Georgetown University Press.

Madaus, G. (1994) A technological and historical consideration of equity issues associated with proposals to change the nation's testing policy. *Harvard Educational Review* 64: 76–95.

McDonough, M. and W. Wolf (1988) Court actions which helped define the direction of the competency-based testing movement. *Journal of Research and Development in Education* 21: 37–43.

Messick, S. (1980) Test validity and ethics of assessment. *American Psychologist:* 35: 1012–1027.

Messick, S. (1989) Validity. In R. Linn (Ed.), *Educational Measurement,* 13–103. London: Macmillan.

Norton, B. and P. Stein (1998) Why the 'Monkeys Passage' bombed: tests, genres, and teaching. In Kunnan: 231–249.

Pullin, D. (1994) Learning to work: The impact of curriculum and assessment standards on educational opportunity. *Harvard Educational Review* 64: 31–54.

Ramsey, P. (1993) Sensitivity review: The ETS experience as a case study. In Holland and Wainer, 367–388.

Rawls, J. (1971) *A theory of justice.* Cambridge, MA: The Belknap Press of Harvard University Press.

Ryan, K. and L. F. Bachman (1992) Differential item functioning on two tests of EFL proficiency. *Language Testing* 9: 12–29.

Sadker, M. and Sadker, D. (1994) *Failing at fairness.* New York, NY: Touchtone/Simon and Schuster.

Shohamy, E. (1984). Does the testing method make a difference? The case of reading comprehension. *Language Testing* 1: 147–170.

Shohamy, E. and O. Inbar (1991) Construct validity of listening comprehensive test of oral proficiency. *Language Testing* 8: 23-40

Taylor, C., Jameison, J., Eignor, D. and I. Kirsch (1998) The relationship between computer familiarity and performance on computer-based TOEFL tests tasks. [*TOEFL Research Report No. 61*]. Princeton, NJ: Educational Testing Research.

Wainer, H. and L. Steinberg, (1992) Sex differences in performance on the mathematics section of the Scholastic Aptitude Test: A bidirectional validity study. *Harvard Educational Review* 62: 323–336.

Wall, D. and C. Alderson, (1993) Examining washback: The Sri Lankan impact study. *Language Testing* 10: 41–69.

Zeidner, M. (1986) Are English language aptitude tests biased towards culturally different minority groups? Some Israeli findings. *Language Testing* 3: 80–95.

Zeidner, M. (1987) A comparison of ethnic, sex and age biases in the predictive validity of English language aptitude tests: Some Israeli data. *Language Testing* 4: 55–71.

Appendix A
Selected list of US Court Cases with sources

Albermarle Paper Co. v. Moody, 422 US (1975)

Debra P. v. Turlington, 474F. Supp. 244 (1979); aff'd in part, rev'd in part, 644 F. 2d 397 (5th Cir. 1981)

Firefighters Institute v. City of St. Louis, 616 F. 2d 350 (8th Cir. 1980)

Golden Rule Insurance Co. v. Mathias, (1984)

Griggs v. Duke Power Co., 401 US 424 (1971)

Hobson v. Hansen, 269 F. Supp. 401 (1967)

Larry P. v. Riles, 495 F. Supp. 926 (1979); aff'd in part, rev'd inpart, 793 F. 2d 969 (9th Cir 1984)

Mandhare v. LaFargue Elementary School, 605 F. Supp 238 (1985), rev'd, (5th Cir. 1986)

McNeil v. Tate, 508 f. 2d 1017 (5th cir. 1975)

PASE v. Hannon, 506 F. Supp. 831 (1980)

Teal v. Connecticut, US, 102 S. Ct. 2525 (1982)

Washington v. Davis, 426 US 229 (1976)

2 Fairness in language testing

Elana Shohamy
Tel Aviv University

Introduction

Most language testers would claim that there is ample research on fairness in testing, that in fact much of the research conducted by language testers focuses on fairness, that testers have developed a series of procedures to ensure that tests are fair and that testers are consistently on guard for fairness. They would also claim that the on-going research aimed at identifying the various sources of unreliability and invalidity is in fact a means through which testers examine fairness. Thus, testers ensure that test takers receive the same scores on tests administered on two separate occasions and from two parallel forms of the same test, that all questions on a test are testing the same construct, that if one type of test is substituted for another, the test taker will still receive a similar score and that the tests will be based on an accepted theory of what it means to know a language. In this regard attention is given to issues of fairness.

Yet, fairness needs to be examined not only on the test level but also in the broader context of 'test use'. It is in the 'use' of language tests that fairness needs to be watched and observed. The reason one would ask questions about fairness in relation to the uses of tests in society is that tests are very powerful instruments which can determine the future of individuals and programs. Decision makers are aware of the power of tests and therefore may be tempted to use them to promote various agendas. It is the power of tests that can lead to unfair behaviour on the part of test users. This situation, therefore, requires an examination of tests in reference to social, educational and political contexts as the actual uses of tests may be different from the purposes they were intended for.

In a number of studies conducted over the past few years on the use of tests several questions were asked. Specifically:

- How are tests being used by decision makers?
- How are scores being interpreted?
- Are language tests used according to their intended purposes?
- What are the consequences of tests?

- Are tests used fairly?
- Do they create biases?
- What is the impact of tests on learning and teaching? and,
- Who are the users and instigators of language tests?

The results of these studies from Israel (reported in Shohamy 1994; Shohamy, Donitsa-Schmidt and Ferman 1996; Shohamy 1997) demonstrate that tests were used for a variety of purposes, the least of which was to measure language. Language tests become the vehicle for a variety of agendas rather than instruments for measuring language knowledge. While language testers design tests to measure language, this use is in fact secondary as the main use of tests by decision makers is to promote political and educational agendas and to obtain power and control of academic systems. The bureaucratic bodies who introduced tests for such purposes provide an illusion of action, a feeling of bureaucratic control and often an excuse for not undertaking meaningful pedagogical actions, which at times could be the agenda for introducing tests in the first place.

In one study (Shohamy 1994), major differences were found between the intended and unintended uses of a reading comprehension test. While the declared purpose of the test, as stated in the official document, was to track the achievements of 4th and 5th grade children for a variety of pedagogical purposes, the actual purpose of conducting the test was to introduce the topic of reading comprehension into the national educational system and thus to 'shake up' the system, and for the Ministry of Education to demonstrate its authority. It was clear to the decision makers that once a powerful device such as a test is introduced it will 'discipline' teachers and students and the test will become the vehicle through which national agendas will be executed.

In another case (Shohamy 1994; Shohamy *et al.* 1996), the national language test of Arabic was introduced for measuring Arabic proficiency of Hebrew speakers learning Arabic as a second language. The purpose of introducing the test was not to measure language but rather to raise the prestige of the subject matter (only what is being tested gets high prestige), to standardize the levels of learning, to force teachers to increase the rate of their teaching and the motivation of teachers to teach.

In yet another case, a new oral test of English as a foreign language was introduced nationally, the main purpose being to divert teachers' attention to the teaching of oral skills, an area believed by the national inspectorate to be overlooked in teaching English. In these cases the purposes of introducing and using language tests were not to measure language. In none of the tests was there any attention given to the results in terms of language proficiency, in none of the cases were students or teachers given any feedback or diagnosis that could have had input into language performance. Rather, all these language tests were used as triggers and vehicles through which bureaucratic agendas could be carried out. Not only is that an unfair and unethical way of doing, it is also ineffective.

In the example of introducing the oral test, it was learned that teachers in fact spent substantially more time on teaching oral skills. Yet, the teaching tasks that were included were only those very tasks that appeared on the test and thus it was 'test language' that got taught and not 'real language'; 'test language' is substantially narrower than real 'oral language'. In addition, many of the teachers whose students were subject to the test reported high anxiety, fear and pressure to cover the material as they felt that their students' success or failure was a direct reflection on them. It should be noted that no changes in the curriculum, teacher training or teaching content were introduced. The test was expected to fulfil all these roles as it became the *de facto* new curriculum, new model of teaching methods and new teaching material, which were very different from what was stated in the official curriculum. In that way the tests provided the educational authorities with a low-cost device that required no investment in any other educational components as the test had the power to trigger and impose a new policy and practice. Is that a fair use of tests?

The use of language tests for other agendas is not limited to the educational context but takes place also in the political context. Politicians, as well, have discovered what a useful tool language tests can be for solving complex political issues that cannot be resolved through regular policy making. It should also be noted that one feature that makes tests so attractive to politicians is that they allow the user to determine cutting scores in an arbitrary way and thus create quotas in a flexible manner.

The current proposal by President Clinton to introduce national tests in grades 4 and 8 in mathematics and reading in order to rescue the failing US educational system is another example of an attempt to control the system with tests and thus to obtain an illusion that as complex a phenomenon as the US educational system can be healed and repaired with as simple a device as a test. It is an attempt to use the powerful device tests to deter teachers. There is a built-in assumption that teachers are not doing their jobs, and that students are not studying hard enough and, if they will only be given a strong push or a whip (a test), the educational system will improve. It is similar to measuring the temperature of a sick person and hoping that repeated measurements will provide the cure. In the political levels tests are used to create *de facto* language policies, to raise the status of some languages and to lower that of others, to control citizenship, to include, to exclude, to gatekeep, to maintain the power of the élite and to offer simplistic solutions to complex problems. Is that a fair use of tests?

Furthermore, using tests in these ways results in two parallel systems, one manifested through politically correct curriculum and policy documents, and the other reflecting bureaucratic aspirations. These two systems are often in contradiction with one another. There is policy and testing policy. The testing policy which is exercised through tests and pushed by bureaucrats, usually unknown to the public, is the *de facto* policy. Is that a fair use of tests?

Using tests to introduce policies is undemocratic, unethical and unfair. The agenda represents those in power, the élite, often not declared publicly and openly and dictated from above, rather than including those who are affected by the test – teachers and test takers. The test becomes the single most influential pedagogical source and the *real* knowledge. Teachers are reduced to 'following orders', a frustrating role as their responsibility increases while their authority diminishes. The test then becomes the device through which control is exercised authoritatively, legitimizing the power of bureaucrats and related groups. Policy is made with no involvement on the part of those who are most affected by the tests. Is that a democratic, ethical and fair way of making policy?

This is not to say that tests should not be used at all. In fact, tests, when used correctly, can provide a most meaningful source for providing information that can be most useful for teaching and learning. There are many exciting developments in the field of language assessment including the use of a variety of procedures – portfolios, self-assessment, peer assessment, etc. to assess language. Then there are models where power is shared with the test takers, where testers and test takers discuss the assessment results in a dialogical way, and thus the power of the tests is transferred from élite and executive authorities who are presently in control with the local groups. Test takers, students and teachers share their power by collecting their own assessment evidence using multiple assessment procedures such as portfolios, self-assessment, projects, observations and tests. This information becomes the evidence of their language proficiency based on a broader representation of agents and materials which together engage in a process of contextualization by obtaining evidence from different sources. Through constructive interpretive and dialogical sessions, each participant collects language data and demonstrates them an interpretive and contextualized manner. This approach can be applied on the national, district or classroom level. Such methods are more time consuming and costly. Yet, fair practices are not chosen because of their efficiency or cost but because of their principles. This is why central bodies and testing agencies often make efforts to reject such proposals.

For the language testers who realize that the products they create are misused, this poses a threat to the ethicality of the profession. Language testers therefore must be engaged in the discussion. They must assume an active role of following the consequences and uses of language tests, and offer assessment models which are more educational, democratic and ethical in order to minimize the misuse of tests by others. Language testers cannot remove themselves from the consequences and uses of tests and therefore must also reject the notion of neutral language testing. Pretending it is neutral only allows those in power to misuse language tests with the very instrument that language testers have provided them.

Language testers must realize that much of the strength of tests is not their technical quality but their use in social and political dimensions. Studies of test use as part of test validation, on an on-going basis, are essential for the integrity and fairness of the profession. Language tests provide a reflection of the complexities and power struggles of society. They fall in the crossroads of all these conflicts and therefore should be studied, protected and guarded as part of the process of preserving and perpetuating democratic cultures, values, ethics and fairness.

References

Shohamy, E. (1994) The use of language tests for power and control. In Alatis, J. (Ed.) *Georgetown University roundtable on Language and Linguistics.* Washington, DC: Georgetown University Press: 57–75.

Shohamy, E. (1997) *Critical Language Testing and Beyond.* Plenary paper delivered at the AAAL Conference, Orlando, Florida, March 1997.

Shohamy, E., Donitsa-Schmidt, S. and I. Ferman, (1996) Test impact revisited: Washback effect over time. *Language Testing* 13: 298–317.

3 Writing assessment: Language, meaning and marking memoranda

Bonny Norton
University of British Columbia

Introduction

In this chapter, I critically examine the marking memoranda or scoring guides used in the assessment of writing skills in pre-university contexts in South Africa, the USA and Canada. The three marking memoranda (respectively) were or are currently being used in school-leaving Matriculation Examinations (South Africa), the Test of Written English (United States) and the Canadian Language Benchmarks Assessment (Canada). My familiarity with these marking memoranda is drawn not only from existing literature, but also from my own practical and research experience with these instruments (Norton Peirce 1990, 1991; Norton Peirce and Stewart 1997). It is important to note that the three memoranda are not necessarily representative of the multiple forms of writing assessment found in each of the three respective countries. Rather, these memoranda provide a window through which assumptions about language, meaning, writers and readers implicit in a variety of essay marking memoranda can be analyzed and critiqued.

What does a marking memorandum have to do with debates on fairness and ethics in language testing? In this article, I demonstrate that marking memoranda are not 'neutral', 'practical' artifacts; they are used to determine the life chances of individuals and assume theories of language and meaning that are rarely made explicit. If test developers and markers are to be ethically accountable (Hamp-Lyons 1997; Norton 1997; Shohamy 1993), we need to examine more closely the assumptions implicit in the marking memoranda we use, the decisions that we make on the basis of such memoranda, and the consequences these decisions have for the life chances of test takers.

It is not my intention to provide detailed analyses of the essay tests in which these memoranda are used. Readers are referred to other literature for this purpose (Educational Testing Service 1989; Greenberg 1986; Norton Peirce 1990, 1991; Norton Peirce and Stewart 1997; Raimes 1990; Stansfield 1986; Stansfield and Ross 1988). Furthermore, it is not my intention to assess the validity of the marking memoranda with respect to the purposes for which the tests were constructed. My more modest intention is to determine what insights can be gained by a cross-comparison of marking memoranda used in the assessment of essay writing tasks – a very common task used in the assessment of writing skills. Comparative analysis is a useful methodological tool because the search for similarities and differences often uncovers hidden assumptions and implicit theories. In this spirit, the questions I will address in this chapter are as follows:

1 What are the similarities and differences among the three marking memoranda?
2 What assumptions about language and meaning are implicit in each of the memoranda?
3 How are writers and readers theorized – either implicitly or explicitly?

In the first section of the chapter, I compare the three essay-marking memoranda; in the second section, I provide a summary comment on the comparison and contrast, highlighting the relevance of the analysis for debates on fairness in language testing.

Comparison of three marking memoranda

In the interests of brevity, acronyms will be used for the three essay-marking memoranda. The one that was used in South Africa (at least during the *apartheid* years) will be referred to as the DEC – from the Department of Education and Culture; the one used in the United States will be referred to as the TWE (from the Test of Written English); and the one used in Canada will be referred to as the CLBA (from the Canadian Language Benchmarks Assessment). Copies of the three marking memoranda are available in Appendices A, B, and C in this chapter.

Central assumptions of the DEC marking memorandum

The DEC marking memorandum (Appendix A) was used in the marking of the essays written by black South African students in their national school-leaving examinations during the *apartheid* years. Essays were marked out of 70, on the basis of two ratings: a 'language' rating (see column 1) and a 'content' rating (see column 2). The highest mark, A, represented a mark of 56–70, and H, the lowest mark, represented a mark of 4–13. It has already been noted (Norton Peirce 1990) that a discrepancy existed between the language curriculum designed for black students, and the way student essays were actually marked in national examinations. The central assumptions about language and meaning – as reflected in the DEC marking memorandum – are as follows:

The theory of language implicit in the memorandum is that language represents – and is primarily limited to – knowledge of grammar, punctuation, vocabulary, and sentence structure, i.e. language is equivalent to linguistic competence and meaning is assumed to be contained within linguistic units. A clear distinction between 'language' (Column 1) and 'content' (Column 2) is drawn. As Norton Peirce (1990: 7) notes, markers are advised that: '*The general principle applied is that the symbol to be awarded (A–H) is dependent on the use of language … You must distinguish between major and minor errors.*' Norton Peirce notes that markers are given specific instructions to circle the major errors and underline the minor ones, and to take lexis and structure into account in determining what 'language' rating the writer should get. Once the writer's 'language' rating has been determined, markers are then required to assess the 'content' of the essay. The quality of the content is determined with reference to the following questions (Norton Peirce 1990: 7):

- How well did the candidate relate to the topic?
- Is the topic introduced and concluded effectively?
- Does the essay hold the reader's attention through interesting description, or imaginative writing, or perceptive ideas?
- Is it generally coherent?

Markers are warned not to become so distracted by the language that they forget the content. Rather, markers are advised to '*read quickly over the essay again after marking the language*' (Norton Peirce 1990: 7).

It is important to notice that 'language', as depicted in the DEC memorandum, is significantly more important than 'content', when their respective weightings are considered. Thus once a writer's 'language' has been pegged at a particular level, the marker has very little opportunity to exercise judgement about the writer's 'content'. For example, if a writer's language has been deemed to be 'patently below standard' (14–22 out of 70), then regardless of how interesting the essay is, the marker may not give the writer a mark above 22, i.e. the marker has to remain within the 9-mark range from 14 to 22 (i.e. a 12% range).

A writer whose language is weak is deemed incapable of producing content that is both interesting and impressive. A 'doubtful' essay, for example, is assumed to have 'dull' content, and may, at best, arouse 'some interest'. The corollary of this assumption, as demonstrated in the marking memorandum, is that a writer whose language is deemed 'competent' is incapable of producing 'dull' content. Thus a writer with a C symbol for language is assumed to produce either 'ordinary' or 'interesting' content.

In this memorandum, the weaknesses of writers are considered more important than their strengths. Although writers are ranked from A–H, the top of Columns 1 and 2 focuses attention on the H rating, after which the focus shifts to G, F, E, D, C and (finally) B and A. Markers are not encouraged to 'bias for best' (Swain 1985).

Central assumptions of the TWE marking memorandum

The TWE is the essay component of the Test of English as a Foreign Language (TOEFL) used by over 30,000 institutions in the USA and Canada to assess the English proficiency of pre-university candidates whose native language is not English (Educational Testing Service 1989). The TWE marking memorandum (Appendix B) is a 6-point holistic scoring guide. The assumptions implicit in this marking memorandum are as follows.

Content and language – framed broadly as 'rhetoric' and 'syntax' respectively – are understood to be distinct, though related categories. A score of '4' for example, 'demonstrates minimal competence on both the rhetorical and syntactic levels.' A paper with a score of 3 'demonstrates minimal competence in writing, but remains flawed on either the rhetorical or syntactic level, or both.' Thus, in contrast to the DEC memorandum, the control of grammatical structures, syntactic variety, and word choice are assumed to be no more important than the organization, development, and effectiveness of the writing. A paper in the '6' category, for example:

• effectively addresses the writing task
• is well organized and well developed
• uses clearly appropriate details to support a thesis or illustrate ideas
• displays consistent facility in the use of language
• demonstrates syntactic variety and appropriate word choice

Meaning is assumed to be contained within the text, but is not confined to linguistic units – as is the case with the DEC marking memorandum. As in the DEC marking memorandum, however, readers are assumed to be outside the process of meaning construction. They are rarely invited to exercise judgement, but instead are expected to 'assign' scores to papers that 'demonstrate' competence, 'display' consistent facility, and 'address' the topic. In this view, a paper assumes a life of its own, independent of both writer and reader.

In contrast to the DEC memorandum, the strengths of writers are assumed to be more important than their weaknesses. Thus the memorandum states explicitly: '*Readers should focus on what the examinee does well.*' It states, furthermore, that a candidate with the highest score (6) is not expected to produce an error-free paper – the paper may have 'occasional' errors. In addition, the highest score is given prominence at the top of the guide, with the lowest score relegated to the bottom of the guide.

Assumptions of the CLBA Scoring Guide

The CLBA is a task-based assessment instrument used to place new adult immigrants in Canada in language programs appropriate for their level of competence in English (Norton Peirce and Stewart 1997). The test is divided into a Stage I (beginner) and a Stage II (intermediate). There is a writing test, a reading test, and a listening/speaking test in each stage. There are four writing tasks in each of the two stages, and the most challenging writing task is one in which writers are expected to express 'complex' ideas in English (Norton Peirce and Stewart 1997: 24). Each task is marked on a 4-point scale and is assessed with the help of a decision tree that distinguishes between 'primary objectives' and 'secondary objectives' of the task. The assumptions implicit in the marking memorandum (Appendix C) are described below.

In contrast to the DEC and TWE memoranda, where 'content' and 'language' are either divorced (the DEC) or integrated (the TWE), there is an assumption in the CLBA that the 'content' and 'expression of ideas' are of primary importance in written communication, while the syntax, spelling, mechanics, and lexis of the text are deemed to be of secondary importance. This is evident in the distinction between 'primary' and 'secondary' objectives.

In this memorandum, the relationship between the reader and the writer is of central importance in the construction of meaning. Thus meaning is not assumed to be contained within linguistic units (the DEC), nor is it assumed to be 'buried' in the text, to be ferreted out by the reader (the TWE). Unlike both the DEC and TWE marking memoranda, meaning is assumed to be co-constructed by both the writer and the reader. This relationship is captured in the 'primary objectives':

• The writer addresses the purpose of the task in paragraph form
• The writer demonstrates an appropriate sense of audience
• The writer organizes and expresses ideas clearly
• The reader can follow and understand the writer's message
• The reader is appropriately informed by the content of the task

There is an assumption that the marking of essays requires judgement on the part of the reader. While the DEC memorandum reduces marking to an accounting process in which major and minor errors are added up and recorded, and the TWE assumes that the worth of an essay is largely self-evident and simply needs to be 'discovered' by the reader, who then assigns an appropriate score, the CLBA foregrounds the importance of the reader's judgement in the assessment process, and provides a decision tree to facilitate the decision-making process.

Discussion

Having examined the assumptions underlying the three different marking memoranda, I would like to provide a summary of the central issues, and then discuss their relevance for fairness in language testing.

1   The marking memoranda have different assumptions about the relationship between language and meaning. The DEC takes the position that meaning can be separated from language, and that ideas are less important than the words that convey them. In this view, meaning is conveyed through language, but separate from language. The TWE takes the position that language and meaning have a complex interrelationship, but meaning is stable in written form. In this view, meaning is 'contained' within texts, and recoverable by the reader. The CLBA assumes that meaning and language have a complex interrelationship, but that meaning is not stable in written form. It is co-constructed by both reader and writer, and subject to change.

2   As an extension of 1, the three memoranda have contrasting approaches to the relationship between 'content' and 'language'. Although all three memoranda (implicitly or explicitly) draw distinctions between language and content, they frame them differently, and establish different priorities in their assessment. The DEC distinguishes between 'language' (error-free words and sentences) and 'content' (organization and ideas). Content is considered of secondary importance to language. The TWE distinguishes between 'rhetoric' and 'syntax' and generally considers them equally important. In the CLBA, appropriate 'content' is understood with reference to a given task in the context of a relationship between the writer and the reader, and is given primary importance in the assessment process. Syntax, spelling, mechanics, and vocabulary are considered to be of secondary importance.

3   It follows from 1 and 2 that the three marking memoranda have different assumptions about competent writers and readers. In the DEC marking memorandum, a competent writer is deemed to be someone who has few errors in grammar, spelling, and vocabulary; competent readers are people who effectively decode text at the level of the sentence. In the TWE, competent writers can communicate ideas effectively in written form; competent readers can decode and comprehend both rhetoric and syntax. In the CLBA, competent writers can express ideas clearly with reference to a given audience; competent readers can make appropriate judgements about the quality of the writer's message.

4 Points 1, 2 and 3 have important implications for fairness in language testing. The same essay marked in accordance with each of the three marking memoranda could be assessed very differently and, potentially, have vastly different consequences for the life chances of test takers. The central point is that theories of language, meaning, writers and readers are not abstract and divorced from the practical decisions that language testers, teachers, and administrators have to make on a daily basis. Such theories need to be made explicit, carefully examined, and rigorously defended on ethical grounds. Such scrutiny might shed some light on an intriguing question: are different theories of language equally fair?

References

Clapham, C. and D. Corson (Eds.) (1997) Language Testing and Assessment: Volume 7, *The Encylopedia of Language and Education.* Dordrecht: Klewer Academic Publishers.

Educational Testing Service (1989) *Test of Written English Guide.* Princeton, NJ: ETS.

Greenberg, K. L. (1986) The development and validation of the TOEFL writing test: A discussion of TOEFL Research Reports 15 and 19. *TESOL Quarterly* 23, 3: 531–544.

Hamp–Lyons, L. (1997) Ethics in language testing. In Clapham and Corson.

Norton, B. (1997) Accountability in language assessment. In Clapham and Corson.

Norton Peirce, B. (1990) Student writers, the DET syllabus, and matric marking: A critical evaluation. *ELTIC Reporter* 15: 3–11.

Norton Peirce, B. (1991) Review of the TOEFL Test of Written English Scoring Guide. *TESOL Quarterly* 25: 159–163.

Norton Peirce, B. and G. Stewart, (1997) The development of the Canadian Language Benchmarks Assessment. *TESL Canada Journal* 14: 17–31.

Raimes, A. (1990) The TOEFL Test of Written English: Causes for concern. *TESOL Quarterly* 24: 427–442.

Shohamy, E. (1993) The exercise of power and control in the rhetorics of testing. In Huhta, A., Sajavaara, K. and S. Takala, (Eds.), *Language Testing: New Openings.* University of Jyvaskyla, Finland.

Stansfield, C. (1986) A history of the Test of Written English: The developmental year. *Language Testing* 3: 224–234.

Stansfield, C. and J. Ross, (1988) A long-term research agenda for the Test of Written English. *Language Testing* 5: 160–186.

Swain, M. (1985) Large-scale communicative language testing: A case study. In Savignon, S. and M. Berns, (Eds.) *Initiatives in Communicative Language Teaching.* Reading, MA: Addison-Wesley: 185–201.

Appendix A

DEC Essay Memorandum   Total possible mark = 70

Column 1 Language Rating		Column 2 Modified by Content Rating	
H. 4-13 (6-19%)	Extremely weak almost unintelligible	1. Extremely poor 2. Entirely dull 3. Arouse a faint interest	4-6 7-10 11-13
G. 14-22 (20-32%)	Patently below standard	1. Very poor 2. Dull 3. In measure	14-15 16-18 19-22
F. 23-27 (33-39%)	Doubtful	1. Dull 2. Some interest	23-24 25-27
E. 28 -34 (40-49%)	Passworthy	1. Ordinary 2. Interesting in parts	28-30 31-34
D. 35-41 (50-59%)	A comfortable pass	1. Ordinary 2. Interesting	35-38 39-41
C. 42-48 (60-69%)	Competent	1. Ordinary 2. Interesting	42-44 45-48
B. 49-55 (70-79%)	Very competent and pleasing	1. Ordinary 2. Interesting 3. Interesting with flashes of impressiveness	49 50-53 54-55
A. 56-70 (80-100%)	Outstandingly good use of vocabulary and structures	1. Interesting 2. Interesting with flashes of impressiveness 3. Superb	56-60 61-63 64-70

Appendix B

Test of Written English (TWE) – Scoring Guide

TEST OF WRITTEN ENGLISH (TWE)
SCORING GUIDE

Readers will assign scores based on the following scoring guide. Though examinees are asked to write on a specific topic, parts of the topic may be treated by implication. Readers should focus on what the examinee does well.

Scores

6   **Clearly demonstrates competence in writing on both the rhetorical and syntactic levels, though it may have occasional errors.**
A paper in the category
- is well organized and well developed;
- efficiently addresses the writing task;
- uses appropriate details to support a thesis or illustrate ideas;
- shows unity, coherence and progression;
- displays consistent facility in the use of language;
- demonstrates syntactic variety and appropriate word choice.

5   **Demonstrates competence in writing on both the rhetorical and syntactic levels, though it will have occasional errors.**
A paper in this category
- is generally well organized and well developed, though it may have fewer details than a 6 paper;
- may address some parts of the task more effectively than others;
- shows unity, coherence and progression;
- demonstrates some syntactic variety and range of vocabulary;
- displays facility in language, through it may have more errors than does a 6 paper.

4   **Demonstrates minimal competence in writing on both the rhetorical and syntactic levels.**
A paper in this category
- is adequately organized;
- addresses the writing topic adequately but may slight parts of the task;
- uses some details to support a thesis or illustrate ideas;
- demonstrates adequate but undistinguished or inconsistant facility with syntax and usage;
- may contain some serious errors that occaisionally obscure meaning.

3   **Demonstrates some developing competence in writing, but it remains flawed on either the rhetorical or syntactic level or both.**
A paper in this category may reveal one or more of the following weaknesses:
- inadequate organization or development;
- failure to support or illustrate generalizations with appropriate or sufficient detail;
- an accumulation of errors in a sentence structure and/or usage;
- a noticeably inappropriate choice of words or word forms.

2   **Suggests incompetence in writing**
A paper in this category is flawed by one or more of the following weaknesses:
- failure to organize or develop;
- little or no detail. or irrelevant specifics;
- serious and frequent errors in usage or sentence structure
- serious problems with focus.

1   **Demonstrates incompetence in writing**
A paper in this category will contain serious and persistent writing errors, may be illogical or incoherent, or may reveal the writer's inability to comprehend the question. A paper that is severely underdeveloped also falls into this category.

Papers that reject the assignment or fail to address the question in any way must be given to the Table Leader. Papers that exhibit absolutely no response at all must be given to the Table Leader.

[Reprinted by permission of Education Testing Service, the copywrite owner.]

Appendix C

CLBA Scoring Guide

**CLBA Scoring Guide
Writing - Stage II - Task D:2: Express Complex Ideas**

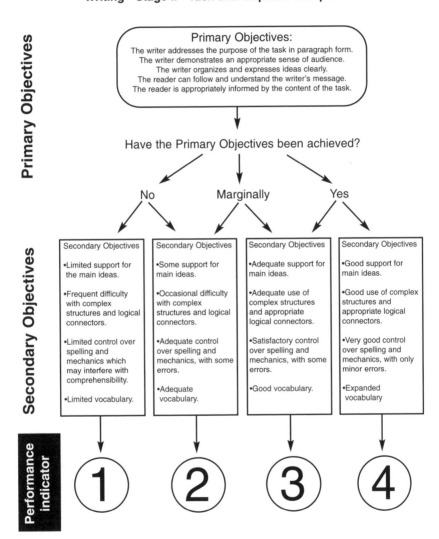

Primary Objectives

Primary Objectives:
The writer addresses the purpose of the task in paragraph form.
The writer demonstrates an appropriate sense of audience.
The writer organizes and expresses ideas clearly.
The reader can follow and understand the writer's message.
The reader is appropriately informed by the content of the task.

Have the Primary Objectives been achieved?

No   Marginally   Yes

Secondary Objectives

Secondary Objectives	Secondary Objectives	Secondary Objectives	Secondary Objectives
•Limited support for the main ideas.	•Some support for main ideas.	•Adequate support for main ideas.	•Good support for main ideas.
•Frequent difficulty with complex structures and logical connectors.	•Occasional difficulty with complex structures and logical connectors.	•Adequate use of complex structures and appropriate logical connectors.	•Good use of complex structures and appropriate logical connectors.
•Limited control over spelling and mechanics which may interfere with comprehensibility.	•Adequate control over spelling and mechanics, with some errors.	•Satisfactory control over spelling and mechanics, with some errors.	•Very good control over spelling and mechanics, with only minor errors.
•Limited vocabulary.	•Adequate vocabulary.	•Good vocabulary.	•Expanded vocabulary

Performance indicator

(1)   (2)   (3)   (4)

[Reprinted by permission of the Centre for Language Training and Assessment, Peel Board of Education, Canada.]

29

4 Fairnesses in language testing

Liz Hamp-Lyons
Hong Kong Polytechnic University

There has recently been considerable debate in educational measurement about 'fairness'. What is fairness? What makes a test fair? How do we know when a test is unfair? I find these questions increasingly difficult, increasingly beyond my wit to answer. But I do feel that they all imply, and assume, some ideal model of 'fairness' that is somewhere 'out there', waiting for us, if we only knew where to look. In this chapter, I don't propose to look for that ideal model: rather, I want to consider some other kinds of fairness that I came across while I was searching vainly for that ideal model.

1 Language teaching as a field has not agreed what is the right way to teach or learn, and has not established a single dominant model for language teaching. Therefore, students should be free to discover and then follow their own learning styles and learning strategies. Similarly, because language testing has not discovered a single dominant model of how to test a student's learning, ability or performance, students should be free to consider their own learning history, their learning styles and strategies, and choose test and item types that best match their own learning profile. Tests, then, would need to exist in multiple forms so that each student could select a unique, appropriate pathway to demonstrate mastery, one which would be uniquely fair to her or him.

2 Students' judgements of their own performances are heavily influenced by their teacher's degree of harshness or leniency toward error, and by the performance targets their teachers set for them and accept from them. Therefore, teachers need to be benchmarked so that students will have better self-knowledge, so that they will not be misled by their teacher's encouragement to view themselves as more successful than they are, or by their teacher's criticisms to view themselves as less successful than they are. The concept of teacher benchmarking implies that teachers would be tested to ensure that they comprehend and can consistently apply the appropriate criteria and standards to learners in their classes. Teachers entering new teaching situations – new school years, new kinds of learners, teaching new skills – would need to take a re-benchmarking course and would be required to pass the course before teaching this new kind of learner. This kind of fairness places the needs of the teacher below the needs of the learner, because it states that standards and criteria are not negotiable. It does not, however, contradict the previous kind of fairness, because standards and criteria are distinct from styles and strategies, which, when the teacher is in turn a rater, she or he can still choose freely.

3 Language testing has embraced post-modernism. It has now accepted the fact that raters have personal philosophies and belief sets, and that it is a fiction to suppose that they can 'check these at the door'. It follows that formal judgement systems should acknowledge this and figure out how to accommodate assessment systems to the rating styles and strategies of raters. Tests, then, would need to have multiple scoring alternatives so that each rater could select a unique, appropriate approach to scoring, one that would be uniquely fair to her or him.

4 Teachers are educated and trained in many different ways; every teacher, through education, experience, personality, interests and skills is different: classes by different teachers are not the same, even if the syllabus is. Therefore, teachers should be free to teach according to their own personal 'style'. It follows that they should be free to assess, and have their students assessed, by their personal style also; when assessments match instruction, not only in content but in style, there will be least dissonance for the teacher, and therefore for the learners. Tests, then, would need to exist in multiple forms so that each teacher could select a unique, appropriate pathway for her or his students to demonstrate mastery, one which would allow students and teacher to be seen in their best light by assessing in areas and in ways where they have the most strength.

5 Parents know their children best of all. They have a set of social values, and they have expectations of what their children should be able to do and how they should be doing it. Parents also want to understand what happens in the classroom and the school much better than they do now. Most kinds of tests are alienating for parents; they are done in technical ways that exclude the parents, and they are reported in technical language, or simply with number scores not attached to actual examples of their child's performance. All this is clearly unfair to the parents. Tests would be fairer to parents if they were directly related to the content the children had been learning and that parents had been seeing in the homework assignments; they would be fairer to parents if they were scored in ways that parents could completely understand, and if parents were able to take part in the design of the test and its scoring method. Because parents understand their children's learning needs and problems so well, it would be fairer to parents if they could take part in test design and could be trained as raters of the tests. Tests will only be fair to parents if test results/reports make complete sense to them, either because the reports are transparently descriptive, or because parents have been trained in test report interpretation in their own children's context. There needs to be an appeal system parents can use to challenge their child's test score or the way the child was tested.

Each of the fairnesses I have portrayed above focuses on being fair to one group of stakeholders: learners, raters, teachers, parents. There are other stakeholder groups too: taxpayers, national and state Education Department officials, big business, political parties, and governments. I feel slightly guilty at not giving a voice to the taxpayers but only slightly, because I am one – we are all taxpayers, as are all the parents; there are taxpayers with different views about the uses of testing, but in general those groups are vocal enough without my help.

It doubtless seems to many of you that I have gone outrageously too far in creating the voices and views of these different groups of stakeholders. I will agree with you that some of the suggestions I have voiced seem outrageous to us, as language testers, perhaps as teachers, perhaps even as parents, but only if you will agree with me that such suggestions are real, that you too have heard these and comments like them discussed in parents' meetings or teachers' common rooms. It seems to me that none of them should be taken too lightly. Once language testers accept that there is no single 'right answer', we also have to listen seriously to all views. 'Fairness' is such a difficult concept because there is no one standpoint from which a test can be viewed as 'fair' or 'not fair'. The language tester has no more inherent right to decide what is 'fair' for other people than anyone else does. But the language tester does have the responsibility to use all means to make any language test she or he is involved in as 'fair' as possible. As our technical skills expand, as our definition of 'a test' is refined, as our political consciousness of the power of tests is heightened, we raise our expectations of ourselves. The time has arrived when we are obliged to look critically at everything that we do, and to take that critique onward and look at the legacy we have given to test takers, other stakeholder groups, and indeed society, and we must not flinch from accepting some responsibility if we do not like what we see when realizing what the tests we have been involved with have become.

As for myself, I was ambivalent about the first revision of the ELTS that I worked on in the early 1980s: while I felt the test purposes, the assessment of the English skills of applicants for (mainly postgraduate) places at British universities were appropriate, I was made uneasy by what test candidates told me during oral interviews, about the inappropriacy of test content for their personal background. It was that unease that motivated the focus in my PhD dissertation on whether specific content testing (of writing, as it happens) would advantage students compared to more general academic content testing. But I didn't bring what the students were telling me into my research, to my dissertation: I looked for textual and statistical evidence only. I wouldn't do that now – I don't think any of us would.

I was more worried about the *access*, the Australian test for aspiring adult migrants. Test scores would play a part in the decision whether or not they could migrate; do the stakes come any higher than that? The goalposts kept shifting: cut scores were changed, the test first had to serve one function and then two. The test was to be used as part of a numbers game, yet gave the impression of being criterion-referenced. The subtleties of Rasch analysis were used to manipulate numbers in different reporting categories tied to visa categories. Though my own role was minimal, a brief visit as a consultant on the writing sub-test scales, I was uneasy about my participation. Later still, it seems, again under governmental instructions, not as a language testing decision, the test was adumbrated as the STEP and recalibrated to keep in the country as many Tiannanmen refugees as possible. The good news was that the test manipulations were with benevolent intent; but that tests should be used as alibis to make politicians' jobs easier is troubling to me. My Australian testing friends liked this a lot less than I did, because they were more deeply involved: but they did their jobs. I hope that now, in the era of critical language testing, in a time when the dominating and colonizing power of tests is beginning to be recognized; in the time of the International Language Testing Association and the development of standards for language testing, none of us would do it.

I was proud of the Michigan Writing Assessment, the writing test that I designed and developed for the University of Michigan's full cohort of freshman students. I tried to do everything right. I even thought for a while that I had. But when we got to the last stages of development, I was compelled to manipulate the score data to make it easier for transfer students to test out of basic writing, for political reasons: the University didn't want to jeopardize its relationship with the area community colleges from which some students transferred. It wasn't the principle of transfer students getting a break that I had trouble with: it was the fact that this was to be done covertly. These students' actual performances would generate descriptions of performance which were tied to scores, and these scores would then be shifted through a computer program that would raise them a few points; the resulting scores would then be fed back through the program and would re-generate descriptions of performance – but, of course, these would no longer be descriptions of the true performance of these students. I fought hard, but I lost. I described the problem and the way the data were manipulated in the official report; but I didn't describe it in papers or conference presentations. Was I ashamed? I don't think so, but I sure wasn't proud.

When I was invited to join the Test of Written English Committee, I was very ambivalent indeed. What I learned from my three years on that Committee was that everyone involved tried really hard to create the very best writing test they could within the constraints set by ETS; and that the constraints set by ETS were the inevitable consequence of the most extreme form of positivist paradigm in practice. Reliability was God, and we worshipped it four times a year. The 'best possible test' meant a test that was unfair to no one, and that meant very high reliability and tasks that neither disadvantaged nor offended anyone. If a task was on sports, we had to add non-physical options so as not to offend or disadvantage the physically disabled or the obese; no prompts on smoking, alcohol, sex. We reviewed essays from pilot tests for evidence of anxiety or offense in writers as well as for score behavior. Within the positivist paradigm, we did everything we could for excellence. And so, ironically, the TWE turned out to be the best test I've worked on, for having clear standards and sticking to them, even in the face of some swingeing criticism.

My purpose in these personal reflections is a simple one: to pause for a moment, and to look critically at a few of the testing projects I've been involved in from the standpoint of this conference theme: fairness. Was I fair to the students who took ELTS, when I didn't let their voices speak in my dissertation? Was I fair to those who would take the *access*, when I remained associated with it (though only as the most minor of consultants) after I learned the unethical ways it was to be used? Was I fair to freshman students at Michigan, when I kept silent about the fact that transfer students had a special statistical advantage on the test? Was I fair to teachers in TOEFL preparation courses around the world, when I didn't publish a revision of my book on the Test of Written English, after I knew how it really worked? And, notice that I have directed all my questions at the question of fairness to the test takers. Similar questions can be asked about fairness to all the other stakeholder groups. What about the freshman composition teachers at Michigan, for example, who were continually surprised by students who had been exempted from basic writing entering their classes at basic writing level?

Yes, there is more than one fairness, and judging what is fair is not so simple. But what is important is that we have begun to recognize that fact, and have begun to care about all the fairnesses that we, as language testers, must be accountable for.

5 Enhancing fairness through a social contract

Mary Spaan
University of Michigan

'Fairness' is, to my mind, a man-made concept; a philosophical ideal which does not exist in the natural world. We all know that 'life isn't fair', that all people are not equally endowed, nor are they presented, in the natural world, with equal opportunities or chances to develop the talents they have at birth. Yet people have ideals, among them the concept of fairness, in which opportunities are equal.

A test is an artificial logical construct created by people. An ideal test would measure something accurately (be unbiased and free of error), consistently, and completely (possess construct and content validity, and obtain a sufficient sampling of the domain). Furthermore, it would always be used for its appropriate, intended purpose and would always be easily and correctly interpreted. Again, we all know how difficult it is to achieve this, how short we have fallen in attempting to reach this ideal. An operationalized test takes only a representative sampling of the complex real world domain to be tested. Examinees of different language backgrounds and with different educational backgrounds may be advantaged or disadvantaged in a foreign language test. Different performance might be due to native language distance from the target language, or might be due to unfamiliar format, or to emphasis on a skill area that is not emphasized in the educational system of the examinee's home country. It would seem then, that in the natural world, test writers and developers cannot be 'fair', in the ideal sense, but that they can try to be equitable.

This equitability implies the joint responsibility of the test developer, the test user, and the examinee, in a sort of social contract, in which the developers promise to maximize validities (construct, content, etc.), reliability, and practicality of application. It is the developer's responsibility to educate the users by providing readable, understandable interpretations and guidelines for use of their products, including the provision of norms and/or scoring criteria. The developer must be able to justify any claims made about the test; and furthermore, the developer must also solicit feedback from users and examinees. In this social contract users do not abuse tests by applying the wrong test to the wrong population, or by running the test through a 'chop shop' in which they remove parts from one or more tests and insert them into new tests. If they have erroneously assumed that the parts are equal to the whole, they may believe they have retained validity. In this social contract, examinees inform themselves about the test content and methods beforehand, so as to avoid negative task effect; they try to match the level of the test to their skill level. And of course, as a member of this circle, it is the developer's responsibility to inform the users and examinees about the test level, method, and content, and to standardize test delivery as much as possible so that various forms of test abuse are discouraged.

The focus of this short chapter will be on the test developer, and how the developer can enhance fairness, or equitability, in language testing. The *ILTA Code of Practice* (1997) refers to validity, reliability, and practicality as three essentials of good language testing; it states as a goal the promotion of synergy between language test developers and users. The idea behind this synergy is to bring the user into the process of test development before the actual product is on the market. The developer seeks information from the user about the examinee population: what are the specific skills they will need to perform what tasks? As we move from a skills model (the traditional four skills of listening, speaking, reading and writing) towards a competencies model (linguistic, pragmatic, sociolinguistic and strategic competencies), we find general purpose skills testing somewhat inadequate and we seek instead to match test content and tasks more closely to the specified examinee population. This implies the increased use of task-based specialized tests over general proficiency tests, as well as criterion-referenced tests over norm-referenced tests. The interaction between the test taker and the task is important in the task-based test. A special purpose task-based test for international business office workers might require them to listen to telephone messages and write brief notes to their 'boss'. This task requires the examinees not only to utilize their listening and writing skills, but also to summarize, get the gist of the message, and convey information accurately.

Test developers have increasingly turned to examinees as well as to users for information about their tests. What was their impression of the test? Did it accurately measure what they knew? Did it accurately reflect the kinds of tasks they would be required to perform? Did it seem to use an appropriate elicitation method? Was it engaging?

It seems what we as test developers must do is to encourage test users and examinees to buy into the system, to co-operate with us at the very first stages of test development and to continually ask for more feedback. The first step can be to clarify the purpose(s) of the test to be constructed and to determine the domain which is to be sampled. What kinds of tasks will examinees be required to perform in the real world that we can try to mirror in the artificial world of the test? If users are applying tests incorrectly or seem to be applying scoring criteria incorrectly, we need to clarify the meaning of the construct by linking concepts to actual observations (Zumbo 1993; Leung and Teasdale 1997) in order to reformulate the operational definition of the criterion, making it grounded in real-world observation.

Problems arise and cries of 'Unfair!' are heard when this synergy breaks down, when a communication gap occurs. For instance, teachers may complain that their pupils failed one test, while they passed another test which the teachers believe is either comparable or even more advanced in difficulty level. This may be due to either a mismatch between the two tests (they may not be highly correlated, or may in fact be at two different levels; possibly outdated or incorrect concordance tables are being used), or an incomplete understanding of the methods, goals and expected performance criteria for the two tests. Another type of complaint is that of the teachers who argue that they have been tutoring or teaching students in a specific area, e.g. writing, and cannot understand why their students, who have been working very diligently, have not passed the writing section of a test. This may be due to different understanding of expected performance criteria on the part of the test developer and the teacher. The *ILTA Code of Practice (1997)* recommends a '*direct and logical relationship between* [performance criteria] *and the manner in which they are operationally represented in the test*'.

Examinees, teachers, and users might question grading methods, doubting that an evaluative system (as opposed to 'objective' scoring) can be reliable and accurate. In this instance, the developer may wish to provide extremely detailed information about scoring methods, criteria and rater training, and built-in safeguards such as multiple ratings. Sometimes examinees question the perceived content validity, as when an Electrical or Systems Engineering student balks at writing a general essay test, saying that this type of task will never be required in the student's Engineering course of study. Creating a task-based writing test specifically for the Engineering student can bring the student back into the test development circle.

The goal of all these developments is enhanced fairness in testing through improved validity, reliability, and interpretability. These features can be enhanced through a type of social contract: a synergistic, co-operative communication cycle among the test developers, users and examinees.

References

ILTA (1997) *Code of Practice for Foreign/Second Language Testing* (Draft). International Language Testing Association.

Leung, C. and A. Teasdale, (1997) *Raters' understanding of rating scales as abstracted concept and as instruments for decision making.* Paper presented at language Testing Research Colliquium, Orlando, Florida.

Zumbo, B. (1993) The role of validity theory in the resolution of observational indeterminacy. *Carleton Papers in Applied Language Studies.* Ottawa: Centre for Applied Language Studies, Carleton University.

6 What, if any, are the limits of our responsibility for fairness in language testing?

Lyle F. Bachman
University of California, Los Angeles

Having just read through the most recent draft of the International Language Testing Association (ILTA) 'Code of Practice for foreign/second language testing', I was surprised, to say the least, that there is no mention at all of 'fairness', or 'equity', or any discussion of how the practical activities that are described in this document might be related to assuring fair and equitable test use. Furthermore, there is only one mention of the word 'responsibility' in the entire 19-page document, and this pertains only to the test developers '*responsibility for the ongoing monitoring of the testing process and, as appropriate, revision of the tests and/or development of increasingly useful interpretive information*'. It would thus appear that, as reflected in this code of practice, a concern for fairness has yet to arrive in language testing, while responsibility for assuring fairness is something we language testers have all been mercifully spared.

My purpose in these comments is not to make sweeping generalizations or to sketch a broad framework, and certainly not to provide answers for addressing issues of fairness in language testing. Rather, my purpose is simply to raise some questions about the nature and extent of our involvement and responsibilities, as individual language testing professionals, and of ILTA and the Language Testing Research Colloquium, as a professional association, in helping to assure fairness in language testing.

Issues of fairness arise in a variety of areas of practical test development and use. The following are a few of the issues and questions that have come up during various test development projects on which I have worked with practitioners and in my mentoring of students in the craft of language testing, over the past twenty-odd years.

- **Utilization of human resources in test development**
  Is it fair to expect practitioners to develop, administer and score tests when they have had little or no education or training in this?
  Is it fair to require practitioners to write types of test items or tasks for which they have little or no training or experience?

What are the consequences, in terms of fairness to test takers and test users, of this practice?

- **Identification of individuals who need or will be required to take a language test prior to an educational program**
  Which applicants should be required to take a foreign language screening test for admission to a university? Who decides?
  Of the students who have been admitted to a university, which ones should be required to take a foreign language placement test? Who decides?
  Who should bear the costs of this placement testing? The students? The departments that admit them? The university unit responsible for administering the test? Who decides?

- **Washback/impact on instruction**
  To what extent do the differential effects of impact on individuals (students, teachers, administrators) introduce inequities into an educational system?
  Who is responsible for assuring that washback, or impact on instruction, in its various manifestations, is equitable to the individuals affected?
  Can we draw a neat line distinguishing the systemic effects of testing from those of what Messick refers to as 'other forces operative on the educational scene' (Messick 1996: 242)?

- **Educating practitioners in language testing**
  Who is responsible for educating practitioners about fairness issues and considerations, and providing them the tools and knowledge needed to deal with these on a practical day-to-day basis?

My point is not to imply that language testing practice in these areas is unfair, but simply to suggest that these are areas in which I believe language testers not only should, but must be involved. Although most of us are educators, we nevertheless frequently find it convenient to adopt the pose that we wear different hats – one for testing and one for education – and that these hats can be kept distinct. I for one find myself less and less convinced by this illusion and feel impelled to become increasingly involved as an advocate for fairness, not only for test takers, but also, as a teacher trainer, for practitioners as test developers and, as an educator, for students of language testing as future test developers. The advocacy for fairness by language testers and language test developers is thus, in my view, a critical element not only in the design and implementation of language assessment systems, but also, and perhaps more importantly, in the education and mentoring of those who will carry the field forward in the years to come.

References

Messick, S. 1996. Validity and washback in language testing. *Language Testing* 13: 241–56

Section Two
Fairness: Standards, Criteria and Bias

The four empirical chapters in this section deal with two concerns of fairness: test standards, criteria and test bias. Peter Lowenberg challenges the assumption that the norms for Standard English around the world used in assessment are limited to those that are accepted and followed by educated native speakers of English. Dan Douglas and Ron Myers investigate the 'indigenous assessment' criteria used by veterinary professionals and applied linguists to evaluate the interviewing skills of veterinary students. Catherine Elder examines the policy of assessing native speakers and foreign language learners of Italian with the same instruments in two Australian language certificate examinations and the implications of this for fairness. Yong-Won Lee discusses two approaches in the identification of suspect items that can be bundled together for an analysis of differential bundle functioning in reading tests.

7 Non-native varieties and issues of fairness in testing English as a world language

Peter Lowenberg
San Jose State University

Abstract

In the assessment of non-native proficiency in Standard English, an implicit, and frequently explicit, assumption has long been that the norms for Standard English around the world are limited to those which are accepted and followed by educated *native speakers* of English.

This chapter challenges that assumption, and thus the fairness of tests based on that assumption, by presenting data from domains of Standard English in the *non-native* varieties of English, which have developed in many former colonies of Britain and the United States, such as Nigeria, Ghana, Zambia, India, Malaysia, Singapore, the Philippines, and Fiji. In these countries, Standard English is used daily as a second, often official, language in a wide range of *international* domains, including government, the legal system, commerce, the mass media, and as a medium of instruction in education.

Analysis of the data from these varieties reveals numerous systematic morphosyntactic divergences in these varieties from 'native-speaker' varieties (e.g. count/mass distinctions in nouns, phrasal verbs, prepositional collocations). In their non-native contexts of use, many of these linguistic changes are so widespread that they have become *de facto* local norms for English usage.

In light of this evidence, acceptable models for Standard English can be seen to vary between native-speaker and non-native norms, depending primarily on the usage and attitudes of educated English speakers in each speech community where English is used.

A major implication of this research for language testing is illustrated by examining selected items from a high-stakes test of English as a world language. The keys to these items, though in accord with the norms of the native-speaker varieties, violate norms for Standard English in one or more non-native varieties which have been described to date. These items could therefore be particularly difficult to answer for users of non-native varieties, thereby putting them at an unfair disadvantage with other examinees.

Introduction

With the spread of English as a world language, several applied linguists, most recently David Crystal (1997), have observed that English is currently used by many more non-native speakers than native speakers. In fact, the late Peter Strevens (1992: 27) estimated that native speakers now comprise 'a fifth or less' of the world's English users. A corollary of this development is that by far the majority of English-language interactions in the world today are solely between non-native speakers, without even the presence of native speakers.

However, in tests of English as an international language, an implicit – and frequently *explicit* – assumption continues to be that the universal target for proficiency in English around the world is the set of norms which are accepted and used by highly educated *native speakers* of English.

This assumption may still be accurate in countries where English is mainly used as a 'foreign language' in largely *inter*national domains with few in-country uses, as in Thailand, Indonesia, and Japan. However, this chapter will demonstrate that this assumption is no longer valid in a large number of settings where institutionalised *non-native* varieties of English are used (Kachru 1992a). These are varieties which have developed in countries formerly colonized by Britain or the United States – including, for example, Nigeria, Ghana, Zambia, India, Malaysia, Singapore, the Philippines, and Fiji – where English continues to be used by substantial numbers of non-native speakers as a second, often official, language in a broad range of international domains. In many of these post-colonial settings, English is widely used for some of the legislative, administrative, and judicial functions of government, and, more significant for the spread of English, it is the principal medium of instruction, especially in secondary and post-secondary institutions.[1]

In these countries, English is used daily by non-native speakers in the absence of native speakers, in non-Western sociocultural contexts, and in constant contact with other languages in multilingual speech communities. As a result, English often undergoes systematic changes at all linguistic levels, from phonology and morphology, to syntax and semantics, to pragmatics and discourse. Many of these changes would be considered deviant if used in countries where the more established, 'native-speaker' varieties of English are used, such as Australia, Britain, Canada, or the United States. However, in their non-native contexts, these linguistic innovations and modifications are so widespread that many have become *de facto* local norms for English usage. In fact, attitudinal research reported in Shaw (1981), Sahgal (1991), and Kachru (1992a), indicates that in at least two countries, India and Singapore, between forty and fifty per cent of college-educated English users believe at least some local innovations should be included in local norms for English use and teaching.

The remainder of this chapter examines a number of such innovations taken from domains of Standard English in several non-native varieties. It will be seen that many differences between non-native and native-speaker norms result from variation in a limited number of types of morphosyntactic constructions which are also highly variable in and often produce differences between native-speaker varieties.[2] This analysis will be followed by a discussion of how familiarity with the types of normative variation across varieties of Standard English can be applied in preparing ESL tests that will be valid for assessing proficiency in English as a world language.

On the characteristics of standard English

Standard English, like the standard dialect of many languages, has always been extremely difficult to delimit. In this paper, based on Trudgill (1983), Tay and Gupta (1983), and Tickoo (1991a), the standard model of a variety of English – native-speaker or non-native – is operationally defined as the linguistic forms of that variety that are regularly used in formal speaking and writing by speakers who have received the highest level of education available in that variety. Standard English is the accepted model for official, journalistic, and academic writing; for public speaking before an audience or on radio or television; and for use as a medium and/or subject of instruction in the schools. A crucial tenet of this perspective is that the features of Standard English in any variety, native-speaker or non-native, are not what any outsider thinks they should be. Rather, based on Hymes' (1972) notion of communicative competence, they are the linguistic forms that are actually *used* by institutions and individuals that have power or influence in the above domains of Standard English use.

In the absence of language corpus planning academies for any of the world's English-using speech communities, such as exist for French, Spanish, Swedish, and several other languages, the identification of particular normative features of Standard English in any non-native variety becomes extremely problematic. Fortunately, previous research by established scholars familiar with specific varieties has identified many normative features for these varieties; much of the early research on this topic is summarized in Platt, Weber and Ho (1984). In other cases, non-native norms have been institutionally codified by the same types of authorities who make such decisions in the native-speaker varieties, such as occur in newspaper style sheets, grammar and ELT textbooks, and examinations which are widely used for each variety. A heuristic for identifying still other features as possible variety-specific norms is their use by English speakers with high sociolinguistic status in the relevant speech community or the appearance of these features in texts likely to have been prepared and edited by speakers who are highly proficient in English (in journalism, for example, in the front-page news rather than in 'Letters to the Editor'), especially when these features are used repeatedly in domains of Standard English.[3] Data in the following analysis are taken from all of these sources in both the non-native and native-speaker varieties.

Actually, the many domains in which English is used with mutual comprehensibility in international communication among both native and non-native speakers suggest that Standard English differs only minimally across varieties, basically sharing a large set of common norms. Examples of such global norms are rules concerning the derivation of adverbs from adjectives, subject–verb agreement, and the use of the past participle in the perfect verb tenses. Violations of these norms in domains of Standard English occur in examples (1) to (3), taken from both native-speaker and non-native major daily newspapers.

1 But a U.S. district judge in New York *temporary banned* railroad machinists from honouring picket lines ...
   (*Washington Post*, March 6 1989: A4)
2 *They* [World Wide Web mirror sites] *speed up* readers' access to information *and reduces* the overall load on the network.
   (*The Straits Times* (Singapore), September 17 1996: 2)
3 Maciu on the other hand just couldn't fulfil his fans' expectations but *had succumb* to Atu's deadly punches.
   (*The Daily Post* (Fiji), May 10 1994: 26), cited in Lotherington-Woloszyn 1994)

These examples would be considered deviations from Standard English in all native-speaker and non-native varieties that have been identified to date.

Variation in morphosyntatic constructions

Nevertheless, there are a number of ways in which Standard English frequently *does* diverge across varieties, and these differences, as will be discussed below, can be very significant for the construction of ESL tests. Many non-native norms develop in types of morphological and syntactic co-occurrences that also frequently differ between the native-speaker varieties.

One of the most frequently occurring of these differences is the conversion to countability of noncount nouns which semantically comprise an aggregate of countable units. Examples of variation in these constructions between native-speaker varieties appear in items (4) and (5).

4 British: two *lettuces*
   American: two *heads of lettuce*
   (Trudgill and Hannah 1985: 62)

5 British: Good *accommodation* is hard to find here.
American: Good *accommodations* are hard to find here.
(Trudgill and Hannah 1985:62)

Lettuce, which is countable in (4), from British English, is a noncount noun in American English, whereas American English *accommodations* as used in (5) would not be countable in British English. In items (6) and (7), this same process is extended in the Philippines and Malaysia, respectively.[4]

6 Number of *Luggages*
(*'Daily Service Report'* form, Century Park Sheraton Hotel, Manila, April 1996)
7 Thank you for upkeeping the *equipments* and facilities provided on this train.
(*Permanent metal sign rivetted to the interior of railway passenger carriages*, Malaysian National Railway, December 1997)

The innovative productivity of this process is demonstrated in (8) and (9), from the United States. Example (8) illustrates how innovations usually begin in particular domains, such as electronics, from which they may or may not spread to other domains.

8 West said they used *a digital equipment* that was capable of transmitting both video and still images.
(*San Jose Mercury News*, July 17 1997: 16A)

Item (9) demonstrates that the acceptability of an innovation can be influenced by the status of its user in the domain of use, in this case Jean Berko-Gleason in the field of child language acquisition.

9 Parents' eagerness to teach their 6-month-old children the prelinguistic routine 'bye bye' is *one evidence* of their desire to show that their baby is on its way to being a socialised person.
(Berko-Gleason 1988: 276)

Other divergences across varieties of Standard English frequently occur in verb phrase collocations. An example of such variation between native-speaker varieties appears in (10), taken from a handout that accompanied a lecture by a British linguist at the 1992 TESOL Convention in Seattle.

10 Options open to us are: … choosing to *miss out* a particular listing.

The phrasal verb *miss out* also occurs in American English, but not with the transitive meaning of 'omit' that it has in British English.

A similar difference between native-speaker and non-native varieties appears in (11), from the Arrival-Departure Card that is issued to foreign visitors by the Malaysian Immigration Department.

11 Citizens and permanent residents of Malaysia with valid entry permits and re-entry permits are not required to *fill* this card.

Travellers to the United States would more likely be requested to *fill out* a similar document; those entering Britain might be asked to *fill in* such a form (Schur 1987:135). Another possibility in Malaysian English, which occurs in neither British nor American English, is to *fill up* a form, as in (12), from a leading Malaysian English-language newspaper.

12 That way the forms would be *filled* and processed within minutes, rather than have the passengers *fill up* all the details while at the checkpoint.
(*The Sunday Star* March 31 1985: 2)

Similar cross-varietal differences occur in certain verb-plus-preposition collocations. This is illustrated by British English *approximate to* and *agree* in (13) and (14), taken from texts written by respected British scholars in the field of second language teaching.

13 The learner will only be able to show that his 'knowledge' of the text is *approximating to* that of the teacher through tests, reproduction, and answers to 'higher inference' questions.
(Porter and Roberts 1987: 182)
14 Examples at task level would include such things as *agreeing a* definition of the problem.
(Breen 1984: 56)

Synonymous sentences in American English would require only *approximating* in (13), but would require *agreeing on* in (14).

Once again, the same type of variation occurs between native speaker and non-native varieties, as illustrated by (15), from Zambia, and (16), from Singapore.

15 They were *discussing about* the proposed opening of a gym at the school when the head arrived.
(Chisanga 1989: 65)
16 China yesterday gave a cautious response to news that a Hong Kong protester drowned soon after jumping into rough seas from a tanker to *protest against* Japan's claim over the Diaoyu islands.
(*The Straits Times*, September 27 1996: 1).

The use of these prepositions after *discuss* and *protest* would be considered redundant by most speakers of Standard English in the United States. Yet some of these constructions are widespread across non-native varieties, such as *discuss about*, which is also reported as being commonly used in Nigeria, India, Malaysia, and the Philippines (Platt, Weber and Ho 1984).

Collocations of prepositions and nouns likewise diverge at times between British and American English, particularly in temporal and locative phrases, such as the British constructions with *at* and *in* in (17), (18), and (19), for which American English would substitute *on* in all three cases.

17 Closed *at the weekend.*
   (sign on door of Library, British Council, Brussels, April 1989)
18 Entrance *in Sherwood Street.*
   (Algeo 1988: 13)
19 Man: I'm looking for the nearest post office.
   Woman: There's one *in St Andrews Street.*
   (*Focus*, p. 17 [ESL coursebook prepared in collaboration with the Council of Europe, no date], Zurich: Eurocentres.)

Such variation also occurs in the non-native varieties. Examples (20) and (21), from Standard Singapore English as codified in the style sheet of Singapore's leading English-language newspaper, *The Straits Times*, follow the British form in (20) and reflect a further innovation in (21).

20 She lives *in 6th Avenue.*
   (Straits Times Press 1985: 4)
21 I live in an apartment *at Belmont Road.*
   (Straits Times Press 1985: 177)

Implications for testing non-native English proficiency

This analysis clearly suggests limits on how far it can be assumed that norms of Standard English in any one variety, native-speaker or non-native, extend to other varieties, native-speaker or non-native. A practical implication of this fact arises in the field of testing English proficiency. Awareness of the types of divergence that can occur between normative features in non-native varieties of English and corresponding norms in the native-speaker varieties is essential for accurately evaluating non-native speakers' proficiency in English in the world context. Since most speakers of non-native varieties acquire these varieties as a second language, examiners must try to distinguish *deficiencies* in the second language acquisition of English by these speakers (errors) from varietal *differences* in the speakers' usage resulting from their having previously learned and used such non-native normative features as those discussed above. This is particularly significant in the case of high-stakes, norm-referenced tests that are administered and heavily relied upon in international settings.

The importance of this distinction between deficiencies and differences becomes evident in assessing the international validity of certain test items on the Test of English for International Communication (TOEIC), which the Educational Testing Service (ETS) and, more recently, an ETS subsidiary have been administering since 1979. In its informational brochures, the TOEIC describes itself as 'designed to test the English language as it is used internationally in business, commerce, and industry' (Educational Testing Service 1990: 2). With over 800,000 candidates currently sitting for it annually, the TOEIC claims that it 'has become the international standard for measuring English-language proficiency' (Educational Testing Service 1992: 3).

Steven Stupak, who directed the TOEIC from 1983 to 1990, explains that the TOEIC 'is for people working internationally who need to be able to communicate in English with both native and non-native speakers' (Stupak nd: 1). Concerning the linguistic norms for this communication, Stupak continues, 'International English, for purposes of the TOEIC, is the English that one non-native speaker uses to communicate in English with another non-native speaker, in the context of business, commerce, and industry.' With a few exceptions, 'the language of the TOEIC is natural, native-speaker English' (Stupak nd: 3) which, according to Matthew Sindlinger, Associate Director of the TOEIC in 1989 (personal communication), strives to represent all of the native-speaker varieties.

However, this assumption that communication between non-native speakers is necessarily based on native-speaker norms raises problems of validity for the TOEIC. For example, in 1992, of the thirty countries in which ETS had established TOEIC administration sites, in five – Pakistan, Malaysia, Singapore, the Philippines, and Hong Kong – non-native varieties of English have been identified and described (Educational Testing Service 1992: 3). As the following examples demonstrate, certain items in past tests have not reflected the above findings that normative features in these varieties frequently diverge from native-speaker norms.

Example (22) is an item that appeared in a form of the TOEIC that has been retired. The candidates task here is to identify the italicised word or phrase that is ungrammatical.

22 The new *equipments shipped* from Hong-Kong will be *the only* items *on sale* this week.
(Educational Testing Service 1980: 28)
The segment that ETS considers ungrammatical here is *equipments*.

However, this construction results from the same process yielding (4) to (9) above, and, as reflected in (7), may well be acceptable to educated speakers of the Malaysian non-native variety of Standard English. Moreover, the possible acceptability of *equipments* in at least one domain of Standard American English is suggested in (8).

A similar problem occurs in item (23), taken from the same retired form of the TOEIC, in which the candidates task is once again to identify the italicised portion of the sentence that is ungrammatical.

23 *To obtain a full* refund on your purchase, you must *return back* the merchandise *within ten* days.
(Educational Testing Service 1980: 28)

In this case, the incorrect segment is *return back*, reflecting the fact that in Standard American English, the combination of *back* with *return* would be considered redundant. But as illustrated in (10) to (16) above, permissible collocations of verbs with particles or prepositions differ considerably across both native-speaker and non-native varieties. Again, it is possible that *return back* is a feature of Standard English in one or more non-native varieties, and would not appear ungrammatical to candidates who speak those varieties.

Yet another possibility of an item having questionable validity arises in (24), taken from a different retired form of the TOEIC.

24 Please *fill out* the enclosed form *to tell* us *how* you think *about* our service.
(Educational Testing Service 1989: 18)

The ungrammatical item here is *how*. However, the construction *fill out* might well also be unacceptable to a candidate accustomed to being requested to *fill* or *fill up* a form, as in (11) and (12) above. For such an examinee, (24) could be extremely difficult since it would contain two ungrammatical constituents.

Further empirical investigation is needed to identify the non-native varieties in which these problematic constructions in (22) to (24) occur regularly. But pending such research, it is reasonable to assume that each of these constructions *could* be considered acceptable in certain domains by educated speakers of Standard English in particular non-native varieties. Therefore, as measures of proficiency in Standard English around the world, these items cannot with much confidence be assumed to have content validity.

To get some idea of the difficulties that speakers of non-native varieties might have with (22) to (24), the reader is invited to supply the correct prepositions in items (25) to (27), which are taken from preparation materials for the standardised Primary School Leaving Examination (PSLE) in Singapore.

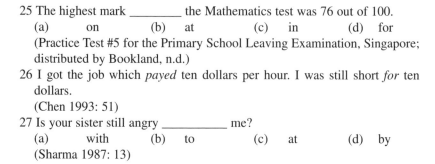

25 The highest mark _____ the Mathematics test was 76 out of 100.

    (a)   on   (b)   at   (c)   in   (d)   for

    (Practice Test #5 for the Primary School Leaving Examination, Singapore; distributed by Bookland, n.d.)

26 I got the job which *payed* ten dollars per hour. I was still short *for* ten dollars.

    (Chen 1993: 51)

27 Is your sister still angry _____ me?

    (a)   with   (b)   to   (c)   at   (d)   by

    (Sharma 1987: 13)

The correct answer to (25) is (c) *in*, but the norms for prepositions in Standard American English would dictate (a) *on*. Similarly, in (26), a speaker of Standard American English would realise that *paid* has been misspelled, but probably wouldn't know that the preposition that should replace *for* in Standard Singapore English would be *of* rather than *by* or no preposition at all, which would be the acceptable possibilities in the United States. In (27) the right answer is (a) *with*. However, Standard American English would allow either *with* or (c) *at* in this collocation; thus, a speaker of Standard American English encountering item (27) on a test would have two acceptable answers, the same dilemma that could confront some speakers of non-native varieties in answering item (24) above, from the TOEIC.

Clearly, items (25) to (27) would not be valid on a test of Standard English as used around the world. The point here is that just as clearly, items (22) through (24) likewise reduce the content validity of the TOEIC as a test to English as used internationally. Granted, it is likely that only a small percentage of the items included in any TOEIC form are affected by cross-varietal differences in norms; most items test features that are normative in Standard English in all native-speaker and non-native varieties, as in examples (1) to (3) above. But given the importance attributed to numerical scores in norm-referenced testing, only two or three items of questionable validity on a test form could jeopardise the ranking of candidates in a competitive test administration.

What is to be done? Actually, two short-term solutions are suggested in currently available ETS materials. The first solution is simply to identify problematic items and rewrite the stems or distractors so that only one answer is likely to be correct among educated English speakers around the world. This has been done in item (28), a revised form of item (24) that appeared on a subsequent form of the TOEIC.

28 Please return the *enclosed* form *to tell* us *how* you think about *our service*.
(Educational Testing Service 1993: 9)

In contrast to (24), this improved item is more likely to have only one grammatical error, regardless of the variety of Standard English in which the examinee has been educated. It is therefore probably a more valid measure of English proficiency than is item (24).

The second solution is to combine criterion-referenced, holistically-scored assessment with the current discrete-point format of the TOEIC in order to compensate for any remaining discrete-point items of questionable validity. An example of this occurs in (29), from an ETS-published set of range finders for the Test of Written English (TWE).

29 Contrary to the belief that it is safe, nuclear power has a way of destroying whole cities. It is not like a fire that can be put out with water or CO_2, but

special *equipments* have to be used.
(Educational Testing Service 1996: 41)

This paper received the highest possible score, a '6', despite its use of *equipments*, for which the same candidate could have been penalised on item (22) above.

Conclusion

The description of non-native varieties of English is still in its early stages. However, the data presented here and in the references cited provide substantial evidence (a) that many normative features of Standard English in these varieties differ from corresponding norms in the native-speaker varieties in the same ways that these constructions diverge across the native-speaker varieties, and (b) that such cross-varietal differences between native-speaker and non-native norms can have significant consequences for the testing of Standard English as a world language.

To date, relatively few linguistic features in specific non-native varieties have been determined to be actual norms on the basis of the still limited data that are available. Research on non-native varieties has not yet advanced to the point of being able to identify all, or even most, of the nativized features in any one variety. In some varieties particular features appear to be so systematic and widespread that, as Serpell (1982, in Chisanga 1989: 79) says of some features of English in Zambia,

> they are sufficiently well established in general usage to qualify for recognition as standard conversational idiom. Nothing more than a tradition of orthodoxy stands as an impediment to the accepting of these forms in suitable contexts within the school curriculum.

However, in other cases, as Kujore (1985:94) observes about English in Nigeria,

> *the situation in Nigeria at present is a far cry from the stage where it can be said that the norms, generally accepted, of what can be called 'Standard Nigerian English' (spoken and written) have been firmly established; the picture now seems to suggest that any such standard is, at best, in process of evolution.* (parentheses in original)

Nevertheless, despite the great deal that remains to be learned about the dynamics of change in norms for Standard English, the research that has been completed calls into question the validity of assuming in English proficiency assessment that certain features of native-speaker English are universally normative, and suggests strategies that can be used to improve the validity of these assessment instruments.

On a broader level, what has been learned thus far about non-native varieties clearly indicates that as the global spread of English continues and the percentage of the world's English speakers who use English non-natively increases, the forms and functions of English in non-native sociolinguistic contexts will continue to diversify. This diversification on a societal level is clearly a significant variable that can no longer be ignored in the measurement of English proficiency.

Notes

1 Among other countries where English serves in one or more of these domains are Bangladesh, Botswana, Brunei, Cameroon, Ethiopia, Gambia, Israel, Kenya, Lesotho, Liberia, Malawi, Malta, Mauritius, Myanmar, Namibia, Nauru, Pakistan, Seychelles, Sierra Leone, South Africa, Sri Lanka, Sudan, Swaziland, Tanzania, Tonga, Uganda, Western Samoa, and Zimbabwe (McCallen 1989: 7–9; Crystal 1997: 55–60).

2 Bamgbose (1998) observes that native-speaker and non-native varieties also differ significantly at the levels of pragmatics, style, and discourse. For a discussion of such differences, see B. Kachru (1986, 1997), Smith (1987), Cheshire (1991), and Y. Kachru (1992, 1997). For implications of these differences for assessing English proficiency, see Lowenberg (1993).

3 For further discussion of these heuristics for identifying non-native norms, see Lowenberg (1990, 1992).

4 Also of interest in example (7) is the innovation *upkeeping*, probably resulting from the same process that has produced *inputting* in the native-speaker varieties.

Suggested further reading

Cheshire, J. (Ed.) (1991) *English Around the World: Sociolinguistic Perspectives*. Cambridge: Cambridge University Press.
A geographically comprehensive collection, this volume includes separate sections on the varieties of English used in the UK and the USA, Ireland, Canada, New Zealand, Australia, South Asia, Southeast Asia and Hongkong, East Africa, Southern Africa, West Africa, the Caribbean, and the Pacific. Every section consists of a survey paper of the status and domains of use of English in the region, and three data-based case studies on particular varieties of English in the region. All of the surveys and case studies are written by authors with extensive research experience on the use of English in the region.

Kachru, B. B. (Ed.) (1992) *The Other Tongue: English Across Cultures* (2nd edition). Urbana, IL: University of Illinois Press.
This volume provides a thorough treatment of crucial theoretical and practical issues surrounding the spread of English as a world language. The nineteen chapters are organised according to six themes: Directions and Issues (including testing, second language acquisition research, and cross-varietal intelligibility); Forms and Functions (covering both second language and foreign language varieties of English); Question of a Standard; Literary Creativity; Discoursal Strategies; and World Englishes in the Classroom. Many of the chapters are written by authors who speak a non-native variety of English.

Platt, J., Weber, H. and Ho, M. L. (1984) *The New Englishes*. London: Routledge and Kegan Paul.
This is one of the few book-length examinations to date of the types of linguistic features and communicative strategies that are shared by the institutionalised non-native varieties of English. The volume's contents are based on the authors' own extensive research on English in Singapore and Malaysia and, for other regions, on their painstaking review of more than 150 other studies, over half of which have been written by speakers of non-native varieties. Separate chapters summarise research at the levels of phonology, morphology, lexis, syntax, style, and literature. Other chapters discuss the communicative functions and sociolinguistic status of non-native varieties, including implications for teaching English as a world language.

Smith, L. E. and Forman, M. L. (Eds.) (1997) *World Englishes 2000*. Honolulu University of Hawaii's Press. [Literary Studies East and West, Volume 14]
This volume is largely composed of the keynote and plenary papers presented at the Third International Conference on World Englishes, organized by the

International Association for World Englishes (IAWE), at the East-West Centre, Honolulu, in December 1996. The papers explore many of the crucial issues involving English as a world language at the end of the twentieth century, including concerns about the possible hegemony of English over other languages with which it comes in contact; political considerations that are often intertwined with attempts to maintain the dominance of native-speaker standards; strategies for identifying norms in non-native varieties of English and for compiling dictionaries incorporating these norms; the status of English-based pidgins and creoles; controversies surrounding the forms and functions of English in foreign-language contexts, particularly Japan; and challenges faced in native varieties. The final paper, 'World Englishes 2000: Resources for research and teaching', by Braj B. Kachru, 'is a state-of-the-art survey of the history and conceptualization of world Englishes, and a selected guide to the available resources on the various dimensions of this topic for research and teaching' (p. 209), including a comprehensive, fourteen-page bibliography current up to the end of 1997.

Tickoo, M. L. (Ed.) (1991) *Languages and Standards: Issues, Attitudes, and Case Studies*. Singapore: Regional Language Centre. [Anthology Series 26] This volume focuses almost exclusively on the variables and challenges involved in identifying the norms of Standard English in the institutionalized non-native varieties. The first section, 'Issues in Theory and Pedagogy', includes six chapters on the concept of Standard English, procedures for identifying norms, and implications for education. The second section, 'Issues in Implementation', contains five case studies from the Philippines, Singapore, Malaysia, India, and Australia, all written by users of these varieties. The third, and final, section, 'English in the World', consists of carefully articulated position papers from an on-going debate between Braj B. Kachru and Sir Randolph Quirk on the international status and consequences of norms for Standard English in non-native varieties.

References

Algeo, J. (1988) British and American grammatical differences. *International Journal of Lexicography* 1(1):1–31.

Bamgbose, A. (1998) Torn between the norms: Innovations in world Englishes. *World Englishes* 17(1):1–14.

Berko-Gleason, J. (1988) Language and socialisation. In Kessel, F. K. (Ed.) *The Development of Language and Language Researchers: Essays in Honour of Roger Brown*. Hillsdale, NJ: Lawrence Erlbaum Associates, Publishers: 269–80.

Breen, M. (1984) Process syllabuses for the language classroom. In Brumfit, C. J. (Ed.) *General English Syllabus Design*. Oxford: Pergamon Press. [ELT documents 118]

Chen, L. (1993) *Primary Six New PSLE Examination: English Practice Papers*. Singapore: Success Publications.

Cheshire, J. (Ed.) (1991) *English Around the World: Sociolinguistic Perspectives*. Cambridge: Cambridge University Press.

Chisanga, T. (1989) 'Non-problematic Zambianisms' and their implications for the teaching of English in Zambia. In Schmied, J. (Ed.) *English in East and Central Africa*. Bayreuth University. [African Studies Series 15]: 63–83.

Crystal, D. (1997) *English as a Global Language*. Cambridge: Cambridge University Press.

Educational Testing Service (1980) *Test of English for International Communication*. Princeton, NJ: ETS. [items from retired version provided by Educational Testing Service]

Educational Testing Service (1989) *Test of English for International Communication*. Princeton, NJ: ETS. [items from retired version provided by Educational Testing Service]

Educational Testing Service (1990) *Bulletin of Information, Test of English for International Communication*. Princeton, NJ: ETS.

Educational Testing Service (1992) *Test of English for International Communication* (introductory brochure). Princeton, NJ: ETS.

Educational Testing Service (1993) *Test of English for International Communication*. Princeton, NJ: ETS. [items from retired version provided by Educational Testing Service].

Educational Testing Service (1996) *Test of Written English Guide* (4th edition). Princeton, NJ: ETS.

Hymes, D. H. (1972) On communicative competence. In Pride, J.B. and Holmes J. (Eds.) *Sociolinguistics*. Harmondsworth: Penguin Books: 269–93.

Kachru, B. B. (1986) *The Alchemy of English*. Oxford: Pergamon Press. [reprinted by University of Illinois Press, Urbana, 1990]

Kachru, B. B. (1992a) Models for non-native Englishes. In Kachru B. (Ed.) (1992c): 48–74.

Kachru, B. B. (1992b) Meaning in deviation: Toward understanding non-native English texts. In Kachru B. B. (1992c): 301–26.

Kachru, B. B. (Ed.) (1992c). *The Other Tongue: English Across Cultures* (2nd edition). Urbana, IL: University of Illinois Press.

Kachru, B. B. (1997) World Englishes 2000: Resources for research and teaching. In Smith and Forman: 209–51.

Kachru, Y. (1992) Culture, style, and discourse: Expanding noetics of English. In Kachru, B. B. (1992c.): 340–52.

Kachru, Y. (1997) Culture and argumentative writing in world Englishes. In Smith and Forman: 48–67.

Kujore, O. (1985) *English Usage: Some Notable Nigerian Variations*. Ibadan: Evans Brothers Ltd.

Lotherington-Wolozyn, H. (1994) *Unintended pedagogy: Fiji's fledgling English television network as an English as a second language curriculum.* Paper presented at AILA/IRAAL International conference, Dublin, June 1994.

Lowenberg, P. (1990) Standards and norms for World Englishes: Issues and attitudes. *Studies in the Linguistic Sciences* 20(2): 123–37.

Lowenberg, P. (1992) Testing English as a world language: Issues in assessing non-native proficiency. In Kachru, B. B. (1992c): 108–21.

Lowenberg, P. (1993) Issues of validity in tests of English as a world language: Whose standards? *World Englishes* 12(1): 95–106.

McCallen, B. (1989) *English: A World Commodity*. London: The Economist Intelligence Unit.

Platt, J. Weber, J. and Ho, M. L. (1984) *The New Englishes.* London: Routledge and Kegan Paul.

Porter, D. and Roberts, J. (1987) Authentic listening activities. In Long, M. and Richards, J. (Eds.) *Methodology in TESOL*. New York, NY: Newbury House: 177–87.

Sahgal, A. (1991) Patterns of language use in a bilingual setting in India. In Cheshire : 299–307.

Schur, N. W. (1987) *British English, A to Zed*. New York, NY: Facts on File Publications.

Sharma, M. K. (1987) *Cannon 'N' Level Guide: Simulated Papers.* Singapore: Cannon International.

Shaw, W. (1981) Asian student attitudes toward English. In Smith, L. E. (Ed.) *English for Cross-cultural Communication*. New York, NY: St. Martin's Press: 108–22.

Smith, L. E. and M. L. Foreman (Ed.) (1987) *Discourse Across Cultures: Strategies in World Englishes*. Englewood Cliffs, NJ: Prentice-Hall.

Smith, L. E. (Eds.) (1997) *World Englishes 2000*. Honalulu.: University of Hawaii's Press (Library Studies East and West Volume 14), HI

Straits Times Press (1985) *Our Style: The Way We Use Words in The Straits Times*. Singapore: Straits Times Press, Ltd.

Strevens, P. (1992) English as an international language: Directions in the 1990s. In Kachru, B. B. (1992c): 27–74.

Stupak, S. A. (nd) *The TOEFL and the TOEIC Programs: Their Purpose, Design, Language, Scoring, Score Interpretation and Administration*. Princeton, NJ: ETS.

Tay, M. W. J. and Gupta, A. F. (1983) Towards a description of Standard Singapore English. In Noss, R. B. (Ed.), *Varieties of English in Southeast Asia*. Singapore: SEAMEO Regional Language Centre. [Anthology Series 11]: 173–189.

Tickoo, M. L. (1991a) Introduction. In Tickoo (1991b): iv–x.

Tickoo, M. L. (Ed.) (1991b) *Languages and Standards: Issues, Attitudes and Case Studies*. Singapore: Regional Language Centre. (Anthology Series 26)

Trudgill, P. (1983). *Sociolinguistics* (revised edition). Harmondsworth: Penguin Books.

Trudgill, P. and Hannah, J. (1985) *International English: A Guide to Varieties of Standard English* (2nd edition). London: Edward Arnold.

8 Assessing the communication skills of veterinary students: Whose criteria?

Dan Douglas
Ron Myers
Iowa State University

Abstract

A fundamental problem in specific purpose language testing involves the selection of assessment criteria that adequately reflect those employed in the target language use situation and yet are interpretable as evidence of communicative language ability. In this chapter, an ethnomethodological technique was used to investigate the 'indigenous assessment criteria' used by veterinary professionals and applied linguists to evaluate the interviewing skills of veterinary students. Videotapes of the students engaging in a simulated patient/client interview were played for a group of veterinary professionals and a separate group of applied linguists. Each group was asked to discuss the students' performances and to arrive at a group judgement of their proficiency. The resulting commentaries were analyzed to derive a set of assessment criteria. A number of problems in the establishment of specific purposes language assessment criteria are discussed.

Background

A fundamental problem in specific purpose language testing involves the selection of scoring criteria that are interpretable as evidence of communicative language ability in tests that only simulate 'real-world' communicative tasks, yet are representative of the real-world criteria that are employed to judge task fulfilment in the target language use (TLU) situations. McNamara (1996), for example, argues for a continuum of language performance tests, from *strong* to *weak*, based on the degree to which the assessment criteria reflect real-world criteria, of which *language ability* may be only a part. Close to the *strong* end of the continuum would be *work sample* assessments such as the 'Classroom Observation Schedule' employed by Elder (1993) to assess the English proficiency of graduates from non-English-medium universities training to be maths or science teachers in

Australian secondary schools. The assessment criteria were based on an extensive observation and analysis of both native and non-native teachers in maths and science classrooms. Toward the *weak* end of the continuum would be a test such as the *Oral Proficiency Interview* (Clark and Clifford 1988), in which the scoring criteria are entirely linguistic and are based on a theoretical framework of what general abilities second language users should have. Thus, tests may fall at different points on the strong/weak continuum depending on the closeness of the assessment criteria used to the criteria employed for assessing non-simulated, real-world target tasks. The purpose of the present paper is to explore the usefulness of a technique for determining assessment criteria that would fall at an 'intermediate to strong' segment of the continuum: the 'indigenous assessment criteria' employed in the assessment of the communication skills of veterinary students.

Jacoby and McNamara (1996) outline an approach to investigating the criteria used by subject specialists in assessing the communicative performances of apprentices in academic and vocational fields. Performance assessment practices are part of any professional culture, from formal, gatekeeping examination procedures, to informal, ongoing evaluation built into everyday interaction with novices, colleagues, and supervisors (Jacoby 1998). Indeed, professional development is just a specialized form of socialization, a general process long recognized as the vehicle through which culturally specific language, discourse, cognition, and skills are transmitted and developed through social interaction. (See Jacoby 1998 for a review of the literature.) Competent professionals are able to articulate assessments of language performances to colleagues and to the persons being assessed, the criteria employed, and ways in which a performance might be improved. The criteria are accessible to researchers primarily by means of an analysis of the discourse in which they are displayed, and therefore the researchers will need to engage in very careful study of the assessment interaction and discourse in the target language use situation, with help from discourse analysts and from specialists in the target field. For example, Jacoby has studied the indigenous assessment criteria employed in a physics research group preparing for conference presentations; McNamara and colleagues are studying the indigenous assessment criteria articulated by medical practitioners. The investigation of indigenous assessment is still a very new, undeveloped possibility for specific purpose language testing, but the expectation is that by studying various types of assessment activities in professional and vocational settings, we may be able to establish criteria for the specific purpose testing enterprise. Jacoby and McNamara (1996) caution, however, that there are difficult problems associated with applying these indigenous criteria, derived from highly specific, dynamic contexts of use, to language tests, no matter how situationally authentic the tests may be.

The present study is an investigation of the various criteria that are employed by veterinary professionals in performance evaluations of the communication skills of their students in interviewing clients about sick animals, including the 'official' criteria which appear in a college assessment document, and criteria as articulated by the veterinary professionals, by the veterinary students themselves, and by a group of applied linguists. At issue is the question of what criteria can and should be used to evaluate communication skills in specific purpose settings.

The veterinary training program

The College of Veterinary Medicine at Iowa State University runs a 'problem-based' alternative curriculum alongside the more traditional 'lecture/exam' curriculum. In the alternative curriculum, called the Rural and General Practice Option (RGPO), the students begin working with animals and their owners (clients) from their first year and, instead of, as in the more traditional curriculum, attending lectures, reading assigned material and taking written examinations, are given series of animal health-related problems, typically written clinical cases. They must identify, investigate, and learn about pertinent aspects of the problem and present the results in discussion groups, termed 'tutorials'. Periodically, they are evaluated by means of performance assessments called Individual Process Assessments (IPA), in which a simulated client – for example, a cattle producer, a pet owner, or a horse breeder – presents a complaint about a sick animal. Each student must interview the client to elicit a history of the complaint, conduct a physical examination of a live, but not actually sick, animal, and interpret simulated written necropsy and laboratory reports to arrive at an understanding of the case in terms of faculty-generated learning issues. The interview and physical examination are videotaped, and the students are provided both with immediate formative feedback on their performances during the assessment process and later summative assessment at the conclusion of the entire procedure. Following the interview and physical examination, the students must write a summary of the case, including a plan of treatment, present the case orally to the faculty evaluators, and self-assess their oral and written presentations. They receive feedback from the faculty at several stages of the IPA procedure.

The specific focus of the current study is the assessment of 'interviewing skills' during the history-taking phase of the interaction with the simulated client. The research question is the following: what are the relevant criteria for assessing interviewing skills in this specific purpose communicative context? We will consider a number of different perspectives in answering this question: that of the veterinary professionals involved in the assessment, that of the students themselves, and that of a group of applied linguists experienced in the assessment of communicative language ability. Our goal is to explore the notion of indigenous assessment criteria in the context of a particular veterinary client interview situation and to attempt to derive a list of generalized criteria that might be of use in other similar specific purpose language assessments.

ISU 'official' criteria

The IPA used at ISU was based on an assessment program developed at the University of New Mexico School of Medicine (UNM–SOM 1992; see Appendix 1). The student is presented with a brief 'scenario' establishing a context prior to an interview with the simulated client. The scenario used in the current study is reproduced as Figure 8.1. The student conducts a client interview, collecting an appropriate case history. This interview performance is assessed with a view to developing and improving oral communication skills, especially in the context of veterinary medicine. In adapting the UNM procedure, veterinary faculty were asked what characteristics graduates from the curriculum should have. *Learning of content* was certainly desired, 'but a long list of equally desirable traits was also valued, such as problem solving, critical analysis, communication (written and oral), veterinary skills, attitudes, behaviors, reliability and so on' (Flaming and Myers 1995:1). The resulting IPA rating form for interviewing skills contains 16 characteristics (see Appendix 2), namely *introduction, establishing rapport, organisation, transitional statements, question type, duplication, summarizing, use of jargon, verification, challenging the client, client understanding and education, admitting lack of knowledge, closing the interview, tone of voice, eye contact* and *empathetic statements.*

Figure 8.1
Individual process assessment scenario

Individual Process Assessment -- RGPO, Spring 1996

The Scenario:

You are a partner in a mixed animal practice in a small town in southern Iowa. It is August and the weather is hot and muggy. One Friday afternoon you get a call from Tricia Hansen, owner-operator of a cow-calf operation. You do very little work for her, except for occasional dystocias and a few other emergencies, and are surprised to hear from her. She has told your receptionist that she has several cows that aren't doing well and one that is dead and "could you please hurry".

Part 1. Client Interview and patient examination.

In Part 1, you will meet "Tricia Hansen" and will conduct an interview in which you will find out more about the case and elicit from her information you need to deal with her problems. You will also be presented with one of her animals to examine and will use the information obtained (and explanatory information also supplied to you) to proceed with the case.

Your client interview and patient examination will be videotaped and you will receive immediate feedback from the "client" and from an independent evaluator.

This is the 'official' set of criteria. Each skill category is to be rated on a four-point scale: *ideal, acceptable, attempted, not done*. However, in actual practice, it turned out, the professor who actually evaluated the interview skills of the students used the following, quite different system:

- 4 = Superlative
- 3 = Better than competent
- 2 = Competent
- 1 = Cause for concern
- 0 = Unacceptable

He could also select half points, e.g. 3.5. He then converted his score on the above 5-point scale to a percentage scale, and reported the results on a decimal scale:

- 4.0 = 100% = 10
- 3.5 = 92% = 9.2
- 3.0 = 87% = 8.7
- 2.5 = 82% = 8.2
- 2.0 = 77% = 7.7
- 1.5 = 72% = 7.2
- 1.0 = 67% = 6.7
- 0.5 = 62% = 6.2
- 0.0 = 0% = 0.0

The end result, then, was a score on a 9-point decimal scale. One of the researchers asked one of the RGPO informants if he could obtain a copy of the criteria that the evaluator had used to place students on the scale and his reply was: 'I'd like to try, but I don't think he would loan me his brain for copying!' So, we are left with an official set of criteria and an unofficial, and unretrievable, set which was actually used to evaluate the students' communication skills. In order to investigate the main question of the relevant criteria for assessing interviewing skills in this specific purpose communicative context, the current study was conducted.

Current study

Subjects

Seven of the students who were evaluated in Spring 1996 agreed to participate in the study, four men and three women. They were all first-year students in their second semester in the program. The score on the IPA ranged from 9.2 to 7.7. Videotapes of their IPA interviews were obtained and each student reviewed her/his videotape with one of the researchers, providing commentary on aspects of their performances that they found 'interesting, unusual, good or problematic' (See Douglas and Selinker 1994 for a discussion of this methodology.) Of these seven, three were selected, on the basis of their evaluation score, for review by the veterinary professionals and the applied linguists. The top scoring student, a middle student and a low scoring student were selected. All three were men[1]: Bud, who scored a 9.2, Jason, who scored 8.7, and Beavis, who scored 7.7. An excerpt from Bud's interview transcript is provided to follow:

Student interview transcript:

Bud: Time: 6:13   Rating: 9.2

Bud:	Tricia
Tricia:	yes
Bud:	you called about a problem related to a cow dying and other cowsthat aren't doing well?
Tricia:	exactly
Bud:	okay – tell me what you what you noticed on particularly thethat died tell me all the abnormalities you you've seen
Tricia:	well y'know honestly I have the cows out on pasture an' I can't say f'r sure that the cow that died is - was one a the ones that was acting sick
Bud:	okay
Tricia:	but let me tell you the sick ones 'r just sort of lethargic they're hanging back behind the rest of the herd
Bud:	how many are we talkin' about here? - when you say the sick ones
Tricia:	mmm – prob'ly four 'r five=
Bud:	four 'r five out of
Tricia:	three hundred – about three hundred=
Bud:	=out of three hundred – 'n all three hundred all three hundred cows are uh on one pasture?
Tricia:	yeah
Bud:	okay – what uh condition is the pasture in?
Tricia:	real good
Bud:	what type of pasture is it?
Tricia:	uh – it's an improved pasture just uh=
Bud:	=which means?
Tricia:	=we just moved 'em off a more native grass pasture in the last few weeks 'n this pasture that they're on now is uhm brome fescue primarily
Bud:	brome and fescue – and you're sayin' they have not been on this pasture a long time before?

Tricia:	a few weeks=
Bud:	=they – so they were moved like in the middle part of July

Note that Bud began the interview with no introduction, immediately asking for information about abnormalities in the cow that died. He then moved to questions about the number of sick cows, and quickly on to details about the pasture. He was an aggressive interviewer, almost attacking the client in his efforts to extract information quickly. The retrospective commentary provided by each student on his own tape became part of the data, and was analyzed in the same way as that provided by the veterinarians and the applied linguists. An extract from Beavis's commentary on his own performance is shown in Italics below:

> Beavis: okay – uhm – y'said
> they were laggin behind
> – was there any other
> signs 'r anything about
> these in particular you
> noticed

Well I'm asking these questions just to get more specifics – try to reach a better diagnosis with a little more specific science so I know what I'm dealin' with I guess

> Tricia: uh – the only other real
> strange thing was that uh
> the one that I have penned
> up for you to take a look at
> when I got her in the pen
> initially she sort of uh
> started acting real
> belligerent – she was
> chasin' after me 'n running
> into the walls 'n

see if I would've known – if I woulda heard that now I would that that's an anem- possibly an anemic state – that belligerence – what that means – at the time I didn't know that but if I were to hear that now I would know – that that would suggest in my mind some certain diseases maybe

Here, Beavis comments on his reason for pursuing a particular line of questioning, and also on his technical knowledge base, which was at that time not very extensive. In their commentaries, the students often expressed concern about the format of the IPA exercise, noting that it was a bit unrealistic because, as Jason put it, 'I also knew that she knew', referring to the fact that the simulated client already knew what the cows' 'illness' was.

A summary of the students' criteria follows:

Table 8.1

Summary of students' criteria

Categories	Examples
Introduction	I don't know if i introduced myself in that uh in that introduction
Rapport	I maybe should have said who I was or uh commented about the weather or the start of the baseball season 'r NBA playoffs whatever I mean I just went right into asking her a quesyion - I shoulda broken the ice a little bit
Interviewing skill	well I'm asking these questions just to get more specifics - try to reach a better diagnosis with a little more specific science so I know what I'm dealin' with I guess
Structure	I really didn't need to ask that question she told me before that they were on pasture
Phrasing	uh that was kinda stuttered - staggered - it wasn't a kind of well phrased question
Follow-up	I tried to get her to elaborate as much as she could on some major areas
Level	I think I'm doin' a good job talking on her level beacuse that's the same level that i'm at
Pace	I maybe could have slowed the pace down a little bit uh to allow both she and I to thimk a little more about other possibilities
Knowledge	see if I would've known - if I woulda heard that now I would that that's an anem-possibly an anemic state - that belligerence
Coverage	I think I did a decent job of turning over most of the stones that coulda been turned over - the one exception being vaccination

These are issues that appeared to be of importance to the students in reviewing their own performances. Out of a total of 33 comments in ten categories, they made only one or two comments about most topics, but they made 13 comments about their skill at interviewing and six about their level of knowledge. This suggests that they are aware of their problems in these two areas, and *because* they lack such knowledge and skills, they are unable to, and obviously do not, comment very much on such areas as *introduction, rapport, structure,* and *phrasing* – all areas that were commented on by the professional veterinarians and the applied linguists, as we will see – which brings us to a discussion of the research procedure.

Procedure

Four veterinary professionals were asked to review the videotapes of the three selected students. The group included James, professor of Veterinary

Pathology and one of the founders of the RGPO program, Siegfried, professor of Veterinary Clinical Sciences and Chief of the Bovine Section, Tristan, a veterinary immunologist and RGPO Program Co-ordinator, and Helen, a D.V.M. and graduate of the ISU vet school, now doing graduate work in neurobiology. James and Tristan devised the IPA task for this evaluation, Siegfried was the evaluator, and Helen was the simulated client.

The four professionals were asked to watch each of the three videotapes and discuss each student's performance among themselves. They could stop the tape at any point to discuss a particular point and rewind and review as much as they needed to. The researcher asked them to discuss each tape in as much detail as they wished, but to arrive at a group consensus on an evaluation of each student, using whatever scale they wished, before moving on to the next one. In fact they rewound a tape only once to review a concluding section of one interview; they took notes during each interview and discussed the performance based on their notes. The discussions, which were recorded on videotape, lasted from about 30 to 50 minutes. The researcher turned on the recording equipment and left the room for the duration of the discussions so the vets would be talking with each other rather than with the applied linguist.

The same procedure was used with the applied linguist informants. They were all professional applied linguists, all women: Jo, Beth, and Meg are involved in language testing as researchers and practitioners, while Amy is a discourse analyst. Their comments were rather shorter than those of the vets, ranging from 15 to 25 minutes per videotape.

The commentary from all the informants, students, vets, and applied linguists. was transcribed and analyzed as outlined by Jacoby (1998):

1 Each feedback session was analyzed for the various comments raised or alluded to by group members, for the criteria mentioned in relation to specific behaviors during each interview, and
2 list of specific comments was collapsed into a smaller, more generalized list of assessment criteria.

As Jacoby pointed out, the second step is often problematic, since comments tend to focus on each particular performance and are highly context embedded. In the present study, we attempted to use terminology provided by the informants themselves to categorize the commentaries. As Selinker and Douglas (1989) point out, sometimes informants will provide names of domains of talk they are engaged in or which are important to them. Interestingly, the veterinarians provided clearer terminology for categories than did either the students or the applied linguists, as we will see below. In another approach to analyzing the commentary, we used the 16 categories provided by the 'official' IPA rating form as a way of organizing. It proved to be possible to place most of the commentary into the IPA categories, but as we will see later, there were a number of areas in the commentary that did not fit into any IPA grouping.

Results

Here we will look at an excerpt from the commentary provided by the veterinarians and the applied linguists, and the results of the analysis. First, the veterinarians' commentary:

Veterinarians' commentary:

James:	who wants to start?
Helen:	you wrote a lot
Tristan:	I just – usually I keep track of what they did so I c'n – somtn'n that catches my mind I c'n catches my mind 'r eye – jus' make a note of it – In an ideal situation when I saw him come in – he very briefly said who he was'n i've heard you've had some problems 'n I think its b- a good idea to establish more rapport with the client – more chit chat if you will than just – develop a pattern of talking so that there gets to be a relationship established before OK what's your problem sort of thing that's a little bit how I felt that was a little bit more direct than while he was there – he didn't establish eye contact with you for a while an' then once he settled into the interview process he began to
Helen:	would you a w'... this was the first time they ever did anything like this – would you expect that of them – having never been through this before?
James:	uh ... may or may not – I think – I think that's a sort of oil discourse people=
Helen:	='ts like a personal=
James:	=normally should be doing y' know=
Helen:	=right=
James:	=th't – y' know – how's it going – nice day today – that sort of thing – had a heck of a time gettin' up y'r lane here b't [laugh] ... now that I'm here – anything like that to sort of ease into the situation rather th'n to just abruptly start ... uh – uh – otherwise his demeanor was quite professional
Siegfried:	yeah, I think Helen prob'ly has a good point – to my way of thinkin' that's a – that's one of those professional skills prob'ly most of our new graduates lack – they don't develop the gift of blarney 'til they've been out a while=

James:	[laugh]
Siegfried:	='n of course some of the seasoned guys 'r more blarney than actual=
James:	=th'n substance yeah=
Siegfried:	=th'n actual substance but a lot'a times that's what clients are lookin' for too but I think m- the majority of new graduates cut right to the chase immediately because that's where the pressure is y' know – am I gonna be able to solve this problem – I need to get hoppin' on that 'n – regardless of how the Packers did 'r

Notice that an important issue in this excerpt is the interviewer's level of rapport with the client and how the students often lack 'the gift of blarney' and feel pressured to get as much information as rapidly as they can, as indeed we saw in the excerpt from Bud's interview. Below is a summary of the criteria discussed by the veterinarians in their commentary on all three student performances.

Table 8.2

Summary of veterinary professors' criteria

Categories	Examples
Introduction	none of 'em had a very good introduction
Rapport	no time spent on establishing rapport
Demeanor	he displays professional demeanor
Conversational style	a very animated conversationalist
Knowledge base	really competent about his knowledge base
Follow up/ elicitation	really strong follow-up questions
Phrasing	he phrased it very well
Level	didn't talk down to her at all
Pace	just got into it so deep 'n so fast
Clarification	made sure he understood what he was saying
Structure	he'd lost the structure of what he was doing
Coverage	he spent so much time asking about the pasture 'n didn't even touch on vaccination history or reproduction history
Appearance	they all look clean 'n well groomed
Summary/ conclusion	he summarized what the problem was very well

Of 13 categories, and a total of 151 comments, those commented on most by the veterinarians were demeanor (27 comments), rapport (19 comments), and coverage (18 comments). This does not mean that these categories are those that would in fact be given the most weight as indigenous criteria for the assessment of communication skills, but it does suggest that, at least at this level of student training, these are characteristics of the performances that caught the judges' eye, so to speak. It is also worth commenting on the sheer breadth of commentary – how many different categories of characteristics were touched upon by the informants, including some that, as we shall see, were not touched upon by the applied linguists, e.g. level, pace, and appearance.

We now turn to an excerpt from the commentary provided by the applied linguists:

Applied linguists' commentary:

Amy:	I had the sense he got more information
Jo:	he was busy writing – I dunno – all he was writing was pastures – I mean it seemed to take him forever to write whatever it was
Meg:	he looked at her too
Amy:	mm-hmm
Beth:	'n he said okay
Jo:	but the interesting thing to me was that she was saying more to him than she did to the other guy
Meg:	mm-hmm
Jo:	I mean whether that was because he was being more com – y' know – asking the questions more – differently
Meg:	you'd have to go back 'n look at the transcript to see if they asked different – if they asked uh y' know the same question 'n she responded – it's real hard to always respond always the same way
Jo:	oh absolutely – but lagging behind – I don't really know what it means lagging behind
Beth:	when the herd's
Jo:	moving along?
Beth:	yeah 'n some are just goin' a little slow 'n
Jo:	cuz the other guy she said they were depressed didn't she?
Amy:	lethargic – lagging behind – those 'r all good describers
Jo:	it seems to me depressed cattle 'r different
	[laughter]
Beth:	kinda blue
Jo:	right [laugh] I have a great picture of depressed cattle
Beth:	so well this guy was good with his y' know framing kind of language but as far as the substance an' the follow up it was the same thing with the – okay t' sum up 'n then he said almost nothing there

The applied linguists, in this excerpt, discuss a variety of categories of criteria: the amount of information obtained by the student (including 'substance' and 'follow-up'), his rapport with the client ('he looked at her' 'he said okay', and 'this guy was good with … his framing kind of language"), consistency of information provided by the simulated client ('it's real hard to always respond always the same way'), and the meaning of technical terminology ('I don't really know what it means lagging behind'). A summary of their comment on all three students follows in Table 8.3.

Table 8.3

Summary of applied linguists' criteria

Categories	Examples
Opening	that was a nice opening
Framework	he doesn't give any framework t' her
The way he asked the question	how do you do reproduction? i don't think that's the way a vet would ask that question
Getting information	he does get some information
Clarification	he repeated some of her – some things she had said to make sure that he got it straight
Authority/ confidence	he had more authority at the end
Engagement	he doesn't look at all engaged
Appropriacy	inappropriate responses
Follow-up	he doesn't follow-up
Duration	it seemed to me that that was much longer – that interview
Knowledge	he should have known that they are – that they were not milk cows
Content	but the content – he didn't ask about the water
Summary	right at the end he summed it up

Of the 117 comments in 13 categories, the most numerous comments made by the applied linguists were in areas of *framework* (20 comments), *getting information* (20 comments), and *content* (19 comments). Again, of course, we can make no claims about relative importance. Also like the veterinarians, the applied linguists commented on a wide variety of characteristics, including some that the veterinarians did not: *duration* and *appropriacy*.

Table 8.4 presents a summary of the criteria named by the three informant groups – the veterinary professionals, the students, and the applied linguists. Where possible, the names of the categories are those employed by the informants themselves in the course of providing their commentary. Where that terminology varied between informant groups, we have tried to relate them in terms of meaning.

Table 8.4
Summary of criteria

Vet Professionals	Vet Students	Applied Linguists
Introduction*	Introduction	Opening*
Rapport*	Interviewing skill	Getting information*
Demeanor*		Authority/confidence*
Knowledge base*	Knowledge*	Knowledge*
Follow-up/ elicitation*	Follow-up	Follow-up*
Phraseology*	Phraseology	The way he asks the questions*
Level	Level*	
Pace*	Pace*	Duration*
Clarification		Clarification
Structure*	Structure	Framework*
Coverage*	Coverage	Content*
Appearance*		
		Appropriacy*
Conversational style		Engagement*
Summary*	Last section of the interview*	Summary*

* Name provided by participants
Shaded cells: categories most commented on by informants

What is immediately striking about this table is the degree of overlap in categories. All three groups of informants discussed quite similar criteria overall in reviewing the videotaped performances, although, as we have seen, each group had more to say about some categories than others.

Finally, we analyzed the commentary from the three informant groups, using as an organizer the 16 categories in the 'official' assessment criteria in the IPA procedure. The result of that analysis is shown as Table 8.5, with examples of the indigenous criteria shown rather than the names given by the informants:

Table 8.5

Comparison of official and indigenous criteria

"Official Criteria"	Vet Professionals	Students	Applied Linguists
Introduction	none of 'em had a very good introduction	I don't know if I introduced myself in that uh in that introduction	He asked if he could call her Tricia
Establishing Rapport	a good idea to establish more rapport with the client – more chit chat		he doesn't look at all engaged
Oraganization	the interview has various components to it – it's got an overall structure	just knowing what the element of what's good is	it didn't seem to me that he went in with a plan
Transitional Statements	he tied things together well	kinda moved from one point of the interview to another 'n I told her now this is what we're gonna focus on	this guy was good with his y'know framing kind of language
Questioning skills: Type of question	let you elaborate on it rather than givin' you forced choices	instead of let her elaborate from scratch I gave her a suggestion	he really was putting words into her mouth
Questioning Skills: Duplication	there's some redundancy to some of the questions	I really didn't need to ask that question she told me before that they were on pasture	seemed like he kept going back
Questioning Skills: Summarizing	he summarized what the problem was very well	tried to sum up what she said – I think I coulda done that throughout maybe more for each section	right at the end he summed it up
Questioning Skills: Use of Jargon	didn't talk down to her at all	I think I'm doin' a good job talking on her level	
Questioning Skills: Verification	really strong follow-up questions	I kinda clarified my question – tried to get to a specific	he was able to keep pursuing the stuff about the pasture
Challenging the client	he asked it in a fairly non-judgmental way		
Client understanding and education	he like summarized the whole way through	When I say her I mean a producer – a producer who doesn't have a wide 'r a high breadth of experience in diseases	
Admitting lack of knowledge	he asked what the wormer was – I'm not familiar with that;	if I was a practicing veterinarian 'n didn't know something I'd maybe asked to see the package	he does admit later another drug he that he doesn't know what it is
Closing the interview	the wrap-up where he did inquire about do you have any theories	at that last uh section of the interview I didn't know how to interpret it	he said do you have any theories 'n that's a smart thing to do
Tone of voice Eye contact	didn't seem nervous he didn't establish eye contact with you for a while		his tone of voice he looked at her too
Empathetic statement	he has the ability to convey the impression he's very attentive to your problem		he was being reasonably sympathetic

We were struck by the fact that the informants touched upon all 16 of the IPA skill characteristics, although some groups did not comment on all areas. The amount of overlap among the groups is also striking, though again, each group had its own priorities. There were a number of areas not included in the IPA criteria that were commented on by the informants: *demeanor/authority/*

confidence, knowledge base, timing, coverage, phraseology, and *appearance.* This raises the question of whether the 'official' criteria need to be amended to include these categories.

Discussion and conclusion

In a forthcoming book on specific purpose language testing (Douglas, in press), it is suggested that investigations of indigenous assessment criteria be a part of the study of target language use situations in all LSP testing development enterprises. This is a bold, perhaps foolhardy, suggestion since the field of indigenous assessment is still so new and untried. As Jacoby and McNamara (1996) have warned, it is still far from certain that the exercise will bear any useable fruit in the form of generalizable assessment criteria. The present study has gone very little beyond where Jacoby and McNamara left the notion in 1996. However, we have learned something, we believe:

1 We've seen that the methodology can produce a generalized list of assessment criteria. However, the list presented here is quite different from that produced by Jacoby (1998) in her work with a physics research group. This may reinforce the caution expressed by Jacoby and McNamara (1996): the more assessment criteria are derived from task-specific and profession-specific real-world concerns, the more they run the risk of being less generally useful beyond their specific context.

2 We've seen that the criteria articulated by the vets, the applied linguists, and the students emphasize somewhat different characteristics. The vets stressed (1) the professional relationship with the client: *I think he really engages the person; his demeanor was quite professional; didn't talk down to her at all; some clients would balk at some of what he homed in on;* and (2) content knowledge: *he just didn't have the knowledge base on a lot a that; not broad enough in his questioning strategies.*
The applied linguists, on the other hand, focused on language, particularly (1) framework: *it didn't seem to me that he went in with a plan; he doesn't give any framework t' her; he doesn't use any language to show that organization; he did give some backchanneling too*; and (2) the construct to be measured: *he got some information but that's not what we're looking at – we're looking at his – skill in interviewing; are we including in interviewing the amount and kind of information gained?*
The students emphasized their own knowledge base and the authenticity of the test format itself: *it seems like we evaluate these things after we do them but didn't beforehand; if I was really a doctor I should have known – but I also knew that she knew; obviously it's a staged situation but y' know I maybe should have said who I was; you'd better give me a few more clues because I'm obviously lost.*

3 We have seen that while all the 'official' assessment criteria were discussed to some extent by the informants, there were nevertheless areas not covered by the IPA rating form that were mentioned in the feedback commentaries. Thus, our investigation of indigenous assessment criteria has suggested some additional categories of criteria that should be considered in revising the IPA rating form.

4 There is a great deal of similarity in the criteria that all three groups discussed. This is particularly striking in the case of the applied linguists, who had not seen the 'official' criteria at all prior to their commentaries; yet they mentioned criteria in all but three of the 16 categories: use of jargon, challenging the client and client understanding and education.

So, to return to the original question: whose criteria? We believe that we must investigate the possibility that the criteria of all three stakeholder groups might be relevant to the assessment of specific purpose language ability: those of the test takers themselves for what they can tell us about affective and procedural characteristics; those of applied linguists for what they can tell us about the construct to be measured – specific purpose language ability and strategic competence; and those of professionals in the target-specific purpose area for what they can tell us about the importance of content knowledge, the relationship of the professional with the client, and the level of professional socialization evident in the discourse. It is unlikely that we will be able to use any single set of criteria for specific purpose assessment, but rather will have to adapt and blend criteria from various perspectives for differing test purposes. For example, some of the criteria that the informant groups discussed might be considered for inclusion in the Veterinary College IPA Rating Scale. For language testing purposes, however, some of the criteria would appear to be irrelevant. For example, it seems unlikely that a specific purpose language test would ever include 'appearance' as one of its assessment criteria, yet that was an important aspect of the veterinarians' assessment of the students' overall interview performance! Nevertheless, knowing that piece of information may be of help in the interpretations we want to make of language performance in the target situation. How all of these perspectives can mesh in the production of specific purpose language assessment criteria is the work of the new millennium, but we are convinced that we need to make the effort. The more we can learn about the indigenous criteria employed in the target language use situation, the better we will be able to interpret test performance in relation to it. As McNamara puts it, 'the point is to get test developers to be clearer about what they are requiring of test takers and raters, and to think through the consequences of such requirements' (1996: 45).

Notes

1 Since Bud was the only student who scored in the 90s, we decided to select men as the other two subjects as well.
2 In fact, while reviewing his interview performance videotape, Bud referred to the IPA procedure as 'sleuth work' and indicated how much he had enjoyed the challenge.
3 We are indebted to Sally Jacoby (personal communication) for the method employed in this study – though she may be appalled at the use to which we've put her suggestions!

Suggested further reading

Jacoby, S. and McNamara, T. (1996) *Locating Competence.* Paper presented at the Annual Conference of the American Association for Applied Linguistics, Chicago, March.
In this important paper (soon to be published), Jacoby and McNamara discuss the notion of 'indigenous assessment criteria' as they explore possibilities for deriving criteria for assessing specific purpose language test performances so that they reflect what counts as communicative competence in target language use situations. They suggest that locating assessment criteria employed in target professional settings may prove productive for establishing criteria for specific purpose language testing.

McNamara, T. (1996) *Measuring Second Language Performance.* London: Longman.
McNamara introduces the reader to the theory and practice of performance assessment in language testing. He reviews research and development activities in such areas as performance test design, raters and rating scales, test analysis techniques, and the interpretation of test performance. As a model for the design and implementation of performance tests, McNamara refers to the development of the Occupational English Test, an Australian performance test for medical practitioners.

Douglas, D. and Selinker, L. (1994) Research methodology in context-based second language research. In E. Tarone, S. Gass, and A. Cohen (Eds.), *Methodologies for Eliciting and Analyzing Language in Context.* pp. 119–131.
In this paper, Douglas and Selinker elaborate a number of methodological principles for the study of second language acquisition in contexts of use, integrating features from 'grounded' ethnography, subject-specialist informant procedures, and discourse analysis. Three types of relevant data are proposed: primary data collected from the subjects, commentary by the subjects on the primary data, and expert commentary on the data by professionals in relevant fields. They illustrate the application of these principles in two case studies.

Elder, C. (1993) How do subject specialists construe classroom language proficiency? *Language Testing* 10: 235–254.

Elder wrestles with the question of whether 'linguistically naive' subject specialists may be better equipped than language experts to judge the effectiveness of communicative performance in specific fields. She found significant correlations between ratings of maths and science teachers' overall communicative effectiveness by ESL teachers and subject specialists. However, she found differences between the two groups in their ratings of particular dimensions of language use and in the relative weighting of the dimensions.

References

Clark, J. and Clifford, R. (1988). The FSI/ILR/ACTFL proficiency scales and testing techniques: Development, current status and needed research. *Studies in Second Language Acquisition* 10: 129–147.

Douglas, D. (2000) *Testing Language for Specific Purposes: Theory and Practice*. Cambridge: Cambridge University Press.

Douglas, D. and Selinker, L. (1994) Research methodology in context-based second language research. In Tarone, E. Gass, S. and Cohen, A. (Eds.) *Methodologies for Eliciting and Analyzing Language in context:* 119 – 139.

Elder, C. (1993) How do subject specialists construe classroom language proficiency? *Language Testing* 10: 235-540

Flaming, K. and Myers, R. (1995). *A plan for assessment in the RGPO*. Unpublished document, College of Veterinary Medicine, Iowa State University.

Jacoby, S. (1998). *Science as performance: Socializing scientific discourse through the conference talk rehearsal*. Unpublished Ph.D. dissertation, University of California, Los Angeles CA.

Jacoby, S. and McNamara, T. (1996) *Locating competence*. Paper presented at the Annual Conference of the American Association for Applied Lingustics. Chicago, IL, March 1996.

McNamara, T. (1996) *Measuring Second Language Performance*. London: Longman.

Selinker, L. and Douglas, D. (1989). Research methodology in contextually-based second language research. *Second Language Research*, 5.2: 93–126.

University of New Mexico – School of Medicine. (1992). *State of the Art Assessment in Medical Education: A Faculty Development Manual*. Author.

Appendix 1

University of New Mexico History-Taking Scoring Sheets

Student Name: Station #12
Date: History Taking

INSTRUCTIONS TO THE STUDENT: This is Joe Richards. He is an asymptomatic 40-year old male with
a 20 pack/year history of smoking. He is present for the follow-up of acute bronchitis, which has resolved
since being treated in Urgent Care.
He has decided to quit smoking. Review his smoking history and counsel him about smoking cessation.

Instructions to observe: Check appropriate column for each item except for "lined" items without numbers.	Accept-able	Attempted	Not done	Col
‡1. Introduces himself/herself				
‡2. Clarifies the purpose of the visit				
3. Permits expression of emotions and/or concerns				
‡4. Verbally praises the patient's efforts to initiate change				
smoking history				
5. Establishes reasons for quitting				
6. "Have you ever quit before?"				
7. Explores barriers to quitting				
counselling				
8. Discusses resources				
9. Sets a quit date				
10. Reviews strategies to prevent relapse				
11. Provides self-help material				
12. Sets a follow-up date				
13. Brings the interview to a close				
communication/interview style				
14. Demonstrates confidence and a positive attitude toward behaviour change				
15. Empathizes with the patient				
16. Organizes the interview				

FOR OFFICE USE ONLY   Raw score   COMMENTS:

Appendix 2

Individual Process Assessment

Individual Process Assessment
Student: _____
Date: _____
Evaluator: _____

Rural and General Practice Option
College of Veterinary Medicine
Iowa State University

Interviewing skills	Ideal	Accept able	Attempt- ed	Not Done	Not Applicable
1 **Introduction.** *Ideal.* the interviewer introduces himself/herself, shakes the client's hand and explains his/her role; checks with the client before using first name; encourages an provides and opportunity for the client to express his, her view, understanding, and/or experience of the chief complaint and how it has affected him/her.					
2 **Establishing Rapport.** *Ideal.* The interviewer attempts to establish rapport with the client by employing deliberate techniques such as the following: neither avoids nor forces eye contact; remains relaxed and unrushed; uses relaxed, open body posture; arranges positioning so that it is comfortable without great distance and/or barriers between the interviewer and the client.					
3. **Organization.** *Ideal.* The interviewer structures and orgainzes the interview. The purpose, agenda, intent, plan, and/or expectations for today's meeting are made clear as the interview unfolds. History is taken in a logical, organized order.					
4. **Transitional Statements.** *Ideal.* The interviewer utilizes transitional statements when progressing from one subsection in the interview to another, making explicit the necessity of the information, e.g., "Now I'm going to ask you some questions about the herd to help us decide to what extent and what ways the herd might be affected."					
5. **Questioning Skills: Type of Question.** *Ideal.* The interviewer starts gathering information with an open-ended question. When required by the large amount of potential information, this is followed by direct and forced-choice questions which will allow the interviewer to narrow in on the pertinent positive and negative points that need further elaboration.					

Interviewing skills	Ideal	Acce ptable	Attem- pted	Not Done	Not Appli cable
6. **Questioning Skills: Duplication.** *Ideal.* The interviewer does not repeat questions, seeking duplication of information that has previously been provided unless it is for clarification or summarization of prior information.					
7. **Questioning Skills: Summarizing.** *Ideal.* At the end of the major lines of inquiry (e.g., history of chief complaint, past medical history), the interviewer summarizes data for the client to verify and/or clarify.					
8. **Questioning Skills: Lack of Jargon.** *Ideal.* Questions asked and information provided to clients are free of difficult medical terms/jargon. If jargon is used, it is defined immediately for client.					
9 **Questioning Skills: Verification.** *Ideal.* The interviewer always seeks specificity, documentation and verification of the client's responses, (e.g., Client: "My dog is allergic to penicillin". Interviewer: "Can you tell me how you know she is allergic? What reaction have you seen in the past?")					
10. **Challenging the Client.** *Ideal.* The interviewer avoids asking the question "why?" or demanding in any other way that the client provide justification for actions, behaviours, perceptions, beliefs, etc.					
11. **Client Understanding and Education.** *Ideal.* The interviewer uses deliberate techniques throughout the interview to assess the client's understanding of information (e.g., asks for additional questions, poses hypothetical situations, summarizes information up to this point, clarifies for the client any evident misunderstanding). The interviewer attempts to provide the client with education regarding his/her problem or about other issues that may have come up in the interview (e.g., vaccination strategies/management practices).					
12. **Admitting lack of knowledge.** *Ideal.* When asked for information/advice which the interviewer cannot provide, the interviewer says,"I don't know, but would you like me to find out and get back to you?"					
13. **Closing the interview.** *Ideal.* The interviewer summarizes today's meeting, clarifying plans made or particular expectations of the client; checks with the client to make sure she/he understands plans that were made and/or expectations of him/her, encourages and provides an opportunity for the client to ask questions and/or express concerns, and explores these with the client, explores issues of treatment preferences/concerns, remains realistically optimistic and reassuring, offers his/her opinion, clearly identified as such, or defers if the client requests; brings the meeting to a close, but avoids appearing rushed as the close approaches.					
14. **Tone of Voice.** *Ideal.* The interviewer's tone of voice is calm, positive and varied throughout the interview.					
15. **Eye Contact.** *Ideal.* the interviewer maintains a level of eye contact with the client throughout the interview that is neither avoided nor forced.					
16. **Empathetic Statements.** *Ideal.* Throughout the interview, the interviewer lets the client know that he/she understands the client's feelings.					
Comments:					

Modified from University of New Mexico School of Medicine, 'State of the Art' Assessment Manual. May 1996

9 Is it fair to assess native and non-native speakers in common school foreign language examinations? The case of Italian in Australia[1]

Catherine Elder
University of Melbourne

Abstract

This chapter compares the performance of two groups of learners (those with and without home exposure to the target language) on Italian examinations administered at different stages of schooling. It investigates first of all whether those with home exposure to Italian achieve consistently higher scores than those without such exposure. Secondly, adopting bias investigation techniques involving both statistical and content analyses of the relevant foreign language examinations, it considers the implications for test validity of assessing the two types of learner in common.

Results reveal significant differences between those with and without home exposure to Italian in relation to both their overall scores and their performance on particular test items/components, but the nature and extent of these differences vary at different stages of schooling. The bias investigation likewise yields equivocal findings which can be interpreted differently according to how the test construct is defined. It is argued that the current institutional practice of compensating non-native learners for their alleged disadvantage may have consequences more damaging than the inequities it attempts to redress.

Background

This chapter is concerned with the teaching of 'community' (or 'heritage') languages in Australian schools and in particular with the implications for test validity and test fairness of assessing foreign language learners (whose L1 is English) in common with native or 'background' speakers of these languages. The term 'background speaker' in this context refers to the learner from one or other of Australia's immigrant groups who has some degree of home exposure to one of these community languages. As a result of intense lobbying from ethnic rights activists in the late 1960s many such languages (e.g. Arabic, Greek, Italian, Macedonian, Maltese, Serbian, Spanish, Turkish and Vietnamese) are offered for study within the mainstream school system and, in the case of languages with wide appeal like Italian, it is not uncommon to find those with and without home exposure to the target language studying alongside one another. It is moreover standard practice, in some Australian states, for these different types of learner to sit for the same foreign language examinations and to be assessed according to the same criteria regardless of the different types and amounts of target language input that they have received.

This practice is the subject of considerable controversy. Since the background speakers (hereafter BS) are generally considered to be more proficient than the non-background speakers (hereafter NBS) on account of their greater opportunities for target language exposure, their presence within the foreign language candidature is viewed by some (Garnaut 1989; Tuffin and Wilson 1989) as creating unfair competition for NBS. And since, at the end of secondary schooling, scores obtained on examinations in languages other than English (LOTE) have the potential to influence candidates' chances of university entry, tertiary selection bodies in some Australian states have taken measures to compensate NBS learners for their supposed disadvantage. Such measures have been fiercely opposed by those (e.g. Cook and McLean 1994) who have fought hard to have ethnic languages accepted as part of the mainstream education system and who see any advantage enjoyed by BS learners as due compensation for the educational disadvantage they may suffer in other school subjects.

It is unclear however whether BS are as proficient in the target language as is commonly claimed. Those studies which have been conducted in the Australian context suggest that many BS use a non-standard variety or dialect in the home and that their active use of the home language may be quite limited. In the case of Italian there is evidence (e.g. Bettoni 1991a; Rubino 1993; Clyne *et al.* 1997) of an overall shrinking of the language repertoire from a situation of trilingualism (Italian dialect, regional/popular Italian and English) amongst the first generation towards one of bilingualism or even English monolingualism amongst the second and third (who are those most likely to be studying Italian at school). The reduction is not only in quantity of Italian used but also in quality (Bettoni 1991b: 266–267). For many of these BS students the foreign language classroom will be the best (and in some cases the only) source of standard Italian input and, since it is the standard language which is the target of instruction, they will not necessarily be advantaged with respect to their NBS counterparts. Although those who speak dialect (and particularly those dialects which are linguistically close to standard Italian) may find it somewhat easier than English speakers to understand spoken and written input in the target language, there are other psychosocial and socioeconomic factors associated with dialect use which may work to their disadvantage. Dialects, for example, are subject to transfers or borrowings from English and to language mixing – a phenomenon which tends to be stigmatised (Bettoni and Gibbons 1990) by both teachers and the speakers themselves. There is also evidence that home maintenance of Italian or Italian dialect[2] may be inversely correlated to educational status. According to Kipp *et al.* (1995) only 26.1% of census respondents claiming to speak Italian at home have a formal educational qualification.

The aim of this chapter then, is to investigate learner performance on school LOTE examinations in order to establish answers to the following questions:

1 Do BS perform better than NBS ?
2 What are the implications for test validity and for test fairness of assessing the two types of learner in common?

If, as suggested above, there is no clearcut advantage for the BS students, then the practice of compensating NBS for disadvantage on these examinations may be inequitable. On the other hand, if the examinations can be demonstrated to be unfairly biased in favour of the BS, this will cast doubt on the validity of inferences we can draw from their results.

The studies

Although the research project from which my data are drawn seeks answers to the above questions in relation to three immigrant languages, Italian, Modern Greek and Chinese, I focus in this paper on Italian only. Study One investigates the performance of BS versus NBS learners in Year 8 or 9 (i.e. in the second or third year of secondary school) after they have completed at least one year of formal Italian study. Study Two focuses on another cohort of learners in Year 12 (in their final year of secondary school) after they have undertaken several years of formal study of the Italian language.

Instrumentation

The tests

The instruments used to compare BS and NBS performance are public examinations.

For Study One I draw my data from the Italian version of the Australian Language Certificate (now known as the National Australia Bank Certificates[3]) which are tests of beginning proficiency administered nationally (on a voluntary basis) in secondary schools which offer either Italian,

Chinese, French, German, Indonesian, Japanese or Modern Greek as a subject within the school curriculum. The ALC tests are communicative in their orientation in that the stimulus texts reflect real-world uses of language and the items purport to test a broader range of language skills than just vocabulary and grammar knowledge. The listening and reading items are based on culturally appropriate texts with accompanying illustrations and the test paper is presented in the form of a short magazine. Questions (about 30 in total for the reading section and 25 for the listening) are in multiple-choice format. (See Elder and Zammit 1992 for an account of this testing initiative and for some sample test materials.)

For Study Two I use data from the Victorian Certificate of Education (VCE) Italian examination (Board of Studies 1994) which is a set of assessment tasks taken by all students in the Australian state of Victoria who have enrolled for Italian as one of their Year 12 (i.e. school leaving) subjects. In 1994, when this study was undertaken, the four components were as follows:

> Common Assessment Task (CAT) 1 takes the form research report (written in the target language) for which candidates may draw on any kind of resource (including people who might have knowledge of the research area). A revision process allows for surface errors in language form to be corrected before the final version of this CAT is submitted.
> Common Assessment Task (CAT) 2 is a three-part oral examination assessed by a panel of two external examiners. Candidates are asked questions about topics of general interest, engage in a roleplay with one of the examiners, and give a prepared talk on a chosen topic.
> Common Assessment Task (CAT) 3 is presented as a folio containing two extended pieces of writing in the target language. One of these is the final product of a series of drafts presented to the teacher for feedback and the other is a supervised piece which is completed in class time with the aid of a dictionary or word list.
> Common Assessment Task (CAT) 4 is a three-part externally assessed examination in which candidates produce a piece of writing which builds on information contained in a number of unseen reading and listening texts.[4]

While the results of the Australian Language Certificate tests serve primarily to give learners a sense of their progress in the target language and thereby to engender a positive attitude to future language study, the results of the VCE Italian examination serve not only as a measure of school achievement but are also used (along with the results for other VCE subjects) for selection for the university or any other tertiary level institution.

The language background surveys

Decisions about how to categorise learners (i.e. as BS or otherwise) were made on the basis of sociolinguistic data gathered from the test candidates. The data gathered for the Australian Language Certificate tests allow only for a binary distinction between BS and NBS (defined as those who use Italian at home and those who do not). On the other hand, all VCE candidates studying a language other than English (LOTE) at year 12 are issued with an extensive questionnaire which makes it possible to classify the students for each language into four different language background groups. At one end of the continuum are the NBS with no exposure to the target language other than that received in the FL classroom and on the other are the 'fully fledged' native speakers, who use standard Italian (rather than dialect) as the main medium of communication in the home and/or who have been to school in Italy. In the middle are two further groups of BS with varying degrees of home exposure to non-standard dialectal or contact varieties of Italian.

Analysis of the data

To explore the answer to the above research questions I undertake both quantitative and qualitative analyses.

On the Australian Language Certificate tests I examine the overall score differences between BS and NBS on both reading and listening components and then use the Mantel-Haenszel procedure (Holland and Thayer 1988) to investigate the possibility of item bias. A *post hoc* content analysis is then undertaken of those items found to function differentially for BS and NBS in order to establish whether the discrepancies revealed by the statistical analysis could be taken as evidence of test bias.

On the VCE Italian examination I compare the four language background groups (alluded to above) in terms of both their overall rank scores and their performance on each of the component assessment tasks. Then, replicating procedures adopted routinely by the body responsible for tertiary selection in Victoria (the Victorian Tertiary Admissions Centre), I perform a bias analysis whereby the VCE Italian examination scores of each group are regressed against an external measure (the VCE English/English as a Second Language (ESL) examination). This measure is deemed by the institutions concerned with tertiary selection to be measuring a construct of ability similar to that of the VCE Italian exam. The results of this bias analysis are considered in the light of an analysis of the construct of ability which the various components of the examination are designed to measure.

Findings of the above analyses are used to evaluate the validity of the two instruments as measures of both BS and NBS performance and to consider the implications for test fairness of assessing the two types of learner in common.

Table 9.1

Design of the research

Study	No. of groups	Instrumentation	Data	Analysis
ONE	2 BS & NBS	Australian Language Certificate tests (for learners in Years 8 or 9)	Scores (item & aggregate) on Listening & Reading subtests	(i) Mann Whitney test (overall score comparison across groups) (ii) Mantel Haenszel (item bias) analysis (iii) item content analysis
TWO	4 BS (subdivided into 3 groups)	Victorian Certificate of Education LOTE examination	Scores on 4 CATs (i.e. subtests) plus golbal (i.e. aggregrate) score	(i) Kruskal Wallis test (overall score comparison across groups)
		VCE English /ESL examination (as benchmark for comparison)	Global score only	(ii) ANCOVA analysis (for bias in relation to external benchmark) (iii) content analysis of assessment tasks

Results

The Australian Language Certificate

Score differences

Table 9.2 below shows the mean rank score for BS and NBS of Italian on each test component and Figure 9.1 shows the percentage distribution of BS and NBS in each of three performance bands which are used for reporting learner achievement on the ALC tests.

Table 9.2

Score differences on the 1993 ALC by home language background

Test	Category	N	Max	Mean score	SD	Mean rank	Z value	p value
ITALIAN								
Reading	NBS	3441	30	18.94	5.74	2465.06	10.371	<.0001
	BS	402		22.04	5.94	1858.56		
Listening	NBS	3441	22	12.89	4.23	2853.16	17.783	<.0001
	BS	402		17.07	4.35	1813.22		

A Mann-Whitney comparison of group means for BS and NBS yields a highly significant Z value, on both the reading and listening tests. Those with a home background in the target language do better than those who use English only at home, and performance differences are particularly marked in relation to listening, which for most BS is the skill exercised most frequently in the home domain.

The impact of the above proficiency differences is best illustrated by looking at the distribution of BS and NBS across the three band levels which are used for reporting purposes.

Figure 9.1

Percentage of BS and NBS candidates in each performance band

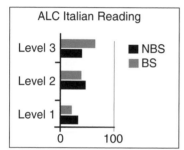 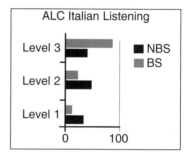

The numbers of BS and NBS in each band level are reported as a percentage of the total number of candidates in each home language group (see Figure 9.1). The distribution across band levels indicates that while the test discriminates effectively between members of the majority group who speak English at home, it is less successful in relation to BS, at least as far as listening skills are concerned. The majority (76%) of those in the latter category achieve listening scores which place them in the top performance band.

Bias analysis

The results of the Mantel-Haenszel bias analysis of test items on the ALC tests (see Appendix 1) are summarised in Table 9.3 below. The analysis reveals that seven of the 30 reading items and five of the 22 listening items are significantly easier for BS candidates, while only two reading items and one listening item favour the NBS learners (in other words they have a higher probability of answering them correctly). The total number of differentially functioning items on the test (30% on the reading test and 27% on the listening) raises questions about the equivalence of test scores for each group. It is clear that the language background of the test takers has a significant effect on the way they tackle a substantial proportion of the test items and hence that a given score on one or other of the test components may have different meaning according to who takes the test.

Table 9.3

Incidence of DIF items across ALC Italian reading and listening tests

	ITALIAN Reading	ITALIAN Listening
in favour of BS	7	5
in favour of NBS	2	1
total DIF items	9	6
% of total items	30%	27%

A content analysis of DIF items undertaken by Italian language consultants produced a number of hypotheses about factors which might be causing discrepancies in item performance across groups.

- The nature of the lexical items used in either the stimulus text or in the test rubric was deemed to be a possible source of DIF on the reading component. Words which proved easier for BS included those referring to household objects (Italian reading: item 28), expressions of time (items 1, 3 and 4) and to food (item 23).

- The DIF effect also appeared more prevalent for particular text types than for others. For example, three items on the Italian listening test (items 14, 15 and 18) based on radio advertisements were significantly easier for BS, perhaps because they are accustomed to listening to Italian radio broadcasts at home.

- BS appeared to do better on items which draw on cultural/sociolinguistic knowledge, presumably because they have greater access to situations where this kind of competence is displayed. Item 3 on the Italian listening test, for example, assumes familiarity with the 24 hour clock, which is seldom used in the Australian context.

- The language of the test question also appeared to be a factor contributing to DIF. Analysis of those reading items which were easier for BS revealed that all but two of them (items 14 and 21) had both an Italian language stem and Italian language distractors. It seems therefore that BS, due to greater familiarity with written forms of Italian, are less troubled by its use in the test rubric.

- Items involving number recognition and recall appeared to be easier for BS. For example, BS scored significantly better than a matched ability group of NBS on Item 18 (Italian listening) which required candidates to listen (once) to a telephone number recorded on the listening tape and match it to the appropriate sequence of numbers on the test paper.

In sum, the investigation of the sources of group difference on the ALC test items suggests that many of the discrepancies favouring BS candidates are due not to bias but rather to real differences in the ability under test (e.g. superior vocabulary knowledge and sociolinguistic competence on the part of the background speaker candidates). The test items on which the corresponding groups of NBS perform better, on the other hand, appear to have less to do with target language proficiency *per se* than with a particular kind of test wiseness or strategic competence (e.g. matching, counting, looking carefully at and drawing inferences from pictures and graphs). For example, one of the items favouring NBS on the Italian reading test (item 8) depends at least in part on visual acuity, in this instance the ability to make sense of diagrams and to match words to symbols on a weather map. Another item involves the ability to count occurrences of a particular word in a school timetable (Italian reading: item 18). These strategic 'noticing' abilities may be indicators of the more sophisticated academic literacy skills which, in the later years of schooling, allow NBS learners to hold their own on school foreign language examinations with respect to their more proficient BS counterparts.

The Victorian Certificate of Education

Score differences

I used the Kruskal-Wallis statistic to compare the four language background groups in terms of their global (aggregate) Italian score, which is what counts for tertiary selection, and on each of the component assessment tasks which make up the VCE Italian examination. Results of this analysis are presented below.

Table 9.4

Kruskal-Wallis analysis of variance in rank scores for VCE Italian (global)

Category	N	Median	Mean	sd	Ave. Rank	Z Value
1	204	30.00	30.348	6.473	302.4	-1.20
2	127	31.00	31.480	7.001	334.9	1.38
3	257	30.00	30.377	5.990	304.9	-1.15
4	41	33.00	32.683	8.241	379.1	2.34
Overall	629				315.0	

H = 8.39   d.f. = 3   p = 0.039

Table 9.4 shows that as far as global scores are concerned, there is a significant difference in mean rank scores according to language background (H = 8.39, DF 3, 629 p = 0.039). Mann Whitney pairwise comparisons reveal that, as we might have expected, the small group of standard Italian speakers in Category 4 outperform all the others and that the NBS candidates (those with no home exposure) perform significantly worse than those in Category 2 and Category 4. What is surprising about these findings is that the majority group of BS, for whom Italian dialect is the main home language, perform just as poorly as the NBS and worse than the other two groups of background speakers. Analysis of performance across the four component parts of the VCE LOTE examination (presented in Tables 9.5 to 9.8 below) sheds some light on this phenomenon.

Table 9.5

Kruskal-Wallis analysis of variance in rank scores for VCE Italian (CAT 1)

Category	N	Median	Mean	sd	Ave. Rank	Z Value
1	203	40.00	39.286	7.569	331.1	1.74
2	126	41.00	39.167	8.803	331.1	1.40
3	256	35.00	36.758	8.990	283.7	-3.38
4	40	42.00	39.875	8.510	345.4	1.17
Overall	629				313.0	

H = 11.62   d.f. = 3   p = 0.009

Table 9.6

Kruskal-Wallis analysis of variance in rank scores for VCE Italian (CAT 2)

Category	N	Median	Mean	sd	Ave. Rank	Z Value
1	204	35.00	32.230	10.704	273.2	-3.95
2	127	35.00	35.157	10.445	326.2	0.82
3	257	35.00	35.545	8.772	325.7	1.28
4	40	42.00	40.375	9.295	415.9	3.65
Overall	628				314.5	

H = 24.54   d.f. = 3   p = 0.000

Table 9.7

Kruskal-Wallis analysis of variance in rank scores for VCE Italian (CAT 3)

Category	N	Median	Mean	sd	Ave. Rank	Z Value
1	204	35.00	37.034	8.179	323.8	0.94
2	127	40.00	37.480	9.061	337.9	1.61
3	256	35.00	35.117	8.248	289.2	-2.85
4	40	40.00	38.375	8.195	349.7	1.29
Overall	627				314.0	

H = 9.02   d.f. = 3   p = 0.029

Elder

Table 9.8

Kruskal-Wallis analysis of variance in rank scores for VCE Italian (CAT 4)

Category	N	Median	Mean	sd	Ave. Rank	Z Value
1	203	35.00	32.488	9.392	284.6	-2.74
2	127	35.00	34.173	9.754	312.2	0.01
3	254	35.00	34.449	9.704	321.3	1.07
4	39	40.00	38.077	10.363	393.1	2.91
Overall	623				312.0	

H = 13.29   d.f. = 3   p = 0.004

On the one hand the relatively poor overall performance of the NBS learners is accounted for largely by the low scores of this group on the oral component of the exam (CAT 2) and to a lesser extent on the written exam (CAT 4). These components share the following features: a) they are externally assessed; b) they require understanding of unfamiliar input in Italian; and c) they emphasise spontaneous language production. What contributes to the low global scores of the Category 3 group on the other hand is their poor performance on the internally-assessed tasks (CAT 1) and (CAT 3), both of which allow opportunities for rehearsal and revision and therefore, it could be argued, place greater emphasis on learning effort or general academic ability than on communicative ability in the target language.

We may surmise that the 'dialect as main home language criterion' used to allocate candidates to Category 3 is in fact a surrogate for another kind of background variable, such as low socioeconomic status. Many of those who continue to use an Italian dialect as the predominant medium of communication at home may do so because they have no choice on account of the fact that their parents a) have remained in relatively low-status occupations where English language is not required and is therefore poorly learned; b) are not fully integrated with the Australian society/culture; and/or c) are unwilling or unable, due to low levels of literacy, to participate actively in their children's school education and to engage in the kinds of language modelling that Cahill (1987) and others have found to be conducive to successful test performance amongst BS of Italian.

Bias analysis

Although we have shown that the BS learners of Italian do not in many cases outperform NBS and that on some tasks they perform worse than them, the bias analysis undertaken routinely by Victorian Tertiary Admissions Centre, the institution responsible for tertiary selection in Victoria, indicates that the scores of all BS learners are overestimated on the VCE LOTE examination with respect to those of the NBS learners. Since this statistical procedure is used to justify the practice of boosting the scores of NBS students to compensate them for comparative disadvantage (with respect to BS) it has been replicated below and an attempt is made to explain its underlying assumptions.

The bias detection procedure in this case takes the form of an Analysis of Covariance (ANCOVA) whereby candidates' Italian scores are regressed against two independent variables: a) their score for VCE English/ESL; and b) the language background category (1, 2, 3 or 4) to which candidates had been assigned. Where there are significant F values from this analysis, the extent and direction of bias is estimated by first calculating the intercepts for each group and then comparing the adjusted mean LOTE scores of candidates in each language background category at any given level of ability in VCE English/ESL using the standard regression formula. (See Reynolds 1982 for an account of this bias investigation procedure.)

The justification for the choice of VCE English as the benchmark for determining whether there is bias in the VCE Italian examination is that, for the purposes of university selection, all VCE subjects are accorded parity of esteem. In other words they are all deemed to be measuring the same thing, namely: academic ability. English has the added advantage of being a compulsory subject, which means that comparative data (i.e. English scores) are available for all VCE Italian candidates. The scoring procedures for VCE English also include a built-in adjustment for non-native speakers (i.e. recent immigrants who have undertaken part of their education in a non-English medium institution) and results on this examination are therefore regarded, at least for institutional purposes, as a 'true' measure of academic ability.

To understand the logic behind this bias analysis it is useful to inspect the raw VCE Italian mean scores for each language background group as against the raw means for VCE English.

Table 9.9

VCE Italian and English/ESL mean scores by category

	VCE Italian	VCE Italian
Category 1	30.4	35.3
Category 1	31.5	32.9
Category 1	30.4	29.5
Category 1	32.7	29.9

Table 9.9 above shows that whereas the Category 1 learners (i.e. NBS) do slightly worse in VCE Italian than some of the other groups, they do better than all of them in VCE English. The reverse is true for the Category 4

learners (i.e. speakers of Standard Italian). The reasoning of the tertiary selection authority is as follows. The English scores of those in Category 1 are a measure of ability. This justifies the subsequent inference that the NBS are a more able group and can therefore be expected to do better in Italian (and all other subjects for that matter) than the NBS. The fact that NBS do not outperform the BS candidates is thus taken as evidence that some aspect of the examination content or format may be biased against them. The regression analysis (findings of which are presented in Appendix 2) bears this out. It shows that the VCE LOTE examination underestimates the ability of NBS learners by between 3 and 6 units depending on which of the BS groups we are comparing them with. Thus, in order to compensate NBS learners for what is perceived to be unfair bias on the VCE Italian examination, university selection officers are instructed to apply a correction factor to the tertiary entrance ranking[6] of those NBS candidates whose overall rank score places them around the cut-point for entry to a particular institution. The validity of this practice will be considered further in the discussion which follows.

Summary and discussion

It appears then that there is no straightforward answer to the first question posed at the outset of this paper:

1 Do BS perform better than NBS on school foreign language examinations?

Results reported above suggest that there are indeed differences in examination performance for the different kinds of learners but that these differences are not always in the predicted direction. While on tests of beginning proficiency (i.e. the Australian Language Certificates), background speakers of Italian tend to outperform NBS (particularly in listening), the mere fact of using the TL (or a related variety of the TL) in the home does not guarantee them a long-term advantage over NBS learners. In fact the majority group of BS taking the end-of-school VCE Italian examination performs no better than, and on some tasks worse than, their NBS counterparts. This may be because, as learners move into the upper school, the content of the foreign language curriculum becomes more academic and less closely aligned to the domains of home language use. What is learned is therefore new to all learners regardless of their language background and it is the academically able, rather than the more experienced (in the sense of having opportunities for LOTE use), who are likely to do better. There nevertheless remain advantages for most background speaker students on those tasks (i.e. the oral and written examination) where there is a greater focus on communicative ability than on academic effort/ability, because it is these kinds of skills that they have had opportunities to practice in the home. However these advantages are not in all cases sufficiently marked to show up when their performance across the whole range of assessment tasks is aggregated. The answer to the second question:

2 What are the implications for test validity and for test fairness of assessing the two types of learner in common?

is also somewhat complex. The question was investigated by means of bias analyses to determine whether the differential performance of BS and NBS was due to factors inherent in the measurement process or rather to real differences in ability resulting from factors external to the test.

The results of the ALC bias analysis showed that when BS and NBS of Italian were matched according to their total listening and reading score, a substantial DIF effect was observable for both reading and listening, with more items favouring BS than NBS. However, the subsequent content analysis suggests that these differences in item-level performance are due to real differences in aspects of the communicative ability which the ALC tests are designed to measure (i.e. superior vocabulary knowledge, sociolinguistic competence, and processing speed on the part of the background speaker candidates) rather than to construct-irrelevant variance.

The results of the VCE Italian analysis likewise revealed marked discrepancies in global scores across the four language background categories, when these scores were adjusted according to candidates' ability on the corresponding VCE English/ESL examination. While these discrepancies differed in size from group to group, they consistently favoured BS. However the choice of English as the external measure of ability, based as it is on the notion that all VCE subjects can be accorded parity of esteem, is, I consider, indicative of a very narrow view of what the LOTE examination is designed to measure. By using English (or any other academic subject for that matter) as the external criterion, the admissions body (VTAC) is placing a greater value on academic ability or learning effort than on proficiency in any language-specific sense. From the brief description of the component assessment tasks described above it is clear that the VCE examination cannot (and indeed should not) be seen as measuring only academic ability, and again, as for the ALC, a case could be made to the effect that the score advantage of BS candidates on CAT 2 (the oral interview) and CAT 4 (the written examination) may be partly due to real differences in the language-specific skills which the VCE LOTE syllabus aims to develop and the examination is designed to elicit.

In sum, for both examinations there are grounds for questioning whether group differences revealed by the statistical analyses are indeed due to bias in the test instruments concerned since bias can only be claimed if performance differences are attributable to factors extraneous to the test construct

(Bachman 1990; Shepard 1987). Thus, although it is clear that neither the ALC nor VCE examinations are functioning homogeneously across BS and NBS groups and that test scores may need to be interpreted differently according to the language background of those taking the test, decisions as to which skills are deemed relevant or irrelevant to the construct, and hence about the presence of bias and its directionality (i.e. whether in favour of background or non-background speakers) are very complex and may be coloured by different opinions about the tests' purpose.

The tests referred to in this paper each have two purposes: the ALC is intended to measure communicative competence and at the same time to provide incentives for LOTE learning, and the VCE is intended to gauge learners' ability to use the target language in 'real-life' situations while also serving as a predictor of academic performance. If the priority of the ALC tests is the assessment of communicative competence, then a case could be made for defining those items measuring 'test wiseness' (e.g. matching, counting or inferencing from context), which are not strictly part of communicative competence as traditionally conceived, as irrelevant to the test construct and therefore biased against the BS (who tend to do worse on them). If incentives for formal LOTE learning are regarded as the primary goal, then test designers should increase the number of items measuring classroom-related abilities or language knowledge (e.g. grammar) which are not typically acquired in naturalistic settings and thereby avoid bias in favour of BS (or at least those BS who have not undergone formal target medium education).

If the chief purpose of the VCE LOTE exam is seen to be the assessment of communicative competence, then some assessment tasks (i.e. CAT 1 or CAT 3) could be treated as biased against BS because they are based on a crafted piece or pieces of writing which are repeatedly revised on the basis of on-going feedback from the teacher and which are therefore a reflection of learning effort rather than of automatised productive ability. If, on the other hand we assume the institutional perspective (i.e. that of the relevant tertiary selection body), and see these academic skills as central to the purpose of end-of-school assessment, then those aspects of the VCE Italian examination measuring communicative skills which can be acquired outside the classroom setting can be regarded as irrelevant to the test construct and hence biased in favour of BS. The consequence of applying a correction factor to compensate NBS for their perceived disadvantage is, in effect, to remove these skills from consideration so that learning in some general (i.e. non language-specific) school sense is all that ends up counting in the university selection process.

In each case I would argue that any alterations to test design or *post hoc* adjustments to test scores run counter to one of the test's goals. To remove those items which those who have learned the target language in classrooms (rather than acquired it automatically) find easier would be to widen the already considerable gap between BS and NBS performance. It might also produce a situation where the level of achievement on the tests may be seen as a function of language background and where learning effort may appear to have little value. To add more such items might tip the balance in favour of NBS but might also reduce the tests' potential for positive, communicatively-oriented washback onto the content of the school curriculum. Likewise if academic aptitude is all that is valued at Year 12, then the VCE LOTE exam may fail to fulfil its other purpose. Communicative skills may end up being given even less emphasis than is currently the case within the VCE LOTE curriculum with consequent negative consequences for NBS (who need to acquire them) and BS (who wish to maintain or develop them).

While adjustments to test items or test scores might, from a measurement perspective, have the effect of restoring the tests' unidimensionality, they might also pose a threat to the tests' consequential validity as conceptualised by Messick (1993) insofar as they could lead to outcomes which are undesirable either from a pedagogical or from a social justice perspective.[7]

The VTAC Special Consideration Scheme has the potential not only to alter the nature of what is being measured by the VCE LOTE examination through *post hoc* adjustments to test scores, but also to create a situation where a home background in the target language is seen as a drawback rather than an asset, with the result that learners suppress information about their home language background for fear of missing out on special consideration in the university selection process. I would propose then that, under the circumstances, technical solutions to the 'bias' problem may have consequences more damaging than the inequities they are intended to redress.

Possible solutions

How then to deal with the fairness issues which emerge when BS and NBS learners are assessed in common? It is tempting to suggest (somewhat facetiously) that, if prediction of academic aptitude is the ultimate goal of foreign language assessment, then we might be better off restricting the range of foreign languages taught to those such as French (or even Latin and Ancient Greek) which are not used on a daily basis within the Australian community. This would, however, be regarded, not least by ethnic communities, as inequitable, given claims about the potential of ethnic or community language study to promote intercultural understanding/ communication, to legitimise or consolidate the status of minority languages within our society and to maintain and develop Australia's existing language resources.

However, what is clear from the findings of the two studies reported here is that, if we accept the value of offering immigrant languages in the context of mainstream schooling, we need to think carefully about the pedagogical implications of offering such languages to all comers. While it is clearly impractical, given the limited resources available to foreign language education, to create a plethora of curriculum and assessment streams for different types of learner, unless these learners are sharply differentiated in their overall level of proficiency, the measures chosen to assess foreign language learners should nevertheless be broad ranging enough for the differing strengths and weaknesses of BS and NBS to be elicited and to allow 'headroom' for those with high levels of ability in particular areas. Where performance patterns across groups are sufficiently diverse to violate the principle of unidimensionality implicit in the measurement process, then separate scaling and reporting procedures should be devised to accommodate these differences.

At upper levels of schooling perhaps the best pedagogical solution to the bias problem and indeed to the university selection dilemma might be to separate the measures used to assess school achievement from those used for university selection (as occurs in the United States). Readiness for future academic study across a range of subjects may be better assessed on norm-referenced scholastic aptitude tests designed and administered by the university so that the two purposes of the VCE exam (that of measuring language proficiency on the one hand and academic ability on the other) are not conflated. This would ease the current tension between the requirements of criterion-referenced and norm-referenced assessment which are linked to the dual purpose of the VCE LOTE examination. The potential for unfairness, which emerges from the findings presented here, stems at least partly from the attempt to combine these competing approaches and purposes.

Notes

1 Some, but not all, of the data presented in this chapter appear elsewhere (Elder 1996, Forthcoming).
2 Census data do not make the distinction between dialects and the standard form.
3 For further information about these tests, readers can contact the Australian Council of Educational Research, 19 Prospect Hill Rd., Camberwell, Victoria 3124, Australia.
4 For further information about the tasks which make up the VCE Italian examination, see the set of sample of materials produced by the Board of Studies (1994).
5 The reader is reminded of what was reported at the outset about the exceptionally low levels of literacy use amongst Italians immigrants and about the low levels of education amongst Italian- (presumably dialect-) speaking members of the Italo-Australian population (Kipp *et al.* 1995).

6   The tertiary entrance ranking is derived from an adjusted average of candidates' scores across a range of VCE subjects.

7   Messick claims that 'the use of test scores in the implementation of social policy falls within the realm of validity inquiry, because the import of scores for action depends on the validity of their meaning and their value implications' (1993: 63).

Suggested further reading

Clyne, M., Fernandez, S., Chen, I. and Summo-O'Connell, R. (Eds.) (1997) *Background Speakers: Diversity and its Management in LOTE Programs.* Canberra, ACT: Language Australia.
This edited volume explores (from a non-measurement perspective) the issue of diversity in foreign language classrooms with particular reference to the 'background speaker' issue, which is the subject of my paper. The sociolinguistics of Chinese, Italian and German immigrant communities in Australia is outlined by way of introduction to the research. The authors go on to document the language behaviours revealed in their interviews with a range of school-age learners of German, Chinese and Italian. Their subjects include recent immigrants who are native speakers of the target language and those of the second and third generation who vary enormously in their language competence depending on the variety of the target language to which they are exposed and the extent to which they have shifted away from their parents' or grandparents' mother tongue towards English. The book concludes with a discussion of the strategies that can be adopted by language teachers in managing classes comprising learners from these very diverse language backgrounds.

Holland, P. W. and Thayer, D. T. (1988) Differential item functioning and the Mantel-Haenszel procedure. In Wainer, H. and Braun, H. I. (Eds.) *Test Validity*: 129–145. Hillsdale, NJ: Lawrence Erlbaum Associates, Publishers.
The book explores the notion of test validity from historical, epistemological, and statistical perspectives. It also considers the challenges which recent developments in cognitive psychology and computer technology pose for the way we think about test constructs and our means of measuring them. The chapter by Holland and Wainer, which I refer to in my paper, presents a lucid account of the use of the Mantel-Haenszel statistic (basically an adaptation of the Chi Square procedure) in the context of testing validity in specific subpopulations. The authors demonstrate the connection between the MH method and other bias investigation techniques based on item response theory.

Messick, S. (1993) Validity. In Linn, R. L. (Ed.) *Educational Measurement*, 3rd edition: 13–104. New York, NY: Macmillan.

Messick's comprehensive and authoritative chapter on test validity has acquired quasi-biblical status in the testing literature and has survived three editions of the *Educational Measurement* volume without undergoing major changes. The section on the consequential basis of test interpretation contains the best discussion of the value implications of test constructs and their associated measures that I am aware of. Messick argues that consideration of the values (and biases) implicit in test constructs is no less important for test validation than exploring the nature of the behavioural domain about which inferences are drawn.

References

Bachman L. F. (1990) *Fundamental Considerations in Language Testing*. Oxford: Oxford University Press.

Bettoni, C. (1991a) Language variety among Italians: Anglicisation, attrition and attitudes. In Romaine, S. (Ed.) *Language in Australia*. Cambridge: Cambridge University Press, pp. 263–269.

Bettoni, C. (1991b) Language shift and morphological attrition. *Rivista di Linguistica* 3, 2: 369–387.

Bettoni, C. and Gibbons, J. (1990) L'influenza della generazione e della classe sociale sugli atteggiamenti linguistici degli italiani in Australia. *Rivista Italiana di Dialettologia* 14: 113–137.

Board of Studies (1994). *VCE LOTE: ITALIAN. Official Sample CATs*. Collins Dove Australia.

Cahill, D. (1987). Bilingual development of Italo-Australian children. In Bettoni (Ed.) *Italian in Australia* (Australian Review of Applied Linguistics Series S, No. 4: 101–127). Canberra: Australian National University.

Clyne, M., Fernandez, S., Chen, I. and Summo-O'Connell, R. (Eds.) (1997) *Background Speakers: Diversity and its Management in LOTE Programs*. Canberra, ACT: Language Australia.

Cook, M. and MacLean, S. (1994) Language study changes discriminatory: Academic. *The Age*, March 1.

Elder, C. (1996) The effect of language background on 'foreign' language test performance: The case of Chinese, Modern Greek and Italian. *Language Learning* 46, 2: 233–282.

Elder, C. (forthcoming). What does test bias have to do with fairness? *Language Testing*.

Elder, C. and Zammit, S. (1992). Assessing performance in languages other than English: The contribution of the Australian Language Certificates. *Vox: The Journal of the Australian Advisory Council on Languages and Multicultural Education* 6: 14–20.

Garnaut, R. (1989) Australia and the Northeast Asian ascendancy: Report to the Prime Minister and the Minister of Foreign Affairs and Trade. Canberra: Australian Government Publishing Service.

Holland, P. W. and Thayer, D. T. (1988) Differential item functioning and the Mantel-Haenszel procedure. In Wainer, H. and Braun, H. I. (Eds.) *Test Validity*: 129–145. Hillsdale, NJ: Lawrence Erlbaum Associates, Publishers

Kipp, S., Clyne, M. and Pauwels, A. (1995). *Immigration and Australia's Language Resources.* Bureau of Immigration, Multicultural and Population Research, Canberra: Australian Government Publishing Service.

Messick, S. (1993). Validity. In Linn, R. L. (Ed.) *Educational Measurement,* 3rd edition: 13–104. New York, NY: Macmillan.

Reynolds, C. R. (1982). The problem of bias in psychological assessment. In Reynolds, C. R. and Guykin, T. B. (Eds.) *The Handbook of School Psychology*: 178–208. New York, NY: Wiley.

Rubino, A. (1993). *From trilingualism to monolingualism: A case study of language shift in a Sicilian-Australian family.* Unpublished PhD thesis. University of Sydney.

Shepard, L. A. (1987). The case for bias in tests of achievement and scholastic aptitude. In Modgil, S. and Modgil, C. (Eds.) *Arthur Jensen: Consensus and Controversy*: 177–190. New York, NY: Falmer Press.

Tuffin, P. and Wilson, J. (1989). Report of an investigation into disincentives to language learning at the senior secondary level. Report to the Asian Studies Council, December. Canberra: Department of Employment Education and Training.

Appendix 1

Mantel-Haenszel DIF Analysis for ALC Italian 1993 (Reading)

```
Matchsets = 7 Cutoffs = 14, 17, 20, 23, 25, 27    Items      (BS= 399 NBS = 3418)
```

Plot of MHDeltas
Easier BS Easier NBS

Item name	MHALpha	MHDelta	Chi-SQ	Prob	Plot (-2 ... -1 ... 0 ... 1 ... 2)
item 1	4.25	-3.40	31.81	.00	@
item 2	1.82	-1.82	6.73	.01	-1 *
item 3	2.22	-1.87	33.03	.00	*
item 4	2.68	-2.32	35.92	.00	@
item 5	1.00	-.00	0.00	.99	0
item 6	.98	.04	0.00	.98	0
item 7	.62	1.13	12.00	.00	1 *
item 8	.45	1.88	17.09	.00	*
item 9	.67	.95	7.34	.01	*
item 10	.89	.29	.81	.37	*
item 11	.70	.85	5.48	.02	*
item 12	.77	.61	4.41	.04	*
item 13	.75	.69	3.57	.06	*
item 14	2.06	-1.70	7.33	.01	*
item 15	.74	.71	5.00	.03	*
item 16	1.56	-1.04	3.74	.05	*
item 17	.85	.39	1.39	.24	*
item 18	.48	1.71	28.11	.00	*
item 19	.85	.38	1.31	.25	*
item 20	.78	.57	3.92	.05	*
item 21	3.48	-2.93	68.81	.00	@
item 22	1.45	-.88	6.09	.01	*
item 23	1.97	-1.59	16.09	.00	*
item 24	.62	1.12	7.11	.01	*
item 25	1.38	-.75	4.65	.03	*
item 26	.69	.87	7.12	.01	*
item 27	1.09	-.19	.43	.51	*
item 28	2.29	-1.94	38.66	.00	*
item 29	.57	1.33	11.19	.00	*
item 30	1.30	-.62	2.34	.13	*

Mantel-Haenszel DIF Analysis for ALC Italian 1993 (Listening)

```
Matchsets = 7 Cutoffs = 11, 14, 18, 19, 20        Items=22  (BS= 399 NBS = 3418)
```

Plot of MHDeltas
Easier BS Easier NBS

Item name	MHALpha	MHDelta	Chi-SQ	Prob
item 1	1.14	-.31	1.27	.26
item 2	.80	.52	2.93	.09
item 3	1.95	-1.57	20.48	.00
item 4	1.00	-.00	.05	.83
item 5	.95	.12	.09	.76
item 6	.55	1.41	6.73	.01
item 7	1.97	-1.60	21.49	.00
item 8	.74	.69	3.33	.07
item 9	.98	.05	.05	.82
item 10	1.25	-.52	1.60	.21
item 11	1.33	-.66	3.22	.07
item 12	1.26	-.54	1.24	.27
item 13	.66	.98	7.37	.01
item 14	2.00	1.63	14.94	.00
item 15	3.40	-2.88	32.46	.00
item 16	1.85	-1.45	7.07	.01
item 17	1.13	-.28	.01	.94
item 18	2.69	-2.33	16.53	.00
item 19	.73	.75	5.84	.02
item 20	1.06	.13	0.00	.97
item 21	1.47	-.90	5.15	.02
item 22	.43	1.99	10.74	.00

Appendix 2

ANCOVA analysis for VCE Italian(1994)

Model 1 (with interaction term included)

F= 1.9 DF 3, 619 P = 0.6 ns

Model 2 (without interaction term)

F= 24.2 DF 3, 622 P < 0.001

VCE Italian scores adjusted for ability in English/ESL

Applying the formula $\hat{y} = a + bx$, where b, the slope of the regression line, is 0.66920 and x is a given English score (let us say 30), the adjusted mean LOTE score for each language background category is as follows:

$\hat{y}$ for Category 1 = 6.74227 + 0.66920(30) = 6.74227 + 20.076 = **26.8**

$\hat{y}$ for Category 2 = 9.4388 + 0.66920(30) = 9.4388 + 20.076 = **29.5**

$\hat{y}$ for Category 3 = 10.58006 + 0.66920(30) = 10.58006 + 20.076 = **30.7**

$\hat{y}$ for Category 4 = 12.70458 + 0.66920(30) = 12.70458 + 20.076 = **32.8**

There is therefore a discrepancy of between three and six units between learners in Category 1 and those in the other categories. Note that if the assumption of homogeneity of regression across groups were tenable we would expect the value of y (the LOTE score) to be the same at any given value of x (the English score) regardless of group membership.

10 Identifying suspect item bundles for the detection of differential bundle functioning in an EFL reading comprehension test: A preliminary study

Yong-Won Lee
Educational Testing Service, Princeton

Abstract

An item bundle refers to a group of related items that are suspected of being locally dependent and recently it has become an important unit of test bias analysis. This chapter addresses two major approaches in the identification of suspect item bundles for differential bundle functioning (DBF) in an EFL (English as a Foreign Language) reading comprehension test. It was found that overall the item clusters based on the reading passages might be the appropriate units of DBF analyses, but that they could be complemented by statistical analyses of dimensional distinctiveness to locate the suspect bundles effectively.

Introduction

To date research on bias in language testing has been mostly directed towards examinees' differential performance on the test that could be attributable to their native language/culture (Angoff 1989; Chen and Henning 1985) and major field differences (Alderson and Urquhart 1983, 1985; Brown 1982; Clapham 1996; Erickson and Molloy 1983; Hale 1988a, 1988b; Henning 1990). These studies in general investigated the impact of the examinees' native languages, prior exposure to American culture, and areas of specialization on their performance on various types of tests including vocabulary, grammar, and reading/listening comprehension tests. As regards methodology, some of these studies used analysis of variance (ANOVA) to examine group x item or group x reading passage interaction effects. Others employed item bias or differential item functioning (DIF) techniques, such as the Delta-Plot method based on IRT (item response theory), item difficulty estimates (Chen and Henning 1985; Henning 1990), and the comparison of IRT item characteristic curves (Linn *et al.* 1981), and the Mantel-Haenszel method (Angoff 1989; Henning 1990).

Over decades, DIF approaches to test bias study have been quite popular, and a considerable number of sophisticated techniques have been developed in psychometrics, which include Delta-Plot (Angoff 1982), Chi-Square (Baker 1981; Scheunemann 1979, 1987), Mantel-Haenszel (Mantel and Haenszel 1959; Holland and Thayer 1988), Standardization (Dorans and Kulick 1986; Kulick and Dorans 1983), and various IRT (Hambleton and Swaminathan 1985; Lord 1980; Shealy and Stout 1993; Thissen, Steinber and Wainer 1988, 1993) procedures. Recently, some of these techniques are being extended for polytomous items, and a lot of new methods are also evolving for the same purposes. (see Millsap and Everson (1993) and Potenza and Dorans (1995) for a comprehensive review). More recently, the research on DIF expanded into another important unit of test analysis called an 'item bundle' (Douglas *et al.* in press) or a 'testlet' (Wainer *et al.* 1991), both of which refer to a cluster of related items that are analyzed as a single unit in the test.

A major rationale for DIF analysis at the item bundle level derives from the recognition that an undetectably small amount of DIF over a number of items can possibly add up to produce an unacceptable level of DIF when those items are organized and analyzed as a bundle (Douglas *et al.* in press; Wainer *et al.* 1991), which is often called 'item DIF amplification' in the literature (Stout and Roussos 1996). In other words, the 'item bundle DIF' or 'differential bundle functioning' (DBF) analysis was proposed as a way to uncover DIF that may be too small to be detected at the item level, if ever, but becomes tangible with some aggregation at the item bundle level (Wainer *et al.* 1991). Greater statistical detection power can also be obtained when testing more than one item at a time for DIF when those items measure a common secondary dimension. Nandakumar (1993), for instance, demonstrated that such a DIF amplification over several items could occur in real data. In this sense, the DBF analysis should be seen as a means to augment the DIF analysis rather than to replace it in the investigation of test bias.

In relation to this, the use of DBF analysis can be also justified on the ground that it enables the model of test analysis to be matched to the model of test construction, especially when 'context-dependent item sets' are used as the building blocks of test construction. In a 'context-dependent item set', usually a series of related items are based on the same stimulus material, such as a reading passage, a table, or a graph (Haladyna 1992). It has been suggested by many scholars in educational measurement that a group of items sharing a common stimulus material are highly likely to be locally dependent and cannot be handled satisfactorily by the major psychometric models that assume the statistical independence of each item in the test (Henning 1989; Rosenbaum 1988; Sireci *et al.* 1991). For this reason, it would be more appropriate in such a situation to treat a group of related items as a basic unit of analysis as in DBF analysis as a way to accommodate the suspected local dependence among items sharing a stimulus material (Wainer and Lewis 1990).

Another rationale for DBF analysis can be found in the DIF cancellation at the item bundle level. In reality, it is quite often very hard to create a test made up of all equally-functioning items for different examinee groups with different backgrounds. Many of the items may be disadvantaging either to a focal or to a reference group. Considering the fact that the final decisions regarding the measurement bias are usually made at the test level, it would be more practical to construct a test in such a way that negative and positive DIFs are cancelled out in item bundles and these DIF-balanced item bundles become the building blocks of a test. In other words, it means that, despite the presence of DIFs at the item level, DIFs may be balanced at the item bundle and test levels, if parallel-form item bundles are used as the units of test construction (Wainer *et al.* 1991). In such a case, DBF could be preferred to the traditional DIF analysis.

As in the traditional DIF analysis, the detection of differentially functioning item bundles in DBF analysis is also dependent upon the use of a construct-valid matching criterion, regardless of whether it is a total test score, a subtest score, or an external criterion. Once a construct-valid matching criterion is used to match examinees in the focal and reference groups on the target ability, it is known that DBF analysis is able to successfully identify the item bundles that function differentially for the two examinee subgroups (Stout and Roussos 1996; Wainer *et al.* 1991). When used alone, however, DBF analysis may not provide much information about individual item performance because either item scores are aggregated into a single item bundle score or the summation of item response functions is used in the analysis. It only reveals the performance of score categories, the magnitude of DIF at the item bundle level, and other item bundle parameters. On the other hand, if DBF analysis is used in conjunction with DIF analysis, they could provide more in-depth information regarding item performance at different levels of analysis than when either of the two is used alone.

In reading comprehension tests, 'passage-based item sets' are often mentioned as a good example of the 'item bundles' (Rosenbaum 1988) or 'testlets' (Millsap and Everson 1993). In the passage-based item set, a reading passage is followed by a series of related items about the passage, and the examinees answer those questions on the basis of their understanding of the passage. Usually, a set of items based on a common passage are suspected of sharing a secondary dimension (i.e. topic knowledge) other than the target trait being measured (i.e. reading comprehension proficiency) and, as a result, of being locally dependent. Such local item dependence may cause a test to be multidimensional and increases the possibility of test bias. (See Henning 1989 for further discussion on local dependence.) For this reason, such passage-based item sets are regarded as a good object of DBF analysis, especially in terms of DIF amplification over several items.

Despite such an assumed perspective, however, it has also been well recognized that the "local item dependence" that provides a rationale for forming item bundles can be caused by a variety of reasons other than merely the sharing of a common stimulus material (Yen 1993). Also, there could be multiple, overlapping factors contributing to the dependency or proximity among items in the test (Rosenbaum 1988; Wilson and Adams 1995). In the context of reading comprehension, for instance, the passage effects on the inter-item dependency structure might be possibly moderated by such factors as cognitive operations or reading subskills required for answering items (Alderson and Lukmani 1989; Pearson and Johnson 1978), the passage-dependency of items (Tuinman 1974; Johnston 1983), item formats, guessing, and so forth. Among them, a variety of reading comprehension subskills tapped by different item types in a test are often mentioned in the literature as a major factor that could possibly create unique cognitive dimensions (Alderson and Lukmani 1989) and, thus, contribute to local item dependence.

The main purpose of this study is, therefore, to find out whether or not reading passages provide reasonable boundaries for partitioning items into dimensionally distinct bundles for aggregate DIF or differential bundle functioning (DBF) analysis and examine whether there could be any other influential attributes of items that contribute to the clustering of items in an EFL reading comprehension test. It should be noted, however, that the research reported here is not a full-scale DBF analysis itself, but just a preliminary study to explore appropriate organizing principles for item-grouping for DBF in an EFL reading comprehension test.

DBF in the measurement of reading comprehension

Measurement bias and item bundle

An item bundle can be defined as a group of related items sharing a secondary dimension other than the target dimension to be measured in the test and thus suspected of being locally dependent (Douglas *et al.* in press; Rosenbaum 1988; Wainer and Kiely 1987; Wilson and Adams 1995). In many cases, the term 'item bundles' is used interchangeably with 'testlets', but the testlets can be regarded as a special case of item bundles. The reason is that the 'testlet' is more often associated with a group of adjacent items sharing a stimulus material (e.g. a reading passage or graph) or a group of related items that can be hierarchically organized in difficulty with a possibility of branching to different paths as in adaptive testing (Wainer *et al.* 1992; Wainer and Lewis 1990). On the other hand, however, the item bundle refers to not only a set of items that are used as the *a prior* unit of test construction and presentation as in the testlets, but also a group of items that turn out to be dimensionally distinct from other remaining items in a test as a result of empirical, statistical analysis.

Usually, a test or an item is regarded as biased if examinees with equal ability but from different groups do not have the same probability of success on the test or item (Shepard *et al.* 1981). Likewise, an item bundle is considered to be biased if two groups of individuals equally able in terms of the target trait measured by a test but from different groups do not have the same probability of success on the item bundle due to the examinees' differential proficiency on the secondary dimension shared by the items in the bundle. For example, let's suppose two examinees John and Scott have equal reading proficiencies but have different academic backgrounds (e.g. business and chemistry respectively). Both of them read a passage and answer six multiple-choice questions about the passage as part of reading comprehension measurement, but John gets a significantly lower score on the item bundle than Scott because the content of passage is specifically about a complex chemical experiment he is not familiar with but Scott is. In this situation, the item bundle can be said to be a biased measure of reading proficiency for John because he is unfairly and reasonably disadvantaged on the item bundle. It should be noted, however, that in reality examinee subgroups but not individual examinees are usually the focus of bias investigation.

DBF analysis and reading comprehension measurement

Differential bundle functioning (DBF) or item bundle DIF can be thought of as a descriptive and statistical term for 'item bundle bias'. It is analogous to the distinction between 'DIF' and 'item bias' made by psychometricians (Angoff 1993; Hambleton *et al.* 1991; Thissen *et al.* 1988). DIF is an abbreviation for "differential item functioning" and refers to a phenomenon in which a specific item functions differentially for different examinee subgroups, as the name implies. DIF does not always, however, indicate the presence of bias in the item. It may be reflective of true ability differences between two groups or of some unknown factors affecting examinee performance. For this reason, DIF is preferred among psychometricians as a neutral and nonjudgemental term for item bias (Thissen *et al.* 1988). In addition, DIF is also distinguished from item bias in the sense that DIF is a piece of evidence gathered in the investigation of bias, and the bias is the judgement based on multiple pieces of evidence (Hambleton *et al.* 1991). In sum, DIF and DBF are more of a statistical issue, whereas 'item bias' and 'item bundle bias' are more of a social and political issue (Angoff 1993).

DBF analysis in reading comprehension tests as a case in point can be justified for the following three major reasons: (1) the wide uses of passage-based item sets; (2) the influence of background knowledge on passage comprehension; and (3) the possibility of item-clustering based on principles other than passage effects.

First, the wide uses of passage-based item sets in reading comprehension tests make it necessary to examine a series of items within each passage as an independent unit of test analysis including DBF. Unlike independent items, in which all necessary information is presented in the stem of each item, the passage-based items usually take the form of 'context-dependent item sets' (Haladyna 1992), in which a series of items are based on the same introductory material (e.g. a reading passage) and are likely to be related to one another to a certain extent (i.e. locally dependent in a statistical sense). Due to such local dependence among items within the passage, the passage-based item sets have caused some major problems for classical and IRT test analysis (Yen 1993) and have not been able to lend themselves well to computer-adaptive testing based on IRT (Wainer and Lewis 1990). Recently, the emergence of the testlet approach (Thissen *et al.* 1989; Wainer and Kiely 1987; Wainer and Lewis 1990) based on polytomous IRT models, however, has made it possible to handle local dependence among items psychometrically and to use the passage-based item sets as the new units of test construction and analysis.

Second, it has been long recognized that readers' background knowledge (e.g. cultural, content or formal schemata) could have a considerable influence on their comprehension of the written text (Carrell 1984, 1987; Clapham 1996; Johnston 1983; Rumelhart 1980), which could possibly be a source of bias in the reading comprehension tests. The act of answering questions about a passage is not directly equated with comprehension of the passage, but those questions are basically intended to be indirect indicators that reveal the level of passage comprehension achieved by the examinees. As long as the examinee responses are indirectly based on the outcomes of passage comprehension, it may be assumed that the examinees' background knowledge could also have an impact upon the way they answer a series of questions within the same passage as a whole.

Third, it may be possible that item clusters can be formed based upon other characteristics of items than the sharing of a reading passage. The significant effect of passage on performance on several items cannot be automatically assumed all the time, especially when the passage-dependencies of items vary according to the type of questions being asked in the items. Although it may be an extreme case, a reading comprehension test can be constructed in such a way that only one question is allowed for a single reading passage. In relation to the passage-dependency of the items, Johnston (1983) argued that passage-independent items tended to be inference-type items in which answers to the items were not stated explicitly in the text and were subject to possible bias due to cultural difference in background knowledge. Washington (1979) also suggested that scriptally implicit items (inference type items) might penalize minority students more than majority students in reading comprehension tests that were purported to be a general measure of reading comprehension.

Identification of suspect item bundles

One important thing to remember in identifying suspect bundles for DBF is that test bias is not only an issue of test fairness, but also of test validity (Ackerman 1992; Shepard *et al.* 1981; Suen 1990). When a reading comprehension test is biased, for instance, it is not only an unfair and partial but also a construct-invalid measure of reading proficiency for a whole examinee population because an unintended construct (e.g. topic knowledge) other than the one being measured (e.g. reading proficiency) is likely to be measured by the test. The construct validity of the test is closely related to the dimensional structure of the test that is not only inherent in the test itself, but is also affected by the characteristics of examinee subpopulations. In this sense, the formation and testing of substantive DBF hypotheses naturally lead to a better understanding of different knowledge structures across different examinee subpopulations (Douglas *et al.* in press).

Currently, there are two major approaches to the simultaneous detection of DIFs among several items in the item bundle: Wainer *et al.* (1991) polytomous IRT and Douglas *et al.* (in press) multidimensional IRT approaches.

The former uses a series of items sharing the common stimulus material (e.g. a reading passage) as the unit of DBF analysis, and basically the passage-based item bundles are prime candidates for DBF analyses. On the other hand, the latter can either use expert opinion or empirically identify suspect item bundles sharing a secondary dimension through statistical analyses including the hierarchical cluster analysis using the computer program HCA/PROX (Roussos 1992; Roussos *et al.* in press) and the dimensional distinctiveness test using the computer program DIMTEST (Stout *et al.* 1993).

What is intriguing is that these two different ways of identifying suspect bundles do not necessarily have to be contradictory to each other, but could be rather compensatory in reading comprehension tests. In this regard, Douglas *et al.* (in press) reported that the structure of the passage-based item clusters was exactly reproduced through the HCA/PROX and DIMTEST analysis used in the second approach in the analysis of a reading comprehension subtest of the Law School Admission Test (LSAT), which consisted of four reading passages and 28 items. This finding has at least two major implications: first, the reading passage-based item clusters could be the most appropriate units for the bundle DIF analyses in both approaches; second, the passage effects might be strong enough to produce secondary dimensions causing biasing effects in reading comprehension in reading comprehension tests in general.

Research questions

The main research question of this study is whether the passage-based item clusters are the most appropriate units for DBF analyses and could be reproduced through PROX/HAC analysis in an EFL reading comprehension test. The specific research questions for this study are as follows:

1 Are the average inter-item correlations higher within passages than between passages and across all item pairs in the test?
2 Are all of the ten passage-based item clusters dimensionally distinct from other remaining items in the test?
3 Does the PROX/HCA analysis augmented with DIMTEST produce an item cluster structure that is close to the structure of the passage-based item sets?

Method

Sample

Participants were 181 twelfth-grade Korean high school students attending a local high school in a central province of South Korea in the Fall of 1996. All of the participants were male and had just taken the Korean Scholastic Abilities Test (SAT) for college entrance when they took the test for this research. However, only 178 students' responses were used because three students who did not answer all 40 questions were excluded in the analysis.

Instrument

The instrument used in this study was a 40-item multiple-choice reading comprehension test that was developed by the researcher for Korean EFL high school students and reviewed by three Korean graduate students studying in the TESL program at the Pennsylvania State University. Ten reading passages were taken from textbooks and magazines for high school children found in the Pennsylvania State University Library. Two reading passages were selected from each of the five subject areas, namely humanity, social sciences, natural sciences, engineering, and arts and sports. (See Table 10.1.)

Table 10.1

Titles, subject areas, and number of words for the passages

Passage	Title	Area	N. of words
P01	Composition	Humanity	148
P02	Yogurt	Natural sciences	166
P03	Piano tuning	Arts & sports	178
P04	Dream	Social sciences	200
P05	Polygraph	Engineering	203
P06	Elevator	Engineering	188
P07	Insects	Natural sciences	181
P08	Means for trade	Social sciences	181
P09	English vocabulary	Humanity	194
P10	Roller skating	Art & sport	193

The length of passages ranged from 148 to 203 words when contracted forms (e.g. *don't*) and compound words (e.g. *Anglo-Saxon*) were counted as single words. Most of the passages underwent a slight revision in order to create the same four item types across all of the ten passages used in the test. Even though there were no established rules regarding the most appropriate number for comprehension items to accompany a single passage, it was helpful to look at Harris's (1969) suggestion that, when a passage ranges from 100 to 250 words, it could be followed by four to seven items.

Four multiple-choice items were constructed for each passage and those four items were of the same item format and arranged in the same sequence throughout all passages. The first item following each passage asked examinees what the main topic for the passage was. The second asked what was mentioned or not mentioned in the passage as a recall of factual detail. The third sought to ascertain which phrase should follow a preceding phrase in the underlined part as a factual inference of details (e.g. *A is B because* _____ .); finally the fourth item, what kind of content would follow this passage as a prediction of content.

The whole content of the test was originally developed in English and then the instructions, stems for the first, second, and fourth questions, and option choices for the fourth questions were translated into Korean in order to help examinees understand the questions easily.

Table 10.2

Reliability of total test

Scoring	N. of items	Scale mean	SD	Mean inter-item correlation	Cronbach-α (KR-20)
Dichotomous	40	25.163	6.445	0.108	0.823
Polytomous	10	25.163	6.445	0.252	0.770

As is shown in Table 10.2, the KR-20 for the 40 dichotomous item test was .82, and the scale mean and standard deviation for the total score were approximately 25.16 and 6.45 respectively. When item scores within each passage were totalled to ten individual scores, the α-coefficient fell to .77. The passage-based scoring produced a lower internal consistency coefficient than the item-based scoring for the same total scores. Sireci *et al.* (1991) and Wainer and Thissen (1996) explain that the first α-coefficient (.82) may be an overestimate of the true α-coefficient (.77) and the difference between the two (.05) may be the inflated portion of α-coefficient due to the local dependence among items within the passages. Superficially, the .05 difference in the coefficient seems to be very small. However, if the Spearman-Brown Prophecy Formula is applied, the length of the current test should be increased approximately 1.7 times. In other words, about 27 more items should be added to the current 40-item test to regain the lost portion of reliability.

Data analyses

First of all, collected data were keyed into the computer program SPSS Windows (6.0). The SPSS reliability procedure was conducted to obtain the descriptive statistics, corrected item-total and item bundle-total correlation, estimates of reliability coefficient (i.e. KR-20 and Cronbach-α) for the whole test and each of the item bundles, and an inter-item correlational matrix of 40 items.

Second, the correlational matrix was imported into the computer program Microsoft Excel (5.0) in order to obtain the average inter-item correlation coefficients across all items and within and between passages. The Fisher-Z and inverse Fisher-Z transformations were conducted before and after all the correlation coefficients were summed and averaged respectively.

Third, the computer program MULTILOG 6.2 (Thissen 1991) was used to obtain the model fit statistics and marginal reliability of one-, two-, and three-parameter logistic IRT models and nominal response IRT model on the current data. MULTILOG is an IRT computer program that is designed for multiple category data and is also quite often used for analysis of testlet data.

Fourth, the computer program DIMTEST (Stout *et al.* 1993) was used to test statistically whether each passage-based item bundle is dimensionally distinct from other remaining items. DIMTEST is basically designed to test the unidimensionality of a test by partitioning the test items into three subtests. In this paper, however, it is mainly used to check the dimensional distinctiveness of the item bundles from the remaining items in the test.

Fifth, the computer program PROX (Roussos *et al.* in press) was used to obtain a matrix of item-pair proximity measures called conditional covariance between items (PCCOV). The computer program HAC (Roussos 1992) was run on the matrix of the proximity measures to conduct hierarchical cluster analysis, and each cluster in the HCA solution was statistically tested for 'dimensional distinctiveness' relative to the remaining items using the DIMTEST procedure. Usually early clusters join with other clusters further up the hierarchy. According to Roussos *et al.* (in press), the proximity measure (PCCOV) used in this study is a matrix of covariance between item residuals obtained after the target ability factor is partialled out, which is known to be very sensitive to the dimensionality of the test but insensitive to the difficulty of the items.

Results

Model fit analyses

Using MULTILOG 6.2, the test data were fitted to four different IRT models: one-, two-, and three-parameter logistic models and Bock's (1972) nominal response model. As is shown in Table 10.3, the three-parameter logistic (3PL) model produced the best fit and highest marginal reliability among the three dichotomous models. It might not be surprising considering the fact that the 3PL model does not exclude guessing error nor multidimensionality due to wide variation allowed in the discrimination parameter.

Table 10.3

IRT model fit

IRT models	Item number	Response category	Marginal reliability	-2log likelihood
1PL	40	(0/1)	0.82	6156.6
2PL	40	(0/1)	0.86	5911.5
3PL	40	(0/1)	0.90	5832.7
NR	10	(0/1/2/3/4)	0.79	3006.9

In this study, there was no testing of whether the reduced amount of –2log likelihood in the nominal response (NR) model is significant in comparison to the reduced degrees of freedom. However, the marginal reliability was lower in the NR model than in the three dichotomous models. It is usually explained by the proponents of the testlet approach (Thissen *et al.* 1989; Wainer and Lewis 1990) that the higher reliability of dichotomous models in comparison to the nominal response model might be attributed to the inflated test information caused by the dichotomous models' inability to account for item local dependence in the test.

Inter-item correlation

First of all, the 40 x 40 correlation matrix produced a grand mean of .11 for 780 inter-item correlation coefficients [(40x40-40)/2], as is shown in Table 10.4. Interestingly enough, the average mean correlation within the passages (r=.19) was higher than either the grand mean (r=.11) or between-passage mean correlation (r=.10). Even the average inter-item correlation within most of the individual passages (7 out of 10) was higher than the grand mean and the between-passage mean. Three exceptions included Passages 1, 5, and 10, which had inter-item mean correlation coefficients of .08, .09, and .07 respectively. However, when malfunctioning items from the fifth and tenth passages (Items 20 and 40) were deleted in the analysis, both passages produced mean inter-item correlations (r=.23,.20) higher than the grand and between-passage means adjusted for this change (r=.12, .11); thus increasing the mean correlation within passages from .20 to .22.

Second, the average mean inter-item correlation within passages (r=.1896) was found to be higher than the average mean inter-item correlation between the same types of items across different passages (r=.1051). The inter-item correlations between passages were further decomposed into two subparts: inter-item correlations between the same and different types of items. There were four types of items in each passage, and the average inter-item correlation mean among the same types of items across passages was .1051, whereas the mean among different types of items was .1100.

Table 10.4

Mean inter-item correlations within and between passages

	P1	P2	P3	P4	P5	P6	P7	P8	P9	P10	Mean	SD
WP												
	.0772	.1541	*.2876*	.2293	.0892	.2346	*.2602*	*.3302*	.1455	.0727	*.1896*	.1771

	IT 1	IT 2	IT 3	IT 4								
BP **S**	.1060	.1276	.1179	.0688							.1051	.1294
D											.1027	.1369
T											*.1033*	.1348
TT											*.1100*	.1403

•WP = within passages; BP = between passages; IT = item type; S = same type; D = different type; TT = grand mean.

Reliability and discriminability of reading-passage testlets

As is shown in Table 10.5, scale mean scores for the passages ranged from 1.94 to 3.02, with Passage 7 being the most difficult and Passage 2 the easiest. In terms of internal consistency among four items in the passage, Passage 8 had the highest reliability (.66) and Passage 1 the lowest (.20). Interestingly enough, out of five item bundles with Cronbach-α values higher than .5, the top three were those passages that had the highest average item–item correlation. It is interesting that the first two passages were found to be relatively easy but had low internal consistency. On the other hand, the last passage (Passage 10) was comparatively difficult and had lower reliability (.24). This may indicate that examinees did not have enough time to read the passages and answer all the questions and might have relied on guessing in responding to the questions for this passage. In terms of discriminability, three item bundles (Passages 4, 5, 6) located in the middle of the test were ranked highest with Passage 10 being ranked the lowest.

Table 10.5

Reliability and discriminability of reading passages

Passage	N. of items	Scale mean	SD	α (KR-20)	Corrected passage-total r	α If passage deleted
P01	4	2.8820	0.9404	0.2019	0.3965	0.7564
P02	4	3.0225	0.9141	0.3804	0.3584	0.7605
P03	4	2.8146	1.1421	0.5924	0.3921	0.7569
P04	4	2.6798	1.1950	0.5178	0.5054	0.7413
P05	4	2.3764	1.0409	0.2586	0.5853	0.7326
P06	4	2.5225	1.2176	0.5554	0.6047	0.7263
P07	4	1.9438	1.3265	0.5836	0.4085	0.7564
P08	4	2.4438	1.3275	0.6548	0.3978	0.7581
P09	4	2.2472	1.1076	0.3865	0.4546	0.7487
P10	4	2.2303	0.9845	0.2357	0.2703	0.7703

DIMTEST analyses for reading-passage testlets

Each of the ten reading passages was tested statistically to examine whether it was dimensionally distinct from the remaining items. As is shown in Table 10.6, only for Passages 3, 7 and 8 was the hypothesis of 'no dimensional distinctiveness' rejected. What is interesting here is that the three item bundles that were dimensionally distinct are those that had the highest within-passage inter-item correlation and the highest internal consistency indices (Cronbach α).

Table 10.6

DIMTEST Analysis for reading passages

Passage N.	Item number				Conservative T	p	More powerful T	p
P01	[1	2	3	4]	-.470	.680	-.700	.750
P02	[5	6	7	8]	.378	.350	.519	.300
P03	[9	10	11	12]	1.797	.036	2.366	.009
P04	[13	14	15	16]	-1.606	.950	-2.058	.980
P05	[17	18	19	20]	-1.272	.900	-1.747	.960
P06	[21	22	23	24]	.597	.280	.773	.220
P07	[25	26	27	28]	2.642	.004	3.074	.001
P08	[29	30	31	32]	2.307	.011	2.520	.006
P09	[33	34	35	36]	.831	.200	1.003	.160
P10	[37	38	39	40]	1.253	.110	1.806	.035

HAC/PROX analyses augmented with DIMTEST

Unlike in the previous analyses, the exploratory HCA/PROX analyses resulted in an item bundle structure that is quite different from the structure of the passage-based item bundles. As is shown in Table 10.7, seven item clusters were identified approximately at the hierarchical level of 27. At this point, Items 16, 40, 8, 9, and 1 did not belong to any clusters. As you move up the hierarchy, more clusters joined together and ultimately all of them were added to Cluster 1, one after the other. Further down the hierarchy, the clusters were divided into smaller subclusters, but only the clusters with two items and above were tested for 'dimensional distinctiveness' using DIMTEST. Among them, Cluster 1 consisting of Items 28, 37, 34, 39, 35, 36, 25, and 33 turned out to be dimensionally distinct from the remaining items through DIMTEST analysis (p=.0002). What is remarkable here is that half the items (Items 33, 34, 35 and 36) included in this 8-item cluster are from Passage 9. Two of the remaining four items (Items 25 and 28) are from Passage 7 and other two (Items 37 and 39) are from Passage 10.

Table 10.7

Hierarchical cluster analysis of the whole test

Cluster N.	Item number	Conservative		More powerful	
		T	p	T	p
C1	[28 37 34 39 35 36 25 33]	3.614	.000 (.0002)	4.37	.000 (.000006)
C2	[26 38 5 14]	-.118	.550	-.181	.570
C3	[22 27 11 29 4 32 31]	-3.259	.999	-4.13	1.000
C4	[17 23 12 30]	.975	.165	1.292	.098
C5	[10 15 3]	-.940	.170	1.251	.104
C6	[19 21 2 13 6 7]	1.241	.110	1.668	.048
C7	[20 24 18]	.270	.390	.393	.350

Further down the hierarchy, Cluster 1 was, as is shown in Table 10.8, again divided into two subclusters 1-1 and 1-2 (made up of Items 28, 37, 34, 39 and Items 35, 36, 25, 33 respectively). The null hypothesis of 'no dimensional distinctiveness' was retained for Subcluster 1-1 consisting of four items from three different passages (i.e. Passages 7, 9 and 10), but the DIMTEST examination rejected the null hypothesis for Subcluster 1-2 (p=.03). Three out of the four items in the second subcluster (1-2) were from the same passage (i.e. Passage 8). Once again, Subcluster 1-2 was further divided into the two smaller subclusters of 1-2-1 and 1-2-2, but the null hypothesis was rejected only for the first subcluster (1-2-1) consisting of the two items from the same passage again. It should be noted, however, that clusters of three items and above are usually considered as objects of investigation in the HCA analysis (Roussos *et al.* 1994).

Table 10.8

Sub-clusters for Cluster 1

Cluster N.	Item N.	Conservative T	p	Cluster N.	Item N.	Conservative T	p
C1-1-1	[28 37]	-1.129	.87	C1-1	[28 37 34 39]	-1.521	.94
C1-1-2	[34 39]	-.823	.21				
C1-2-1	[35 36]	2.098	.02	C1-2	[35 36 25 33]	1.903	.03
C1-2-2	[25 33]	.316	.38				

Discussion

The two main objectives of the current investigation were to find out whether the 'passage-based item clusters' were appropriate units of DBF analyses, especially for identifying suspect item bundles, and to examine whether there could be any other factors that contribute to the clustering of items in an EFL reading comprehension test. Overall, the comparisons of within- and between-passage average correlation and DIMTEST analyses of the ten item bundles indicated that the passage-based item clusters would be very appropriate units of DBF analyses in the EFL reading comprehension test and particularly useful for identifying suspect bundles when augmented by the DIMTEST procedure of the dimensional distinctiveness test. First of all, it was demonstrated that the context effects of reading passages were noticeable in the EFL reading comprehension test through the comparisons of the average inter-item correlation within the passages and between the passages and the comparisons of the average inter-item correlation within the passages and grand mean across all item pairs. Especially, the comparisons of the within-passage average inter-item correlations and between-passage average inter-item correlations among the same type of items seemed to contradict a general view that there might exist universal subskills for reading comprehension that are applicable across different contexts. However, the passages seems to provide support for grouping items together based on the reading passages and treating them as single units.

Second, it was confirmed again that the reading passage had a sizeable impact on the item clustering through the DIMTEST analyses of ten passage-based item bundles. Three out of ten passage-based item bundles (i.e. Passages 3, 7 and 8) turned out to be dimensionally distinct from the remaining items in the test due to the sharing of the reading passages. Especially, the DIMTEST procedure of 'dimensional distinctiveness' based on conservative and powerful 'T' statistics proved to be very sensitive to high average correlation and internal consistency among items within the passage and, as a result, is expected to be useful in identifying suspect item bundles made up of homogeneous items in terms of secondary dimensions.

Third, the exploratory PROX/HCA analyses produced an item cluster structure that is very different from the passage-based item clusters, possibly implying that there might be other important factors that might affect the item-clustering in a statistical sense. Nevertheless, even in one of the clusters produced by the PROX/HCA analysis (i.e. Cluster 1), the passage effect was partially identified. Four of the eight items in Cluster 1 were from Passage 9. One problem was the fact that the DIMTEST analysis did not reject the null hypothesis for Passage 9 in the previous analyses of ten reading passages, but, when Item 34 was excluded in the DIMTEST re-analysis, the null hypothesis was rejected for the 3-item cluster based on Passage 9.

Despite these encouraging results, the findings of this study should be interpreted cautiously for several reasons. First, as was mentioned previously, this study was not the actual DBF analysis study. No focal and reference groups were defined in this study, such as male and female, urban and rural, or humanity and engineering major examinee groups. Furthermore, no DBF analyses were actually conducted upon those item bundles. Moreover, the sample size in this study (n=179) was not large enough for most IRT analyses and DIMTEST significance testing. Especially for the two- and three-parameter logistic models, approximately 200–400 and 1000–2000 examinees respectively are required to obtain stable parameter estimates (Henning 1987). For this reason, the comparison of fit statistics between the models should be interpreted with caution. With a larger sample size, more confidence could have been placed upon the output of the DIMTEST analyses as well. Finally, the four item types used in this study are just a very small subset of a larger pool of item types. The results of this study should be limited only to those four item types, but cannot be generalized to other item types. In a full-scale study in the future, however, it is expected that the first and second limitations will be overcome and valuable information may be obtained regarding DIF amplification and cancellation within and between item bundles in the EFL reading comprehension tests.

Notes

The author would like to express his sincere gratitude to Do-Young Park for his help in data collection, two anonymous reviewers and Grant H. Henning for valuable comments on an earlier version of this manuscript, and Antony J. Kunnan for encouragement and support.

Suggested further reading

Douglas, J., Roussos, L. and Stout, W. (in press). Item bundle DIF hypothesis testing: Identifying suspect bundles and assessing their DIF. *Journal of Educational Measurement.*

Douglas, Roussos and Stout outline two different methods for selecting suspect item bundles for multidimensional IRT model-based DBF analysis: (a) using expert opinion and (b) using hierarchical cluster analysis and dimensionality test along with human judgement. They also suggest that the hierarchical cluster analysis and dimensionality test can be used to confirm the item bundle structure based on passage-based item sets in reading comprehension tests.

Shealy, R. and Stout, W. F. (1993). An item response theory model for test bias. In Holland, P. W. and Wainer H. (Eds.):197–238. *Differential Item Functioning* Hillsdale, NJ: Lawrence Erlbaum Associates, Publishers. Shealy and Stout present the nonparametric multidimensional IRT modelling approach to DIF and DTF (differential test functioning). Through this approach, they provide a mechanism for explaining how several differentially functioning items can be combined together through test scores to produce DIF amplification or DIF cancellation effect at the test level. Such a framework can be also extended for DBF analysis.

Thissen, D., Steinberg, L. and Wainer, H. (1993). Detection of differential item functioning using the parameters of item response models. In Holland P. W. and Wainer H. (Eds.), *Differential Item Functioning*: 67–113. Hillsdale, NJ: Lawrence Erlbaum Associates Publishers.

Thissen, Steinberg and Wainer introduce four different IRT approaches to DIF detection that test the significance of the difference between the item parameters for the focal and reference groups through likelihood ration (LR) tests: (a) general IRT-LR, (b) loglinear IRT-LR (c) limited-information IRT-LR and (d) IRT-D^2. They also extend the general IRT-LR approach to the detection of differential alternative functioning (DAF) in multiple-choice items. A similar framework is used in the polytomous IRT-based DBF analysis.

Wainer, H., Sireci, S. G. and Thissen, D. (1991). Differential testlet functioning: Definitions and detection. *Journal of Educational Measurement* 28(3): 197–219.

Wainer, Sireci and Thissen provide definitions of differential testlet functioning (DTF) and summarize a polytomous IRT model-based approach to DTF (or DBF). They suggest that Bock's (1972) nominal response model can be used to estimate testlet parameters for the two groups and –2log likelihood values for the unrestricted and restricted models. Both internal and external criterion methods can be used in this approach.

References

Ackerman, T. A. (1992) A didactic explanation of item bias, item impact, and item validity from a multidimensional perspective. *Journal of Educational Measurement* 29: 67–91.

Alderson, J. C. and Lukmani, Y. (1989) Cognition and reading: Cognitive levels as embodied in test questions. *Reading in a Foreign Language*, 5(2): 253–270.

Alderson, J. C. and Urquhart, A. H. (1983) The effect of student background discipline on comprehension: A pilot study. In Hughes, A. and Porter, D. (Eds.), *Current Developments in Language Testing*: 121–128. London: Academic Press.

Alderson, J. C. and Urquhart, A. H. (1985) The effects of academic discipline on their performance on ESP reading tests. *Language Testing* 2: 192–204.

Angoff, W. H. (1982) Use of difficulty and discrimination indices for detecting item bias. In Berk, R. A. (Ed.), *Handbook of Methods for Detecting Test Bias*: 96–116. Baltimore: Johns Hopkins University Press.

Angoff, W. H. (1989) *Context Bias in the Test of English as a Foreign Language.* (TOEFL Research Report No. 29). Princeton, NJ:

Angoff, W. H. (1993). Perspectives on differential item functioning methodology. In Holland and Wainer (Eds.):3–23.

Baker, F. G. (1981). A criticism of Scheunemann's item bias technique. *Journal of Educational Measurement* 19: 59–62.

Bock, R. D. (1972) Estimating item parameters and latent ability when responses are stored in two or more latent categories. *Psychometrika* 37: 29–51.

Brown, J. D. (1982) *Testing EFL reading comprehension in engineering English.* Unpublished Ph. D. dissertation. University of California at Los Angeles. *Dissertation Abstracts International* 43: 1129A–1130A.

Carrell, P. (1984) The effects of rhetorical organization on ESL readers. *TESOL Quarterly* 18(3): 441–469.

Carrell, P. (1987) Content and formal schemata in ESL reading. *TESOL Quarterly* 21(3): 461–481.

Chen, Z. and Henning, G. (1985) Linguistic and cultural bias in language proficiency tests. *Language Testing* 2: 155–163.

Clapham, C. (1996) *The Development of IELTS: A Study of the Effect of Background Knowledge on Reading Comprehension*. New York, NY: Cambridge University Press.

Dorans, N. J. and Kulick, E. (1986) Demonstrating the utility of the standardization approach to assessing unexpected differential item performance on the Scholastic Aptitude Test. *Journal of Educational Measurement* 23: 355–368.

Douglas, J., Roussos, L. and Stout, W. F. (in press) Item bundle DIF hypothesis testing: Identifying suspect bundles and assessing their DIF. *Journal of Educational Measurement*.

Erickson, M. and Molloy, J. (1983) ESP test development for engineering students. In Oller, J. W. Jr. (Ed.), *Issues in Language Testing Research*: 280–288. Rowley, MA: Newbury House.

Haladyna, T. M. (1992) Context-dependent item sets. *Educational Measurement: Issues and Practice* 12(1): 21–25.

Hale, G. A. (1988a) *The interaction of student major-field group and text content in TOEFL reading comprehension* (ETS Research Report. No. RR88-1). Princeton, NJ: Educational Testing Services.

Hale, G. A. (1988b) Student major field and text content: Interactive effects on reading comprehension in the Test of English as a Foreign Language. *Language Testing* 5(1): 49–61.

Hambleton, R. K.and Swaminathan, H. (1985) *Item Response Theory: Principles and Applications*. Boston, MA: Kluwer-Nijhoff Publishing.

Hambleton, R. K., Swaminathan, H. and Rogers, H. J. (1991). *Fundamentals of Item Response Theory*. Newbury Park, CA: Sage Publications.

Harris, D. P. (1969) *Testing English as a Second Language*. New York, NY: McGraw-Hill.

Henning, G. (1987) *A Guide to Language Testing: Development, Evaluation, and Research*. Boston, MA: Heinle & Heinle.

Henning, G. (1989) Meaning and implications of the principle of local independence. *Language Testing* 6(1): 95–108.

Henning, G. (1990) National issues in individual assessment: The consideration of specialization bias in university language screening tests. In de Jong, J. H. L. and Stevensen, D. K. (Eds.) *Individualizing the Assessment of Language Abilities*: 38–50. Clevedon, Avon: Multilingual Matters.

Holland, P. W. and Thayer, D. T. (1988) Differential item performance and Mantel-Haenszel procedure. In Wainer and Braun (Eds.): 129–147.

Holland, P. W. and Wainer, H. (Eds) (1993) *Differential Item Functioning*. Hillsdale, NJ: Lawrence Erlbaum Associates, Publishers.

Johnston, P. (1983) *Reading Comprehension Assessment: A Cognitive Basis*. Newark, DE: International Reading Association.

Kulick, E. and Dorans, N. J. (1983) *Assessing unexpected differential item functioning of Oriental candidates on SAT from CSAG and TSWE form E33* (Statistical Report. No. 83-106). Princeton, NJ: Educational Testing Services.

Linn, R. L., Levine, M. V., Hastings, C. N. and Wardrop, J. L. (1981) An investigation of item bias in a test of reading comprehension. *Applied Psychological Measurement* 5: 159–173.

Lord, F. M. (1980). *Applications of Item Response Theory to Practical Testing Problems.* Hillsdale, NJ: Lawrence Erlbaum Associates, Publishers.

Mantel, N. and Haenszel, W. (1959) Statistical aspects of the analysis of data from retrospective studies of disease. *Journal of the National Cancer Institute* 22: 719–748.

Millsap, R. E. and Everson, H. (1993) Methodology review: Statistical approaches for assessing measurement bias. *Applied Psychological Measurement* 17(4): 297–334.

Nandakumar, R. (1993) Simultaneous DIF amplification and cancellation: Shealy-Stout's Test for DIF. *Journal of Educational Measurement* 30: 293–311.

Pearson, P. D. and Johnson, D. D. (1978) *Teaching Reading Comprehension.* New York, NY: Holt, Rinehart, & Winston.

Potenza, M. T. and Dorans, N. J. (1995) DIF assessment for polytomously scored items: A framework for classification and evaluation. *Applied Psychological Measurement* 19(1): 23–27.

Rosenbaum, P. R. (1988) Item bundles. *Psychometrika* 53(3): 349–359.

Roussos, L. (1992) *Hierarchical agglomerative clustering computer program: Users manual.* Department of Psychology, University of Illinois at Urbana-Champaign.

Roussos, L., Stout, W. F. and Marden, J. (1994) *Analysis of multidimensional simple structure of standardized tests using DIMTEST with hierarchical cluster analysis* (Research Report of Office of Naval Research Cognitive and Neural Science. Grant No. N0014-90-J-1940). Department of Statistics, University of Illinois at Urbana-Champaign.

Roussos, L., Stout, W. F. and Marden, J. (in press) Using new proximity measures with hierarchical cluster analysis to detect multidimensionality. *Journal of Educational Measurement.*

Rumelhart, D. E. (1980) Schemata: The building blocks of cognition. In R. J. Spiro, B. C. Bruce and W. F. Brewer (Eds.), *Theoretical Issues in Reading Comprehension*: 33–58. Hillsdale, NJ: Lawrence Erlbaum Associates, Publishers.

Scheunemann, J. D. (1979) A method of assessing bias in test items. *Journal of Educational Measurement* 16: 143–152.

Scheunemann, J. D. (1987) An experimental, exploratory study of causes of bias in test items. *Journal of Educational Measurement* 24: 97–118.

Shely, R. and Stout, W. F. ((1993) An item response theory model for test bias. In Holland and Wainer(Eds.): 197–238.

Shepard, L., Camilli, G. and Averill, M. (1981) Comparison of procedures for detecting test item bias with both internal and external ability criteria. *Journal of Educational Statistics* 6(4): 317–375.

Sireci, S., Thissen, D. and Wainer, H. (1991) On the reliability of testlet-based tests. *Journal of Educational Measurement* 28(3): 237–247.

Stout, W. F., Douglas, J., Junker, B. and Roussos, L. (1993) *DIMTEST manual*. Department of Statistics, University of Illinois at Urbana-Champaign.

Stout, W. F. and Roussos, L. (1996) *SIBTEST manual*. Department of Statistics. University of Illinois at Urbana-Champaign.

Suen, H. K. (1990) *Principles of Test Theories*. Hillsdale, NJ: Lawrence Erlbaum Associates, Publishers.

Thissen, D. (1991) *MULTILOG User's Guide – Version 6*. Chicago, IL: Scientific Software.

Thissen, D., Steinberg, L. and Mooney J. A. (1989) Trace lines for testlets: A use of multiple-categorical response models. *Journal of Educational Measurement* 26(3): 247–260.

Thissen, D., Steinberg, L. and Wainer, H. (1988) Use of item response theory in the study of group differences in trace lines. In Wainer and Braun (Eds.):147–170.

Thissen, D., Steinberg, L. and Wainer, H. (1993) Detection of differential item functioning using the parameters of item response models. In Holland and Wainer (Eds.): 67-113.

Tuinman, J. J. (1974) Determining the passage dependency of comprehension questions in 5 major tests. *Reading Research Quarterly* 9: 206–223.

Wainer, H. and Braun, H. I. (Eds.) (1988) *Test Validity*. Hillsdale, NJ: Lawrence Erlbaum Associates, Publishers.

Wainer, H., Kaplan, B. and Lewis, C. (1992) A comparison of the performance of simulated hierarchical and linear testlets. *Journal of Educational Measurement* 29(3): 243–251.

Wainer, H. and Kiely, G. (1987) Item clusters and computerized adaptive testing: A case for testlets. *Journal of Educational Measurement* 24(3): 185–201.

Wainer, H. and Lewis, C. (1990) Toward a psychometric for testlets. *Journal of Educational Measurement* 27(1): 1–14.

Wainer, H., Sireci, S. G. and Thissen, D. (1991) Differential testlet functioning: Definitions and detection. *Journal of Educational Measurement* 28(3): 197–219.

Wainer, H. and Thissen, D. (1996) How is reliability related to the quality of test scores? What is the effect of local dependence on reliability? *Educational Measurement: Issues and Practice* 15(1): 22–29.

Washington, E. D. (1979) *The classification of reading comprehension items and its relation to the performance of selected racial groups.* Unpublished Ph. D dissertation. University of Iowa at Iowa City, IA.

Wilson, M. and Adams, R. (1995) Rasch models for item bundles. *Psychometrika* 60(2): 181–198.

Yen, W. M. (1993) Scaling performance assessments: Strategies for managing local item dependence. *Journal of Educational Measurement* 30(3): 187–213.

Section Three
Validation: Ratings and Test Development

The four empirical chapters in this section deal with two aspects of validation: ratings and test development. Alfred Appiah Sakyi examines the thinking processes and criteria used by holistic raters to evaluate written compositions. Beryl Meiron and Laurie Schick use both quantitative/statistical and qualitative/discourse analyses of performance on an oral proficiency test and discuss the ratings and rater background. Charles Stansfield, Weiping Wu and Marijke van der Heide describe the methodology used for the development of a performance-based listening-summary Minnan language test for selection and placement of employees of the US Government. Ebrahim Khodadady and Michael Herriman report on the application of schema theory to the construction of selected response item reading tests.

11 Validation of holistic scoring for ESL writing assessment: How raters evaluate compositions

Alfred Appiah Sakyi
University of Toronto

Abstract

This chapter is about the thinking processes and criteria used by holistic scores to evaluate written compositions. Twelve English essays written by first year university students were read and scored independently by six experienced English readers. Analysis of the raters' think-aloud protocol revealed characteristic reading styles used by individual raters to evaluate the essays. These reading behaviours determined what occupied their attention while they read the essays and how the final score was assigned to each essay.

Four distinct reading styles were observed:

1 focus on errors in the text;
2 focus on essay topic and presentation of ideas;
3 focus on the rater's personal reaction to text; and
4 focus on the scoring guide.

For raters who made a conscious effort to follow the scoring guide, the restrictions imposed on them to assign a single score at the end caused them to depend mostly on only one or two particular features to distinguish between different levels of ability. A tentative model showing factors affecting the scoring process was suggested.

Introduction

Statement of the research problem

Concerns about the validity of holistically scored writing samples were raised in 1970 by William McColly. Now after more than 25 years, the concerns are still echoed by many researchers in second language writing assessment (Connor-Linton 1995; Hamp-Lyons 1991a; Sweedler-Brown 1993; Vaughan 1991). Even when similar scores are obtained from different raters, it is difficult to tell whether raters are using the scale descriptors exclusively to classify ESL (English as a Second Language) compositions. Most correlational studies have reported the dominance of linguistic errors on holistically scored ESL compositions (Homburg 1984; Perkins 1980; Rafoth and Rubin 1984; Sparks 1988; Sweedler-Brown 1993). However, these studies have failed to develop any theoretical basis for the continued use of holistic scoring in ESL writing assessment.

The present study goes beyond correlational studies to describe the thinking processes used by holistic raters and to identify factors that influence their decisions during the rating process. The results of these analyses will be used to construct a tentative model of the holistic scoring process of ESL compositions. It is hoped that the outcome of the study will contribute towards the establishment of a theoretical model for measuring ESL writing ability and help clarify some of the issues and objections raised concerning validity of holistic scoring. The study is being conducted in two phases. This chapter presents the results of the first phase which was a preliminary study to define and refine variables and to model parameters to be used in the second phase.

Background

The construct validation of direct writing assessment such as holistic scoring is fundamentally problematic since it involves human 'instruments' whose behaviour cannot be completely understood. Most earlier research on composition evaluation was correlational studies where the researcher usually examined the essays for traits associated with high and low scores. Results of correlational studies collectively show that holistic scores are influenced by both discourse-level and sentence-level features in an essay, and these effect change according to the context of the study. Studies involving university professors' reactions to academic writing show that professors seem to make a distinction between content and language and they tend to focus more on content, development and organization when evaluating both ESL and NS (Native Speaker) writing (Breland and Jones 1984; Freedman 1979; Mendelsohn and Cumming 1987; Santos 1988; Song and Caruso 1996.) In other studies involving ESL writers, sentence level features, especially absence of errors, appear to be the most common factor associated with holistic scores (Homburg 1984; McDaniel 1985: McGirt 1984; Mullen 1980; Perkins 1980; Sweedler-Brown 1993).

Verbal protocol analysis provides direct observational evidence that supports results of correlational studies. This approach involves the use of verbal reports (concurrent or retrospective) to obtain insight into what actually goes through the raters' minds when they rate compositions, particularly key decisions and attention to specific criteria for making judgements. It is based on the paradigm of cognitive psychology (e.g. Ericsson and Simon 1993) and has the potential of providing rich information on the mental processes of holistic raters as they read and score essays. The approach has been used successfully in language testing situations to understand reading and writing process and, on a very limited basis, to study the scoring processes of written composition. The few studies on rater behaviour using this approach show that it is capable of producing rich information about rater behaviour and other factors related to the holistic scoring of written compositions (Cumming 1990; Hamp-Lyons 1991; Huot 1993; Janopoulus 1993; Vaughan 1991; Weigle 1994). All of the studies agree that experienced raters appear to bring well formulated strategies not only about the criteria with which to judge compositions but also about how to conduct themselves during actual rating sessions. This indicates that holistic scoring is a skill that is developed through training and practice (Weigle 1994), though there could still be differences in rating styles among experienced raters. Some of the studies using verbal protocols have suggested tentative models of the holistic scoring process but they all agree that a lot more work needs to be done in order to establish a theoretical basis for holistic scoring (Cumming 1990; Huot 1993; Vaughan 1991; see also Connor-Linton 1995).

Figure 11.1 displays Freedman and Calfee's (1983) information-processing model of holistic raters. They identified three main processes that underlie the rating of a composition: read and comprehend text to create an image, evaluate the text image and store impressions, and articulate an evaluation.

Figure 11.1

**An information-processing model of rating a composition
(Freedman and Calfee 1983)**

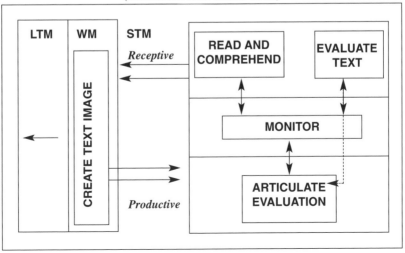

According to the model, a rater constructs an image of the text through reading and stores a set of impressions about that image in his or her working memory. Judgement of writing quality is not determined by the text itself but rather by the image of the text which is stored in the evaluator's memory.

Freedman and Calfee indicated that every evaluator may store a slightly different text image for a given text but for a homogeneous group of skilled evaluators reading a particular text under similar conditions, similarities in their text image should be more important than differences. The relationship between the three processes is more likely to be recursive than linear. After articulating part of an evaluation, the rater continues to read and, as bits of text are comprehended, they are judged. Furthermore, the evaluation of one section of text may change as one comprehends a subsequent section of text.

Cumming's (1990) study of concurrent verbal protocols of ESL instructors observed that expert raters tend to integrate their interpretations and judgements of situational and textual features of the compositions simultaneously, using a wide range of relevant knowledge and strategies, and their decision making appears to involve complex, interactive mental processes that seem to characterize other cognitive aspects of teaching skill and rating complex texts. He identified 28 interpretation and judgement strategies which could not only form the component behaviours of the three processes outlined in Freedman and Calfee's model but also serve as a broader basis for further research in developing explicit and accurate definitions of the knowledge and strategies used in holistic scoring. Cumming observed that both novice and expert raters distinguished between language proficiency and writing ability; however, expert raters reported more self-reflexive behaviours. Classifying errors accounted for a large proportion of the number of behaviours reported by expert raters while the novice group did more editing of errors.

Huot (1993), working with composition instructors of mother-tongue English courses, also observed through verbal protocols that expert raters are satisfied with a particular rating style which revolves more around a method of rating than it does any criteria for judging writing quality. Huot reported that expert raters have a definite guideline on which to base their scoring decisions, and they bring fairly well formulated strategies not only about the criteria with which to judge writing quality, but also about how to conduct themselves during the session itself. The expert raters in Huot's study responded more after reading the text than novice raters. The expert raters also contributed substantially more personal responses, representing many viewpoints besides just evaluative ones. Huot concluded that holistic scoring procedures may actually promote systematic and personal reading of student writing.

In Vaughan's (1991) study, trained raters agreed on the rating criteria outlined in the scoring guide in most cases but fell back on their own style in situations where an essay did not fit well into the pre-defined standards outlined in the scoring guide. Some raters relied on first impressions while others used one or two criteria such as grammar and/or content as the main factor for making decisions. Weigle (1994) also observed from think-aloud protocols that experienced raters tended to weigh additional aspects of the composition (not specified in a scoring guide) and were not guided by a strict literal interpretation of the rating scale.

Freedman and Calfee's model is more generic and focuses on general rater behaviour. The most significant aspect of their model is that evaluation is based on text as image created by the reader of a composition and not by the actual text *per se*. The implication of this model for validation on holistic scoring is that analysis of observable textual features such as Homburg's (1984) funnel model may be insufficient, unless there is an established significant relationship between observable textual features and text image created by holistic raters. Other significant observations that have come up from verbal protocol analysis are as follows:

• there are certain strategies that are effective and which can be developed through training and experience;
• experienced holistic raters are able to interact with text and express their personal impression in addition to the criteria outlined in the scoring guidelines; and
• holistic raters could be influenced by both content and language-related factors as well as their own expectations and personal reactions.

As of now there are very few such studies and the evidence is insufficient to develop a complete theoretical model. In the ESL context for example, there is very limited information on how raters combine different factors to decide the level of writing ability. Questions such as the extent to which errors influence judgement of other components or the effect of other features on error judgement have not been fully answered. There are also very few data on how raters systematically classify ESL compositions in different levels of writing ability.

This study attempts to provide additional information towards the development of a valid and reliable model for the holistic scoring of ESL compositions. It will focus on how holistic raters evaluate and classify ESL compositions in different levels of ability by using verbal protocol analysis as has been the focus of a few recent studies (Cumming 1990; Hamp-Lyons 1991; Huot 1993; Janopoulus 1993; Vaughan 1991; Weigle 1994). The present study will, however, go beyond analyses of the characteristics that distinguish good essays from bad ones to analyze the relationship between these factors and assess their relative importance. It will also provide further description of the interpretation and judgement strategies used by experienced raters and how they distinguish between different levels of writing ability.

The Study

Participants

Six raters were selected. They all had experience in teaching and testing writing ranging from six to 37 years. Three were primarily English first language (L1) instructors, and the other three were primarily English second language (L2) instructors. However, four of them had had experience with both first and second language instruction. All but one of these raters have had considerable experience with holistic scoring.

Procedures

A set of 12 papers representing the range of holistic scores on the Professional Faculty (PROFAC) rating scale[1] was used for the first stage of the project. The essays were randomly selected from English proficiency tests taken by first-year students in Architecture, Engineering and Pharmacy. Engineering and Architecture students summarized a discipline-related text before they wrote the essay. Pharmacy students were given a series of professional scenarios which required an oral response, and were then asked to provide (as their essay) an explanation for their response. They were re-marked using the PROFAC rating scale while the raters thought out loud after being directed to respond in as open and individual a way as possible. Their responses were taped as they carried out this activity and the tapes were analyzed. The raters were not trained for this session so as to ensure that they reacted to the texts naturally without any attempt to agree with other raters. Each rater marked all the 12 essays and assigned a score based on the descriptions on the PROFAC scale. (See Appendix 2 for a table of scores.) Scores on four essays from one rater could not be analyzed due to technical problems during the recording; one rater did not complete his evaluation of one essay because he found it very hard to read.

Results

The following results were obtained only from qualitative analysis of verbal protocols. They describe the reading styles (what raters focused on while reading) and criteria used by the raters to judge essay quality.

1 Reading styles

Analysis of the think-aloud protocol revealed characteristic reading styles used by individual raters to evaluate the essays. These reading behaviours determined what occupied their attention while they read the essays and how the final score was assigned to each essay. Four distinct reading styles were observed from the six raters' think-aloud data. These are described below.

i Focus on errors in the text

One rater read the entire text aloud pointing out mistakes and correcting them throughout the entire process. This person's comments were focused entirely on appropriateness of words, phrases and sentences and the frequency of errors such as omissions, wrong or missing punctuation and spelling mistakes. Judgement of writing quality appeared to be based on the meaning of phrases and sentences and the frequency of errors. The following are excerpts from the rater's think-aloud protocol.

> R2E5[2]: *The falls gives [not give out]. You don't need the word [out] there. Preposition problem there ..... [3] Out of there minds? Major spelling mistake. They are confusing the two: there and their. Anyone ..... There should be a [who] there. Anyone who talks about ..... falls [capitalize]. Immediate [spelling mistake]. ...[4] Wrong sentences, problems with spelling, punctuation, word choice, etc. They should have taken time to proof read it.*

ii Focus of essay topic and presentation of idea

One rater read for a well defined criterion based on essay content in relation to the topic and how the ideas had been presented. This rater usually read the opening paragraph, assessed the extent to which it addressed the topic, and then moved on to read subsequent paragraphs for idea development and organization. Comments were made mainly on content in relation to topics, organization of ideas and paragraphs (opening paragraph/thesis statement, links between paragraphs, and examples) and grammar. The comments were directed mostly at the text and not to the writer. The rater who used this approach was very quick to assign scores and rarely made references to the scoring guide.

The following is an example from the rater's think-aloud protocols.

> R1E6: *The CN Tower. Some very nice distinctions, sort of division of ideas here. CN Tower has physical and spiritual features. Let's see if the writer actually continues that as a point of organization. It seems to be the main idea for the first body paragraph. Yes this paragraph, the first body paragraph, quite nicely follows the ideas of spiritual strength, it has examples about the lights that keep on going and the economy being down but the tower still standing tall and straight and things like that. So that is at least emotionally very appealing and good to read. This paper is well written. It is quite passionate. It is not strictly speaking an essay in that it only really has one body paragraph but it clearly shows the writer's feelings about the CN Tower. No mistakes at all. I would give it 4.*

iii Focus on the rater's personal reaction to text

A third rater reacted personally to each essay. There were reactions to content that focused on whether or not what the writer was trying to say made sense and whether they had adequate English to say whatever they wanted to say. In some instances the rater's own biases were indicated. Sometimes a strong reaction to a specific feature appeared to dominate the rater's assessment of the overall writing quality. There were occasional laughter, comments about the learner and many personal comments. Comments were mainly made on logic, organization of ideas and language (grammar, sentence structure, ESL problems). The following is an example of the rater's think-aloud protocol.

> R4E6: *OK, this might even be acceptable for a preacher in the American South but as language, no, the symbolism is getting out of hand. It's becoming a kind of parody. Now, the problem is to be fair with this because, for me, because I reject this kind of verbiage which really has no thought in it. It's excessive and unconvincing I suppose. The language is reasonably acceptable but I certainly couldn't give it a 4. It's, even allowing for bias, it's the kind of stuff that Sister Mary Theresa in a small Ontario school would encourage their student to write and it has all of the tiresome, excessive, enthusiasm of snowfall over Lake Simcoe in the winter time except we are talking about something which is impressive but certainly doesn't go nearer to God to me. ... OK, so I have admitted my bias. I think it is excessive. I think it is brainless. I don't think it has any thought to it. It is reasonably clearly written and I would give it a 3, 3+ but no more than that and not have a bad conscience about it. So, this would definitely be a 3.*

iv Focus on the scoring guide

Three raters displayed conscious attempts to use the scoring guide provided. There were frequent references to the guide, and comments made on essay quality were mostly direct readings from the scoring guide. There were two different approaches to this reading style. One rater decided on a range from the first paragraph or first few sentences and then used the guidelines for the pre-defined range as benchmarks. The other two raters attempted to obtain a total impression of the essay before deciding on the score range. All three raters read the entire text while commenting along and referring to the scoring guide. They re-read parts or the whole text then summarized strengths and weakness and assigned a score. Comments were made on clarity of the thesis statement, organization of ideas and paragraphs, support/examples, distinctions between main and secondary ideas, vocabulary, grammar, sentence structure, coherence (connections between paragraphs) and how an essay compared with the previously marked ones. Comments were directed at both the writer and the text. The following examples are from one rater's think-aloud protocol.

a) First impression approach

R5E6: *..... This is a good paper. Nice introduction. So either a 4 or a 5, in the upper range. ..... qualities ..... It isn't sophisticated in terms of vocabulary. ..... OK verb tense, so there is some problems with verb tense. ..... provide ... I think it's definitely a 4 essay. It communicates clearly. It is immediately comprehensible to the reader. I think the reason I would give it a 4 and not a 5 is because there are occasional errors in grammar or word choice and because it doesn't have a sophisticated range of vocabulary and it isn't perhaps as formal as the essay I looked at before. ..... As I read it over, though, I find that it is really cohesive. You know, it is nicely organized. So, I would say that it's very, very definitely a high 4. A writing course though for this student is going to deal with minor problems in sentence structure which don't occur too often. It's getting up there. It's getting up to a 5.*

b) Overall impression approach

R6E9: *This person has immediately referred this to own potential career. I expect that this person will take the thesis that there are advantages for working for yourself or advantages in entrepreneurship, that's my expectation. Well, that's not as quite as organized as I had hoped but. Good points on the advantages. Nice swinging back and forth from advantages to disadvantages. This person obviously has a positive attitude to whatever will happen to him. The language in this certainly did not cause interference as I was reading it so I was able to look at the argument of the advantages or disadvantages. It's not perfectly organized in terms of transition words used but a good attempt at it. It's fairly substantive although I think maybe I would put this one in the 4 rather than the 5 area. It's generally well developed and relevant to the assigned topic. ..... The ideas simply are not quite connected as they were in the previous one which I think was definitely a 5 relative to this. So, this one for me falls in the 4 on the PROFAC scale.*

2 Raters' rating criteria and their assessment of essay qualities

Results of the think-aloud protocol analysis revealed some differences and similarities in criteria used to evaluate essay qualities. There were certain features that were associated with essays that received very high marks and other features associated with those that received very low marks. The following is a summary of positive and negative features that were mentioned most by the raters:

Positive features:
- good thesis statement/introduction
- clear/good thesis development
- clearly addresses topic
- good organization (use of transitions/coherence)
- providing support/examples
- good logic/intelligent thinking/knowledgeable
- very few or no grammatical errors
- good/sophisticated vocabulary
- complex/correct sentence structure

Negative features
- poor/unclear thesis statement/introduction
- poor development
- poor organization
- lack of coherence
- poor content – inappropriate/inadequate/no support/examples
- wrong/simplistic sentence structure/short/incomplete
- persistent grammatical errors

Table 11.1 shows comments given by the six raters on essays 3 and 11 which received the highest and lowest scores respectively from five of the six raters. One rater agreed that essay 11 was the poorest but he identified some problems with essay 3 and rated it as his second best.

My impressionistic analysis of comments made on the other essays in this sample shows varying differences in the raters' perception of essay qualities. In most cases there were combinations of 'good' and 'bad' qualities, and raters were at their own discretion to decide which ones were important. Their decisions to focus on certain qualities or characteristics were found to be influenced by certain factors including their reading style and own expectations as well certain distinctive characteristics of the essays. Essay 9 for example, which received scores ranging from 2 to 5 (Appendix 2), was perceived by some raters to be poor in content, but other raters were satisfied with the language.

The negative and positive comments were combined and summarized into three main characteristics that appear to determine these raters' judgements of the quality of these written compositions. (See Table 11.2.)

Table 11.1

Summary of raters' descriptions of a good and a poor essay (numbers in brackets indicate scores assigned by rater on a five-point holistic scale).

Rater	essay 3 ('very good')	essay 11 ('very poor')
1	clearly addresses the problem well organized sophisticated vocabulary good and clear content no serious problems with grammar and vocabulary (score: 5)	does not address the issue at all no clear organization naive vocabulary no support for general statement full of grammatical mistakes unclear thinking (score: 2)
2	awkward sentences punctuation problem verb problem cliche (score: 3.5)	serious ESL problem major senence problem sentence fragmentation logic problem (score: 0)
3	clearly developed clear ability to communicate effectively has an intellectual logic very clear to the reader lacks coherence some repetitive vocabulary well developed paragraphs (score: 5)	grammar is obscuring meaning syntax is off no support/examples for ideas ideas aren't really well developed inaccurate translation of words needs more help with ESL work needed in idea development and grammar (score: 1)
4	quite at ease with the language well organized intelligent totally persuasive nice sentence variety (score: 5)	second language learner brainless thought put together in semi-English random and disconnected ideas short sentences impossible grammar (score: 1)
5	nice choice of vocabulary knowledge of formal and informal good control of the aspects of language coherent and cohesive few minor errors very nice conclusion almost like a native speaker (score: 5)	no clear thesis statement not relevant to assigned topic writing some miss interprutation of information provided incorrect vocabulary surface errors no connection between paragraphs lacks coherence poor sentence sctructure (score: 2)
6	demonstrates knowledge of formal structures complex sentence structure sophistocated vocabulary minor errors an emotional response knowledgeable (score: 5)	problems with vocabulary and sentence structure persistant grammar errors no clear connections between ideas ideas not developed needs ESL arguement addresses topic poorly organized and repetitive

One significant outcome of Phase I is the realization that some experienced raters (especially ESL instructors) made a conscious effort to follow the scoring guide to distinguish between different levels of ability. However, the restrictions imposed on them to assign a single score at the end caused them to depend mostly on only one or two particular features for their judgement decisions.

Table 11.2

**Main characteristics that determined raters' judgements of the quality
of the written compositions**

Characteristics	Positive comments	Negative comments
1 content & organization	well developed & organized (logical, intelligent or persuasive)	poorly developed & organised/not relevant
2 grammatical & mechanical errors	very little	many/persistant
3 sentence structure & vocabulary	correct & sophistocated/complex	incorrect or simplistic

Some essays appeared to fall somewhere in between two scale points, and raters had to decide (sometimes unwillingly) to assign one of the two. To address this problem, some raters came up with their own sub-categories such as a low 4 or a high 3. Others essays were found to be strong on certain qualities and weak on the others. Since there were no weights given for the different criteria, the raters found it difficult to assign a single score that would best describe the person's writing ability. Some raters ended up judging different features separately as indicated in the comments below:

R4E5: ..... *It's a real puzzle. It's hard to force oneself to a 3. I will give it a 2 for content. The language is possibly 3. A course in writing will not help this person. The person needs to be thoughtful. It could be a 3 but I will give it a 2 for my own bias.*

R4E7: ..... *My debate would be between and a 4 and a 5. Yeah, in fact, that is kind of a problem because it is quite well done. There are a few little awkward things but there are also some rather nice turns of phrase. Logic is fine. The person is literate. I would give it a 4+. I am not going to sit on the fence and then after supper I will come back and give it a 5-. So this one is a problem as to location but I'm certainly very, very comfortable with it as a 4. OK, so that is our candidate #7 and I'm not giving it a good mark ..... I think it is quite nicely done and does develop and really we should think perhaps of a 5 but not. Let's keep it at a 4.*

R5E10: ..... *I find though, in terms of development of ideas, it's not quite, so I am saying it is a 5 in terms of language, I think though in terms of the development of ideas and the connection between main ideas and supporting ideas, I think it's not quite a 5. There isn't a clear connection. So, this is where I am at. In terms of language I don't even know if there is occasional minor errors in grammar. I don't know it is a clear 4 because I think the language is good and I think the language is at a 5 range. ..... If you want a commitment, Marian will give it a 4 although I think the language is at a 5 range. ..... I think the language is good. There is a few problems with prepositions but because it is not sufficiently developed in terms of supporting ideas and because there aren't clear connections between ideas, I give it a 4.*

R4E10: *..... In a generous moment I would give it a 4 but the language is pretty good but the organization of the ideas and the logic for the sequence I think is not up to snuff, so I would say 3+, if I had to. It was certainly written in recognizable English and there were certainly thoughts there. He or she took a particular position in favour of the workplace and argued it fairly well. So, I would bow to others who would say it should be a 4 but I would say, in fact, it would probably be a 3.*

These kinds of evaluations, however, occurred in the minds of the raters and would have never been known without a think-aloud protocol. Therefore in an actual scoring situation where raters have to assign only one of the 5 scores, the mark others finally see on the paper could be chosen from among one of two or more possible scores for a particular essay, depending upon certain dominant factors such as:

1 Content-related factors
Content-related factors that were observed include personal reaction to content such as:
- agreement or disagreement with opinion expressed by the writer;
- assumptions about task demand/degree to which content addresses task;
- presentation of ideas (development, organization, support); and
- length of the essay.

Below is an example one of the raters' comments that focused on content:

R4E9: *..... Last paragraph. ..... home as a workplace ..... trend will never cause a problem for any future career. Come on, this is nonsense. ..... creating our own jobs. Well, this is not a very good essay. It bounces all over the place. It really doesn't develop anywhere. It keeps saying the same thing, time and again with a few little examples. In light of all four essays, I might have to revise my analysis of the previous one which I gave a 3 to. Now #9, the essay at hand, is really not very good. I don't think it demonstrates marginal ability so I would have to give it a 2. It demonstrates some limited ability but it's not very good.*

R3E3: *..... The person seem to have good damage control skills. Really a process essay here. A clear sense of development. This essay is quite* *clearly developed. The essay has an intellectual logic, it is written as a process essay and what might even enhance is if the writer were to quote what she said to Susan to show that she was sympathetic to the problem. Very nice, very clear to the reader. Why not a 5? I think coherence is an issue here. ..... Maybe this is the one that I sit on the fence. This could be a high 4 or a low 5. Some of the vocabulary is repetitive and yet the paragraphs are well developed. Yeah, low 5, high 4. Nice length.*

Length was found to be a very important factor only when an essay was unusually short.

The following comments about Essay 2, which was only two paragraphs long, indicate the influence of length on holistic scores:

- *The problem is it simply lacks content. The student does not have anything to say. (score: 2)*
- *It is short but the content is quite clear. It is very well written so that will give it a (4) but unfortunately I have to give it a (3) because there is not enough content. (score: 3)*
- *This person does not lack writing ability. What is there is very good but was not able to say a whole lot – perhaps due the time frame. What is written demonstrates some clear ability in the (4) area, it might be a low (4) but it is better than a marginal ability. (score: 4-)*
- *There isn't enough there to warrant anything higher than (3). Not a well developed paper. Unfinished. Ideas lack connection but there are a variety of sentence types which are not incorrect grammatically. The vocabulary is good too. (score: 3)*

The scores assigned to this short essay ranged from 2 to 4, which indicate that the essay demonstrated adequate or inadequate writing ability depending upon who was rating it. Perhaps some raters perceived it as inadequate simply by its length whereas others saw it as an unfinished process but judged the writer's ability from what they were attempting to do. The effect of length on holistic scores has also been reported in a number of studies such as Charney (1984), Nold and Freedman (1977), Page (1968), Rafoth and Rubin (1984), and Steward and Grobe (1979).

2 Language-related factors

The main language-related factor that appeared to influence raters' decisions was the presence or absence of grammatical errors. Other language-related factors were the scope and complexity of vocabulary and sentence structure and the style or format used by the writer.

The absence of grammatical and mechanical errors appeared to make essays favourable (perhaps, unconsciously) to some readers. Most of the essays that were scored 4 or above were described as having few or no grammatical errors. The following excerpts from raters' think-aloud protocols indicate a possible effect of grammar on the final score assigned to an essay.

R3E9: ..... *There could be some improvement in terms of connectors and even in terms of a little bit of clarity but I think ... maybe I can give it a 5 ... possibly a 4 ... but I am not finding any grammatical errors that stand out and I realized that only 40 minutes were given ..... Yeah I guess the only thing is that I would like to see is more connectors ..... OK so this one I think gets a 5. .....*

R6E12: ..... *More and more I am convinced that this needs some language work ... I am just looking at the scale ..... It is relevant to the assigned topic but not well developed ... Not the range of sentence types that I might expect. I think this one will come on the side of a 3 for me in the language area although there is some attempt at coherence in terms of transitions and what have you ... but my thought is that this probably will be a 3 because of language.*

One significant observation related to errors was the influence of raters' perception of the writer as a second language learner:

R7E1: *... I think this not an ESL person. Why I say that is ... it's interesting, ... It just has all the feeling of a native speaker, a fairly intelligent native speaker talking to someone about a situation that they need to talk to them about. A little bit of a run on there which could be a native speaker simply carrying on without thinking too much about closure on sentences. That's odd and I'm wondering. It's a bit strange expression there. I might be changing my mind. OK some pronoun and references that are not ... Interesting although I still think that this is a native speaker, a native speaker who has not had absolute instruction in the writing of essays ... Just a thought. However, if we are judging it as just an essay, this does not have a real beginning with a thesis nor a real closure but it's well done ... So, I think I am going come down on the side of a 4. Some work could be done to bring this to a beautiful 5 in no time, if this, in fact, is a native speaker. I'm pretty confident that it's not a second language person. I could be wrong but that's why I'm coming down on the side of 4, a high 4.*

R4E11: *... Not a promising beginning, I must say ... Second language learner ... This is not very promising I must say. The idea is pretty lamebrain. If the rest of it is like this, we are in trouble. Second paragraph ... This really is not English. It would be very, very difficult to remediate these sentences because both the grammar and the logic are so badly out of joint. Next paragraph ... Good God, here is the semi-English again ... but this isn't going anywhere, I mean, it's just a series of random rather brainless ideas put together in semi-English. Next paragraph ... Well, home is a place for rest and your office is a place for work, I guess but God help us ... Well, this poor soul has learned one*

*phrase in English or what sounds like English and that's the rallying
call "We are the Engineers." But, apart from that everything else is his
own brand of semi-literate fractured English so I think I would have to
score this the lowest as a 1 simply because the ideas are totally random,
disconnected, the sentences are all short, the grammar is just
impossible. So, a mark of 1 for student #11.*

These comments indicate a possible effect of language proficiency on these
raters' perceptions of essay quality. This finding agrees with the results of
other studies on ESL writing evaluation where English language proficiency,
especially the absence of error, has been found to exert the greatest influence
on raters' evaluation (Homburg 1984; McDaniel 1985: McGirt 1984; Mullen
1980; Perkins 1980; Sweedler-Brown 1993). In another related study Rafoth
and Rubin (1984) found that mechanics was the sole variable affecting
judgements of other essay features including ideas and organization. Huot
(1993) also indicated that raters may focus on errors in grammar and
mechanics because they are so easy to recognize.

There have been other studies which indicate that ESL and native speaker
students are judged by different standards and that the types of errors that ESL
students make are far less acceptable and have more influence on a rater's
perception of overall writing quality than the types of error which are
commonly found in native speaker writing (Sweedler-Brown 1993). Land and
Whitley (1989) suggested that ESL students are implicitly expected to be as
fluent as native speakers of English when they are evaluated by instructors
who have no ESL training and in situations where they must compete directly
with native speakers. Others studies have attempted to move a step further to
classify non-native speaker errors in order of seriousness. Rifkin and Roberts
(1995) reviewed several of these studies and found varying results resulting
from inconsistent methodologies used in the different studies. Santos (1988)
also found out that judgement of error severity tended to vary among different
academic disciplines.

3 Contrast
Contrast refers to the influences of previous stimuli on the evaluation or
judgement of a new stimulus. The order in which essays were read was also
found to have some effect on judgement of essay quality for some raters.
Essay 10 followed two very poor essays in the original pile and some of the
raters kept the same order when scoring (even though they were not
necessarily told to do so). Below are some of the comments made about Essay
10.

- *Initially I am quite impressed with the sentences and the vocabulary in this essay, much higher level than the previous two.*
- *I would move this up to a (5). I think in terms of both the language and the arguments and the coherent organization and the manner with which they were put together, much superior to the other two papers.*
- *I think the reason I would give it a 4 and not a 5 is because there are occasional errors in grammar or word choice and because it doesn't have a sophisticated range of vocabulary and it isn't perhaps as formal as the essay I looked at before.*
- *The ideas simply are not quite connected as they were in the previous one which I think was definitely a 5 relative to this. So, this one for me falls in the 4 on the PROFAC scale.*
- *OK, well this essay is clearly worse than the essay I just read. I mean, ... 12 would have been a high 2, if this is a 2.*

Comments like these suggest that raters' evaluations of an essay may differ depending on how each rater perceived its quality relative to the preceding ones. There have been a few other studies that demonstrate the effect of contrast in the evaluation of essays (Daly and Dickson-Markman 1982; Hughes, Keeling and Tuck 1980; Hales and Tokar 1975) and in other forms of assessment such as visual perception, social judgements, weight estimates, attraction ratings of females, and interview judgements (Dally and Dickson-Markman 1982). This finding emphasizes the importance of research and rating practices having at least two different raters with essays arranged in different orders.

The observations from this study together with what has been reported in the literature have helped me to construct a preliminary, tentative model of the holistic scoring process (Figure. 11.2). The model presented here is only tentative and its validation is beyond the scope of this study. Validation of the model will require a larger sample of experienced holistic raters and a modified design that allows replication and the use of confirmatory factor analysis in addition to think-aloud protocol analysis.

Figure 11.2

A tentative model showing factors affecting holistic scores of written compositions

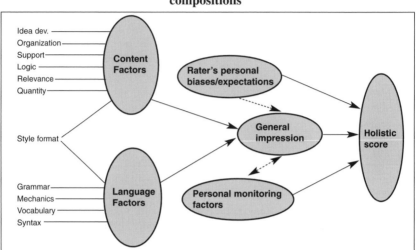

The second phase of the research will provide a more detailed description of the decision-making processes of holistic scores in an ESL context. Twenty raters will rate six samples of Test of Written English (TWE) essays using the TWE scoring guide. Raters' think-aloud protocols will be analyzed both qualitatively and quantitatively to determine: the nature and sequence of evaluation processes typical of experienced and inexperienced ESL composition raters; the aspects of the compositions (i.e. content-related factors or language-related factors) they are most likely to pay attention to; how they distinguish between different levels of writing ability. The second phase will also identify the common problems faced by inexperienced raters when deciding on the final score for an essay and the strategies and implicit criteria used by experienced raters to address these problems.

Notes

1 PROFAC is a 5-point holistic rating scale used to assess the writing ability of first year engineering, pharmacy and architecture students in a Canadian university.
2 These numbers are used to identify the source of each think-aloud protocol. Numbers appearing after R represent raters' identification number. Numbers appearing after E identify the particular essay that was being scored. For example, R2E5 means rater 2's think-aloud protocol on Essay 5.

3 Five dots represent momentary silence lasting more than two seconds. Raters were either reading silently or just pondering on what to say.
4 Three dots appear at places where parts of the think-aloud protocol have been omitted.

Suggested further reading

Freedman, S. and Calfee, R. (1983) Holistic assessment of writing: Experimental design and cognitive theory. In Mosenthal, P., Tamor, L. and Walmsley, S. A. (Eds.) *Research on Writing*. New York, NY: Longman: 75–97.

The article focuses on the application of cognitive theory to understanding holistic assessment of writing. The authors discuss various types of experimental design that can be used to study how raters score compositions. Two studies by Freedman that illustrate the experimental-design approach are described: the effect on holistic scoring of different facets of the rating situation; and the effects of experimentally varied facets of a composition on holistic rating. The authors also describe a model that shows how information is processed through working memory, short term memory and long term memory as raters read and evaluate written compositions.

Cumming, A. (1990) Expertise in evaluating second language compositions. *Language Testing* 7: 31–51.
The author reports a study of novice and expert ESL composition raters using verbal protocol analysis. He identifies 28 interpretation and judgement strategies used by raters which can be a very useful basis for further studies on rating behaviour. Differences between the behaviours of novice and expert raters are analyzed and reported.

Huot, B. (1993) The influence of holistic scoring procedures on reading and rating student essays. In Williamson, M. and Huot, B. (Eds.) *Validating Holistic Scoring for Writing Assessment: Theoretical and Empirical Foundations*. Cresskill, NJ: Hampton Press: 206–36.
This chapter reports on a study of expert and novice English composition raters with verbal protocol analysis. Huot reports that expert raters have a definite guideline on which to base their scoring decisions, and they bring fairly well formulated strategies not only about the criteria with which to judge writing quality, but also about how to conduct themselves during the session itself. Appendix includes a coding grid for the verbal protocols.

Vaughan, C. (1991) Holistic assessment: What goes on in the raters' minds? In Hamp-Lyons: 111–26.

This article focuses on think-aloud protocol analysis of trained raters scoring ESL compositions. The author reports that trained raters mostly agreed on the rating criteria outlined in the scoring guide but fell back on their own style in situations where an essay did not fit well into the pre-defined standards outlined in the scoring guide. Appendix includes comments made by individual readers grouped under 14 categories.

References

Breland, H. M. and Jones, R. J. (1984) Perceptions of writing skills. *Written Communication* 1: 101–119.

Charney, D. (1984) The validity of using holistic scoring to evaluate writing: A critical overview. *Research in the Teaching of English* 18: 65–81.

Connor-Linton, J. (1995) Looking behind the curtain: What do L2 composition ratings really mean? *TESOL Quarterly* 29: 762–765.

Cumming, A. (1990) Expertise in evaluating second language compositions. *Language Testing* 7: 31–51.

Cumming, A. (in press) The testing of writing in second languages, language testing and assessment. To appear in C. Clapham (Ed.) Vol.7, *Encyclopedia of Language and Education*. Dordrecht, Netherlands: Kluwer.

Daly, J. A. and Dickson-Markman, F. (1982) Contrast effects in evaluating essays. *Journal of Educational Measurement* 19: 309–316.

Educational Testing Service (1992) *TOEFL Test of Written English* (3rd edition), Princeton, NJ: Educational Testing Services.

Ericsson, I. K. and Simon, E. A. (1993) *Protocol Analysis: Verbal Reports as Data*. Cambridge, MA: MIT Press.

Freedman, S. W. (1979) How characteristics of student essays influence teachers' evaluations. *Journal of Educational Psychology* 71: 328–338.

Freedman, S. and Calfee, R. (1983) Holistic assessment of writing: Experimental design and cognitive theory. In Mosenthal, P., Tamor, L. and Walmsley, S. A. (Eds.) *Research on Writing*. New York, NY: Longman: 75–97.

Grobe, C. H. (1981) Syntactic maturity, mechanics and vocabulary as predictors of quality of ratings. *Research in the Teaching of English* 15: 175–185.

Hales, L. W. and Tokar, E. (1975) The effect of the quality of preceding responses on the grades assigned to subsequent responses to an essay question. *Journal of Educational Measurement* 12: 115–117.

Hamp-Lyons, L. (1991a) Scoring procedures for ESL contexts. In Hamp-Lyons: 241–78.

Hamp-Lyons, L. (Ed.) (1991b) *Assessing Second Language Writing in Academic Contexts.* Norwood, NJ: Ablex Publishing Co-orporation.

Homburg, T. (1984) Holistic evaluation of ESL compositions: Can it be validated objectively? *TESOL Quarterly* 18: 87–107.

Hughes, D. C., Keeling, B. and Tuck, B. F. (1980) The influence of context position and scoring method on essay scoring. *Journal of Educational Measurement* 17: 131–135.

Huot, B (1990a) The literature of direct writing assessment: Major concerns and prevailing trends. *Review of Educational Research* 60: 237–63.

Huot, B. (1990b) Reliability, validity and holistic scoring: What we know and what we need to know. *College Composition and Communication* 41: 201–213.

Huot, B. (1993) The influence of holistic scoring procedures on reading and rating student essays. In Williamson and Huot: 206–236.

Janopoulos, M. (1993) Comprehension, communicative competence, and construct validity: Holistic scoring in an ESL perspective. In Williamson and Huot: 303–326.

Land, R. and Whitley, C. (1989) Evaluating second language essays in regular composition classes: Towards a pluralistic U.S. rhetoric. In Johnson, D. and Rosen, D. (Eds.) *Richness in Writing.* New York NY: Longman: 207–293.

McColly, W. (1970) What does educational research say about the judging of writing ability? *Journal of Educational Research* 64: 147–156.

McDaniel, B. A. (1985) *Ratings vs. equity in the evaluation of writing.* Paper presented at the 36th Annual Conference on College Composition and Communication, Minneapolis, MN.

McGirt, D. (1984) *The effect of morphological and syntactic errors on the holistic scores of native and non-native compositions.* Unpublished master's thesis, University of California, Los Angeles, CA.

Mendelsohn, D. and Cumming, A. (1987) Professors' ratings of language use and rhetorical organization in ESL compositions. *TESL Canada Journal* 5: 9–26.

Mullen, K. (1980. Evaluating writing proficiency in ESL. In Oller Jr., J. W. and Perkins, K. (Eds.) *Research in Language Testing.* Rowley, MA: Newbury House: 160–170.

Nold, E. and Freedman, S. (1977) An analysis of readers' responses to essays. *Research in the Teaching of English* 11: 164–174.

Page, E. (1968) Analyzing student essays by computer. *International Review of Education* 14: 210–225.

Perkins, K. (1980) Using objective methods of attained writing proficiency to discriminate among holistic evaluations. *TESOL Quarterly* 14: 61–69.

Purves, A. (1992) Reflections on research and assessment in written composition. *Research in The Teaching of English* 26: 109–123.

Rafoth, B. A. and Rubin, D. L. (1984) The impact of content and mechanics on judgements of writing quality. *Written Communication* 1: 446–458.

Raimes, A (1990) The TOEFL Test of Written English: Causes for concern *TESOL Quarterly* 24: 427–442.

Rifkin, B. and Roberts, F. (1995) Error gravity: A critical review of research design. *Language Testing* 45: 511–537.

Ruetten, M. K. (1994) Evaluating ESL students' performance on proficiency exams. *Journal of Second Language Writing* 3: 85–96.

Santos, T. (1988) Professors' reactions to the academic writing of nonnative-speaking students. *TESOL Quarterly* 22: 69–90.

Song, B. and Caruso, I. (1996) Do English and ESL faculty differ in evaluating the essays of native English-speaking and ESL students? *Journal of Second Language Writing* 5: 163–182.

Sparks, J. (1988) Using objective measures of attained writing proficiency to discriminate among holistic evaluations. *TESOL Journal* 9: 35–49.

Stansfield, C. (1986) A history of the Test of Written English: The developmental year. *Language Testing* 3: 224–234.

Steward, M. and Grobe, C. H. (1979) Syntactic maturity, mechanics of writing and teachers' quality ratings. *Research in the Teaching of English* 13: 207–215.

Sweedler-Brown, C. O. (1993) ESL essay evaluation: The influence of sentence-level and rhetorical features. *Journal of Second Language Writing* 2: 3–17.

Vaughan, C. (1991) Holistic assessment: What goes on in the raters' minds? In Hamp-Lyons (1991b): 111–126.

Weigle, S. (1994) Effects of training on raters of ESL compositions. *Language Testing* 11: 197–223.

Williamson, M. and Huot, B. (Eds.) (1993) *Validating Holistic Scoring for Writing Assessment: Theoretical and Erupirical Foundations.* Cresskill, NJ: Hampton Press.

Appendix 1

Summary of the PROFAC scale level descriptors

Level 5:

An essay that scores '5' demonstrates superior ability to communicate effectively in an academic setting. It also evokes an intellectual or emotional response in the reader. A writer at this level needs no further writing instruction.

Level 4:

An essay that scores '4' demonstrates a clear ability to communicate effectively in an academic setting. It is immediately comprehensible to the reader. A writer at this level could still benefit from help in a one-to-one writing laboratory situation or in an advanced writing course.

Level 3:

Papers that score '3' demonstrate a marginal ability to communicate effectively in an academic setting. The reader has to do some work to follow the argument. A writer at this level needs to take appropriate courses in academic writing.

Level 2:

Papers that score '2' demonstrate limited ability to communicate effectively in an academic setting. The reader has to work hard to follow the argument. A writer at this level needs to take appropriate courses in (English as a Second Language) Academic Writing, Grammar or Vocabulary.

Level 1:

Papers that score '1' demonstrate little ability to communicate effectively in an academic setting. The reader is unable to follow the argument. A writer at this level needs intensive English as a Second Language training.

Appendix 2

Table A2.1

Comparison of raters' scores with original essay scores[1]

Discipline	Essay	Origional score	Scores assigned by raters					
			R1	R2	R3	R4	R5	R6
Pharmacy	1	4	5	-	4-	2/3	4	4+
	2	3	4&3	2.5	3	2	3	4
(problem solving)	3	5	5	3.5	5-/4+[2]	5	5	3
	4	3/4	3	2.5	3	3	4	3
Architecture	5	2	2	1	2	3&2	3	-
	6	4	4	4	4+	3+	4++	-
(descriptive)	7	4	4	3	5	4+/5-	5	-
	8	2/3	2	2	2	3	3+/4-	-
Engineering	9	3	3	3/4	5	2	4	4
	10	4	3	3.5	4-	3&4	4&5	4
(arguementative)	11	2	2	0	2	1	1	2
	12	3	2	2	3	2	2/3--	3

Notes

1   Some raters gave two scores to some essays, for example 4 for content and 3 for language.

2   Some rater could not be certain on a single score. 5-/4+ for example means the seeay is either a low 5 or a high 4.

12 Ratings, raters and test performance: An exploratory study

Beryl E. Meiron
Cambridge Examinations and IELTS International
Laurie S. Schick
University of California, Los Angeles

Abstract

The aims of this chapter are: (1) to investigate by means of discourse analysis whether quantitative scores represented qualitatively different performances in an oral proficiency test (OPT); and (2) how a qualitative analysis of performance might account for any quantitative improvement in oral skills scores by test takers. An unexpected finding was that such a qualitative analysis helped account for variability among rater scores. The OPT studied here was administered to 25 Egyptian English as a Foreign Language teachers in an 11-week teacher training program. The OPT was a role-play directly related to the training program and professional interests of the test takers. Four raters were normed and paired to rate videotaped pre- and post-test sessions. Discourse analysis comparing transcripts of pre- and post-test videotapes was used to 'disambiguate [the] gross subjective ratings' (Douglas and Selinker 1992: 327). The discourse analysis indicates that similar quantitative scores do not necessarily indicate similar performances. The investigators hypothesize that this discrepancy occurred because teacher and non-teacher raters were influenced by occupational background, experience, and different features in the discourse. The chapter concludes with a call for rating verbal protocols to study features raters attend to and cognitive processes used when scoring OPTs.

Introduction

The slippery slope of trying to assess oral proficiency has prompted increasing research into the validity and usefulness of oral proficiency testing methods. In his 1989 article, van Lier posed two questions which he deemed 'central' to any discussion of oral proficiency interviews (OPIs) in particular, but which are also important for examining any method of testing oral proficiency:

(a) Are OPIs examples of conversational language use? and
(b) Is conversational language use the appropriate (or the only, or the best) vehicle to evaluate oral proficiency?' (van Lier 1989: 489).

In answering his questions, van Lier makes several observations and comes to several tentative conclusions, not the least among them that: 'Conversation is much more difficult to rate than monologic interviewer-elicited talk' (1989: 501). Thus while there has been considerable research done examining oral proficiency interviews, including van Lier (1989), Ross and Berwick (1992), Young and Milanovic (1992), Young (1995), and Lazaraton (1996), this work has looked primarily at the way in which the native-speaker interviewer, by virtue of her dominant position and linguistic proficiency in the target language, has come to asymmetrically influence discourse features such as topic nomination, ratification and persistence, turn-taking, and goal orientation. This continuing focus on OPIs in particular is understandable in that this has been a prevalent means of testing oral proficiency, and this focus on interviewer–test taker interaction is also understandable given the type of test under examination. However, as van Lier (1989) indicates, one of the dominant problems in oral proficiency testing is the difficulty which evaluating conversational features presents to raters. It is this problem – the problem of rating oral proficiency within a conversational context – to which we turn our attention in this study.

We focus here on the problem of rating and raters rather than on the problem of interviewer–test taker interaction for several reasons. First, the oral proficiency test (OPT) which we are discussing was not designed as an interview but as a role-play involving four to five non-native speaker participants. Second, we are interested in looking at some of the variables which might influence how raters evaluate conversational features as an integral part of oral proficiency.

Rating OPTs depends on the judgement of test-taker performance by human raters. Understanding raters, ratings, and test performance has become an area of research interest for second language acquisition researchers, language testers, teachers, and test users in part because inconsistencies between raters may be a source of bias. Ratings are most frequently determined by trained raters applying a rubric and rating scale to a performance. However, in spite of rater training and the use of rubrics and rating scales, raters can arrive at similar ratings for different reasons (Douglas 1994). That is, test takers can have qualitatively different performances yet obtain similar quantitative scores. This is an important concern because 'the rater is an integral component of proficiency rating scores' (Chaloub-Deville 1995: 255) and variation in rater scoring may call into question the reliability and validity of the resulting score. However, if conversation is, as van Lier (1989) says, an 'appropriate vehicle for the all-around display of speaking ability in context,' (p. 489) then we need to examine the way in which raters are trained to recognize conversational features, and the way in which they actually interpret and assess oral proficiency in conversational test performances.

Three recent studies have addressed the issue of how raters rate as well as how test takers perform in oral proficiency testing by using both quantitative and qualitative approaches. These studies were based on a series of field-specific, semi-direct, tape-mediated OPTs. Douglas and Selinker (1992), determined that a field-specific test, CHEMSPEAK, was a better predictor of field-specific oral performance than a general OPT, and called for 'rhetorical/grammatical interlanguage analysis ... to disambiguate gross subjective ratings on field-specific oral tests' (p. 327). Douglas and Selinker (1993), investigating MATHSPEAK, were unable to determine from evidence in the transcripts that test takers' grammar performances were demonstrably better on the field-specific test than their performances on a more general test. Nevertheless, test takers received higher grammar scores on the field-specific tests. The researchers surmised that rhetorical complexity was higher on the field-specific OPTs, but because raters had no category for such a score, they assigned a higher score to the grammar category. In an investigation to clarify ambiguous holistic ratings, Douglas (1994) qualitatively analyzed test-taker performance by focusing on rater performance on one more field-specific test, AGSPEAK. In this study, he found that there was very little relationship between quantitative rating scores and test-taker performance analyzed qualitatively.

A number of factors may influence the rater in determining the features attended to in the discourse. One of these factors includes the rater's occupational and experiential background. Of importance not only for this study but for any study of raters and their backgrounds are previous findings from research which examine differences between teacher and non-teacher raters of OPTs. Such studies are of great importance because raters are frequently teachers, and both teacher training and experience may influence teacher raters' judgements such that they may differ from non-teaching raters (Chalhoub-Deville 1996). Although Shohamy, Gordon and Kraemer (1992), who examined inter-rater reliability between teachers and non-teachers, concluded that, while rater training had a positive impact on rater agreement, occupational background appeared to have no effect, many other studies have found that there are differences between the way in which teachers and non-teachers rate oral proficiency. These studies do not always agree, however, as to how these two rater populations differ. With regard to harshness, for example, Barnwell (1989) found that native-speaker non-teachers rated more harshly than ACTFL-trained teacher raters, but Galloway (1980) found that teacher raters were harsher than non-teacher raters, particularly on linguistic features, such as pronunciation and speed. Supporting this latter finding,

Hadden (1991) concluded that English as a Second Language (ESL) teacher raters rated oral proficiency lower than non-teachers. Two other recent studies compared the rating differences between teachers and non-teacher subject or occupation specialists. Brown (1995) examined the occupational and linguistic background effect on an occupation-specific oral language performance test, Japanese Test for Tour Guides, focusing on teacher and non-teacher raters, and found a significant difference in ratings between the two rater groups which she attributed to different perceptions of test-taker performances. Elder (1993) found that teacher and non-teacher subject specialist raters correlate on rating communicative effectiveness, but show differences in rating language use and weighting features. In addition, there was evidence of differences in how the two rater groups perceived the rubric and applied the rating scales. Finally, in a study investigating the holistic scoring of three methodologically different OPTs of Arabic as a Foreign Language, Chalhoub-Deville (1995, 1996) found that teacher and non-teacher raters weighted features in the discourse differently. When we performed qualitative analyses on transcripts taken from a videotaped, field-specific OPT, we also found that raters with different teaching and non-teaching backgrounds attended to different features when scoring test-taker performances.

Background

The CSULA Institute for Egyptian Teachers of English as a Foreign Language (EFL) was an eleven-week teacher-training program administered by the TESOL Program at CSULA from April 4 to June 20 1996. The Institute began as a six-week program in the summer of 1995, and was expanded to a longer program for the second year. This teacher-training initiative was sponsored by the United States Agency for International Development and was co-ordinated by the Binational Fulbright Commission, Cairo, Egypt.

The Institute was organized into three complementary components: the EFL teacher development component, the personal development component, and the teacher-in-training component. The teacher development component consisted of five courses taught in two-hour blocks: issues in ESL/EFL, curriculum and materials design, ESL/EFL methods and practicum, assessment, and classroom management. The personal development component comprised two one-hour workshops taught twice per week including written English language development, and pronunciation and communication skills. This component also included a special topics workshop, four educational field trips, five cultural dinners, and five guest lectures. The teacher-in-training component had a twice-a-week classroom observation module and a once-a-week reflective teaching session.

The OPT was administered to the test takers prior to instruction and immediately scored at the beginning of the program in order to advise the Institute instructors regarding curriculum development, and then again at the end of the program, again in order to examine curriculum development. Thus the ratings of the pre- and post-tests were not conducted as blind studies because the test was not originally meant for research purposes but pedagogical ones.

Purpose

The original purpose of this coupled quantitative and qualitative study was threefold:
1 to identify, measure, and compare oral skills gains on a pre-test and post-test of oral proficiency by means of quantitative analysis;
2 to identify those participants whose gains differed from the norm, and investigate by means of discourse analysis whether the quantitative scores represent qualitatively different performances;
3 to analyze the differences in test-taker performance as well as in rater scoring by comparing test-taker performance and scores.

The three research questions with which we began this study were:
1 Do participants make quantitatively measurable gains after an 11-week teacher training program?
2 Will discourse analysis reveal any differences or similarities in performance which are not reflected in quantitative results?
3 Will discourse analysis reveal whether the content-based instruction (CBI) received by participants had any effect on their oral proficiency gains?

Method

Test takers

Twenty-five Egyptian teachers of English as a Foreign Language who participated in an 11-week teacher training program at a large, urban California university were the test-taker subjects of this study. All of the participants were elementary, secondary or preparatory level teachers of EFL from both urban and rural areas of Egypt. The ages ranged between 25 and 40 years (mean = 32); 40 per cent were female. They were all native speakers of Arabic, and had been in the United States for less than one week at the time of the pre-test. All were university graduates with degrees in English at the baccalaureate level. Their pre-institute TOEFL scores ranged from 450 to 530, with a mean score of 483.2.

Raters

Four graduate student researchers were normed and paired as raters. Rater 1 was an ESL instructor with experience in discourse analysis; Rater 2 was an ESL instructor with experience in teaching pronunciation and oral skills, and was also the instructor of the Institute pronunciation and communication skills component; Rater 3 was a novice in the field with no prior teaching experience; Rater 4 was an experienced elementary and secondary EFL/ESL teacher and a non-native speaker of English.

Instrument

The test-taker subjects took an oral proficiency test, one of a battery of three tests designed to assess reading, writing, and oral skills, administered pre- and post-Institute. The test elicited performance based on a role-play simulation task which required test takers to discuss reasons for declining EFL test scores at a hypothetical secondary school and argue either for a literature or grammar-based approach to remedy the situation. The task attempted to elicit content-specific language.

A five-category rubric and rating scale was revised from a prior version to assess the participants' oral performance. Five components were included for evaluation: topic control, pronunciation, grammatical control, lexical control, and conversational control. Topic control was rated on a rating scale from 1 to 3; the other four components were rated on a rating scale of 1 to 5. A final score for the OPT was calculated by adding all the subscores; 23 points was the maximum possible score.

Procedure

A written prompt described a school-related situation that required the subjects to engage in a single-task group oral discussion simulating an authentic speaking situation. The subjects were randomly divided into five groups of four individuals and one group of five. All subjects were tested on the same day in a videotape-lab setting. The written prompt was first read individually by the test takers and then read aloud by one of the test administrators. Each group was then divided into two subgroups; each subgroup was randomly assigned a role to support one of the two differing opinions and given ten minutes preparation time. The discussion was videotaped for fifteen minutes. The test administrators monitored for turn-taking only when necessary, and did not participate in the discussion.

A norming session was held following the pre-test and post-test administration. One videotape of a group of four participants was selected at random from the cassettes and viewed independently by the four raters. The ratings were tallied, compared, and discussed. In cases of disagreement on more than one point on the rating scale, the cases were discussed at length with raters providing a rationale for their score judgements. Raters 1 and 2 were paired together as Pair 1; Raters 3 and 4 were paired together as Pair 2. Each pair then received the same videotapes to be viewed independently, and the scores were computed for the five different speaking components. All scores were reported as a total score both for the pre-test and post-test. The statistical analyses were performed using the Statistical Package for the Social Sciences (SPSS) and Microsoft EXCEL 6.0. We then used quantitative findings to identify which test-taker performances would be used for qualitative analyses.

The taped protocols were transcribed by Rater 1 using discourse analysis notation. (See Appendix B for the transcription key.)

Quantitative results

In order to ascertain the gains achieved by the participants, a descriptive analysis was performed on the pre-test and post-test scores. A further analysis of the different speaking components was done to determine whether the participants improved in any of the specific categories. Inter-rater reliability on both the pre-test and the post-test was determined by a bivariate correlation analysis from the scores given by each rater. To identify whether the gains made were statistically significant, a matched t-test was performed on the mean scores of the speaking category and its different components.

Table 12.1 shows the mean scores and the standard deviations for all subjects on the pre-test and post-test. The difference in the mean, minimum and maximum increased and the standard deviation decreased, indicating that there was an overall tendency of the individual scores to shift to higher scores with the standard deviation spread closer to the mean. The results of the descriptive analysis indicate an overall gain in performance on the post-test.

Table 12.1
Descriptive analysis of pre-test and post-test scores (n=25)

	Mean	Standard Deviation	Minimum	Maximum
Pre test	13.76	1.87	10.5	16.5
Post test	16.04	1.40	13.0	18.5
Difference	2.28	-0.47	2.5	2.0

Inter-rater reliability was computed for each test using Pearson's correlation coefficient. Table 12.2 shows the inter-rater reliability for each pair of raters on the pre-test and post-test. Pair 1 showed a consistently fair degree of inter-rater reliability on both tests. Pair 2 showed relatively high inter-rater reliability on the pre-test; however there is a significant drop to 0.47 on the post-test indicating very little agreement between the two raters.

Table 12.2

Inter-rater reliability (Pearson)

	Pair 1 (Raters 1 & 2)	Pair 2 (Raters 3 & 4)
Pre test Total	0.71	0.82
Post test Total	0.75	0.47

Table 12.3 shows a matched t-test comparing the subject overall score and the differences in the five components of the test.

Table 12.3

Matched t-test of pre-test and post-test ratings by components (n=25)

Components	Pre-test mean	SD	Post-test Mean	SD	Difference in mean (%)		Gain t-value
Topic Control	2.34	0.28	2.72	0.44	0.38	13%	3.37*
Pronunciation	2.62	0.44	3.00	0.63	0.38	8%	3.92**
Grammatical Control	2.86	0.53	3.30	0.46	0.44	9%	4.03**
Lexical Control	2.94	0.49	3.44	0.39	0.50	10%	5.48**
Conversational Control	3.00	0.74	3.58	0.40	0.58	12%	4.42**
Overall Score	13.76	1.87	16.04	1.40	2.28	10%	9.64**

* significant p>.01

** significant p>.001

The results show gains for the mean scores of all five components. The results of the matched t-test indicate that the t-values for four of the five components were significant at 0.001 level; topic control was also significant at 0.01 level. The increases in all five components and overall score were identified as significant.

Table 12.4 shows the distribution of individual gains. Considering the whole range of gain was 22%, from -2% to 20%, we divided the total range into three groups.

Table 12.4

Distribution of individual gains

Range of % gain	# of Cases
13 - 20%	6
5 - 12%	11
-3 - 4%	4
Total cases	21

In order to perform detailed qualitative analyses on portions of the OPT, we chose to focus on participants based on the distribution of individual gains. To compare performances qualitatively, we selected cases from each range. For the purpose of this paper, two test takers, one from the top range, who had increased his score considerably, and one from the bottom range, who had a very small increase in her score, were selected to exemplify the qualitative findings. We call these two test takers 'Mohammed' and 'Fatima'.

Table 12.5 shows the pre-test and post-test scores for Mohammed and Fatima. These results reveal that Fatima had a higher total score on the pre-test than Mohammed, but that they had similar overall post-test scores. From Fatima's conversational control score, it appears that she was slightly better than Mohammed on the pre-test, but they appear to be equally proficient on the post-test. Mohammed increased his scores in lexical, grammatical, and topic control by one point, but remained the same in pronunciation. Fatima maintained the same scores in lexical and grammatical control, and slightly increased her score in pronunciation. Her score in topic control, however, decreased slightly on the post-test.

Table 12.5

Pre-test and post-test score comparisons of Mohammed and Fatima

	Mohammed		Fatima	
	Pre-test	Post-test	Pre-test	Post-test
Conversational Control	2.5	4	3	4
Lexical Control	2	3	3.5	3.5
Grammatical Control	2	3	3.5	3.5
Pronunciation	2	2	3	3.5
Topic Control	2	3	2.5	2
Total Score	10.5	15	15.5	16.6

Qualitative results

Qualitative analyses of the transcripts of the test takers' responses revealed differences in test-taker performance as well as in rater scoring. These findings centre around comparing Fatima's performance and scores with those of Mohammed.

Lexical control

Although the lexical control rubric specified the use of vocabulary 'to address the topic' as one of its criteria (Appendix A), the use of ESL/EFL content-specific vocabulary in the role-play was not necessarily attended to or valued by the raters in the same way.

In Table 12.6, not only did Mohammed's vocabulary in the content area increase, it also became more pedagogically oriented. The focus of the discussion has changed from teaching 'verbs' (four mentions), 'novel' and 'poetry' in the pre-test, to teaching English 'through stories', and (not) as 'an isolated subject' in the post-test. Mohammed's score in lexical control increased from two to three.

Table 12.6

Lexical control, Mohammed's vocabulary use

Pre test		Post Test	
student(s)	5	student(s)	4
grammar-based	2	grammar-based	1
grammar	3	grammar	11
concentrate(d)	2	concentrate on grammar	3
teach/teacher	7	teacher(s)/teaching	9
school	1	school(s)	3
English	1	English	1
vocabulary	1	vocabulary	1
verbs	4	verbs	1
meaning	1	meaning	2
answers	1	answers	3
test	1	achievement test	1
(grammar) mistakes	1	English as a second language	1
sentence	1	scores	2
novel	2	exam	3
poetry	2	question(s)	6
mastered	1	translat(ion)	3
		dialogue	1
		learn	1
		write	1
		rules	1
		(through) story/ies	2
		(not as an)isolated subject	1
		first language	1
		literature	1
		textbook	1
		speak	2

Fatima's lexical control score is more problematic. While her score did not change, having started and remained at the 3.5 level, it is higher than Mohammed's. However, looking at her topic-related vocabulary use (Table 12.7), this score seems high when compared to Mohammed from the point of view of ESL/EFL topic-related vocabulary.

Table 12.7

Lexical control, Fatima's vocabulary use

Pre-Test		Post-test	
grammar	5	grammar	8
literature	1	literature	1
students	1		
vocabulary	9		
express(themselves)	3		
speech speech patterns	2		
enable(s)	4		
conversation	1		
		grammar-based	1
		be fluent	1
		helps	2
		structure of sentence, structured	2
		accurate	1
		sentence(s)	1
		formal situations	1
		final draft	1
		mark a paper	1

Grammatical control

According to the rubric (Appendix A), for a score of two, the test taker will show 'a limited range of syntactic structures' and 'frequent and systematic errors in syntactic structures which may cause misinterpretation of message'. Examining an excerpt from Fatima's pre-test (Excerpt 1), there are grammar-related problems that can cause difficulties in interpretation.

Excerpt 1: Pre-test (Fatima)

29	Fatima	/ they can express themselves
30		according to'
31		eh the (the negative)
32		especially when writing
33	===>	they can express about something'
34	===>	when they whe- when it happens
35	===>	when it correctly or rightly happens
36	Ahmed	yea
37	Fatima	and at the same time also understand'
38		the other(s) speech uh and the (t———)
39		ah: th(is/ese) ah::: ah: ah speech pattern
40		(or) will happen or happened is happening and so on

Even in sections where her grammar has shown improvement, for example in her first of two post-test excerpts (Excerpt 2) described in this paper, the sentences still show 'a limited range of structures', thus calling into question the 3.5 rating for both pre-test and post-test.

Excerpt 2: Post-test (1) (Fatima)

20	Fatima	okay
21		but eh: eh:: you can't say that
22		literature is more important than uhm
23	Karima	yes
24	Fatima	or or grammar is more important than the other
25		because I think eh oh eh
26	===>	literature leads to grammar
27	===>	and the grammar leads to literature . eh um
28		in o- in other words'
29		I think w- . I I mean
30		when you: . read literature'
31		you need to know about grammar and uh::
32		the: structure of sentences ah:::
33		tenses . many grammar . many aspects (of) grammar
34		in during the reading literature

The problem with Mohammed is that although he is attempting to use fairly sophisticated sentence structures (Excerpt 3), using 'if', 'so', and 'because' clauses, he does not have good control over the accuracy; however, their use is contextually appropriate.

Excerpt 3: Post-test (Mohammed)

21	===>	( ) if we look at uh: the (specification)
22		of the Ministry of the (of the) Education
23		we will find' about ninety per cent of the
24		(st-) of the teachers concentrate on grammar
25		ah translation vocabulary grammar
26	===>	so' eh if we didn't uh:
27		concentrate on grammar in our teaching'
28		I think eh the result of ah:: all the students'
29		will be declining and declining
30	===>	so' we should give more attentions
31		toward grammar
32	===>	because ( ) students didn't uh::
33		didn't learn grammar'
34		they didn't know how to (write)
35		uh they didn't know how to answer questions'
36	===>	because for example you find that uh::
37		the first question of the exam
38		is ah a dialogue
39	===>	uh if the students (they) don't know
40		how to answer questions
41		and how to form the question'
42		they can't answer th(ose) questions
43		eh: the the last question
44		that's a translation
45	===>	if they don't know grammar
46		eh ah also they don't know
47		ah how to translate'

While it does appear that both Mohammed's and Fatima's gains are warranted, the discrepancy between the scores of the two test takers, with Fatima receiving higher scores, does call into question inter-rater reliability with respect to Pair 2, who scored Fatima, and Pair 1, who scored Mohammed. There appears to be a relationship between this finding and the previous findings of Douglas and Selinker (1992) that raters of a field-specific test who had difficulty agreeing on scoring may have been responding to something else in the discourse and scoring it under the category of grammar. Further, there appears to be a relationship, with the findings of Douglas (1994), who noted that a subject receiving a higher grammar score was found to have made more grammar errors than a subject receiving a lower score when transcripts of the performances were examined qualitatively.

Conversational control

The problem of scoring with respect to Fatima and Mohammed is perhaps best illustrated by the conversational control category. Since both Mohammed and Fatima scored a four on the post-test in this category, it is particularly instructive to compare their performances.

First, a look at the rubric for scores three and four (Appendix A) reveals that Section 2, 'the ability to open and close discussions', has not been included in Score 3. Different problems are posed by other sections of the rubric. For example, Section 3 emphasizes the use of language to perform speech acts like agreeing, apologizing and criticizing, but couples these with rhetorical strategies like 'argue-counter argue', 'state [and] propose solutions to problems', and 'hypothesize'. This arguably places this rubric in the domain of discourse and academic genre more than in the domain of 'conversation' as studied by conversation analysts, who would look not only at speech acts but also at turn-taking issues, for example.

Unfortunately, we do not have a record of what the raters attended to in order to arrive at their score decisions. Specifically, we do not know definitively if raters were concentrating more on rhetorical control features related to discourse and academic genre, or if they were concentrating more on features related to conversational control such as the use of turn-taking devices (Sacks *et al.* 1978), openings and closings (Schegloff and Sacks 1973), and the co-construction of sentences (Goodwin 1984). But we can make some informed hypotheses.

First, let us look one more time at Mohammed's post-test excerpt (Excerpt 3). He has structured a fairly sophisticated argument based on the requirements of the prompt, using detailed examples to state the problem, hypothesize what might happen if grammar is not taught, and even criticize the *status quo*. Rhetorically, it is logically structured; the register is properly academic. It is, however, a monologue.

Now, let us look at the second excerpt from Fatima's post-test (Excerpt 4).

Excerpt 4: Post-test (2) (Fatima)

69	Fatima	oka:y what about uh formal situations
70		and (the) writing
71		especially the last the final drafts' for writing
72		whe- when you when you::: mark ah a paper
73		or a writing piece'
74		okay you can you can't / eh:=
75	Karima	(you say the final)
76	Fatima	YES
77	Karima	so (the teacher has to)
78	Fatima	SO: you prepare your students=
79		=to write (without ....)
80	Karima	(to express themselves)
81	Fatima	without (caring eh)=
82	Karima	=to grammar
83	Fatima	grammar
84		you you
85	Karima	( )
86	Fatima	you should eh eh be CAREful . with grammar

Notice that she begins the excerpt with 'okay', and then she uses 'okay' once again within the same turn. In fact, Fatima uses 'okay' at least four times each in both the pre-test and post-test in order to initiate turns or signal a transition of theme or topic within a turn. This use of 'okay' raises the issue of appropriateness from the point of view of the academic context posed in the rubric. By the same token, however, despite the relative narrowness of both the language and the argument being constructed, she has not constructed her argument as a monologue. Rather, she has co-constructed the argument with another participant, whom we are calling Karima, thereby demonstrating an ability to be persuasive through involvement rather than through overt argumentation.

Discussion of qualitative findings

Let us review. Both Mohammed and Fatima received the same score for their post-test performance in conversational control. However, the details of their performance are very different. Mohammed's performance more closely resembles an academic approach to rhetorical control; Fatima's more closely resembles a dialogic approach to conversational control. It appears as though, like Douglas' (1994) finding that raters arrive at similar quantitative scores which represent qualitatively different performances, the two pairs of raters were arriving at an identical score for qualitatively different performances by attending to very different features in the discourse. It further appears as though this overall difference in what the raters heeded may also be the key to understanding differences in scoring in other features, such as lexical and grammatical control. If one pair of raters holds the more academic–rhetorical interpretation of the rubric as primary, this would also no doubt create a disparity in the way they scored lexical and grammatical control as well as conversational control, since they would also be attending to much more content-specific vocabulary.

Although we will never really know, it seems likely that Pair 1, who rated Mohammed, was indeed attending more to content-specific features than Pair 2, who rated Fatima. Although Fatima displays much less control of the content-specific lexis, she was rated as superior to Mohammed. The only explanation would be that Pair 2 was not necessarily looking at content-specific lexis as a major criterion. Thus, they were probably not looking at language functions which were directly related to the topic of the role-play *per se* as a major criterion for their scoring in other categories as well, also explaining Fatima's relatively high scores in conversational and grammatical control.

It is difficult to speculate without more evidence from transcripts of other test takers rated by Pair 1 (who rated Mohammed) whether for them the opposite was true – that the specificity of the role-play content had more influence on their rating strategy. However, given the occupational and experiential backgrounds of the two rating pairs, this hypothesis has some merit.

Pair 2, who rated Fatima, matched one novice rater with no teaching experience with one non-native speaker of English with primarily secondary school EFL teaching experience. Pair 1, who rated Mohammed, matched two native-speaker ESL instructors with significant training and experience teaching adults in university contexts, including content-based instruction contexts. It is thus much more likely that the fact that the test takers were adults participating in what was a content-based, field-specific learning experience in EFL, had a greater influence on Pair 1's scoring than on Pair 2's. This finding seems to be related to that of Chalhoub-Deville (1996), who found that teacher and non-teacher raters weighted features in the discourse differently.

While the correlation coefficients for both pairs on the pre-test and for Pair 1 on the post-test indicated a fair degree of inter-rater reliability, Pair 2 had a significant drop on the post-test indicating very little score agreement between the two raters in the pair. In this connection it is especially interesting to note that, although we chose Fatima as an example completely independently of Pair 2's inter-rater reliability results, her score had been one of four flagged as representing particularly high disagreement between the two raters in Pair 2. Whether there is indeed a relationship between this fact, and any difference between what features the two raters were attending to while interpreting the rubric and rating scales is open to question – but the question is still there.

Summary and conclusion

To review then: in answer to our first research question, we found that participants did make statistically measurable gains in their oral skill performances after the eleven-week training program. Those results, in and of themselves, however, were expected and rather unremarkable. The qualitative analysis of the transcriptions was then carried out to answer the second and the third research questions. In answer to the second question, we found that similar quantitative scores reflected qualitatively different performances, as Douglas (1994) had hypothesized, and we showed that at least two participants with similar scores on the OPT demonstrated markedly different performances when the transcripts were examined. Looking at the third question, we found very specific evidence that CBI had a demonstrable effect on the lexical control of the participants. An unexpected finding, however, indicated that the CBI context of the OPT may have had different effects on different raters.

As a result of our preliminary findings, we propose that rater background had a significant influence on how test-taker performance was assessed. Because the test takers in our study came from a common speech community, and because there was no native-speaker interviewer, observations concerning cultural differences between interlocutors were less salient. However, when we look at differences among the raters in our study, we find that background may help explain variability in rater judgement of performance.

When looking at cultural differences, Young (1995), for example, used Hymes' (1974) definition of speech community to identify the influence which a test taker's cultural background may have on her conversational style. In this study, we use Swales' (1990) definition of discourse community to understand the influence which a professional and/or academic background may have on raters. According to Swales (1990), while a speech community is more of a 'sociolinguistic grouping', a discourse community is more of a 'socio-rhetorical one' (p. 24). Thus while a speech community tends to share a common culture, 'an archetypal discourse community tends to be a Specific Interest Group' (Swales 1990: 24). From a linguistic point of view, discourse communities acquire not only 'some specific lexis' but also specific communicative genres. Moreover, it is these communicative genres which dictate 'discoursal expectations' concerning features such as the 'appropriacy of topics' and 'the form, function and positioning of discoursal elements' (Swales 1990: 26).

For this study, one of the most important discourse community-related issues raised is related to how the raters may heed different features in the discourse and apply the rubric differently based on their particular genre expectations. We saw that even though the raters did not keep a record of what they attend to in a test taker's performance, we can speculate that some raters may have concentrated more on rhetorical control features related to the use of academic genre, and others may have been concentrating more on features related to conversational control, the use of turn-taking devices, and the co-construction of arguments. That is, raters may have attended to and been influenced by different aspects of the discourse, and thus they may also have applied the rubric differently as well. Douglas (1994) points out that 'interlocutors' interpretations of the message vary owing to which facets are being attended to' and that 'no two listeners hear the same message' (p. 134). Additional research on raters of oral proficiency tests has also established that rater occupational and experiential backgrounds may have an effect on ratings, with teacher raters and non-teacher raters in particular varying in features in the discourse they attend to and the assignment of weights to those features. (See the Introduction re: Galloway 1980; Barnwell 1989; Hadden 1991; Elder 1993; Brown 1995; Chalhoub-Deville 1995; 1996.) We may also have seen evidence of this occurrence in Pair 2, one of whom had no teaching experience.

The results of our study highlight some important issues and pose several important questions for future research on rater variability and OPT scoring. For example, Douglas and Selinker (1992) point out that ratings are often ambiguous because raters may utilize widely different thought processes to arrive at their scores. In order to disambiguate such scores, Douglas (1994) suggests that raters perform a think-aloud protocol. Such verbal protocols have been used by Vaughan (1991); Huot (1993); Milanovic and Saville (1994); and Milanovic, Saville and Shen (1996) to study raters of writing. Similar studies of OPT raters may shed light on what elements raters attend to in the discourse, what thought processes they use, and how they apply the rubric to the test taker's performance. If the results of such verbal protocol studies prove useful in determining how raters attend to and evaluate specific discourse features, should these observations be incorporated into rater training sessions?

Another issue that also pertains to the raters involves the question of pairing or grouping of raters. While maintaining the same pairs for both the pre-test and post-test allowed for a more accurate statistical assessment of inter-rater reliability in this study, especially given the small numbers involved (only four raters and 25 test takers), would a different pairing have led to greater fairness? Were the raters in Pair 1, the experienced college-level ESL teachers, too similar in occupational and experiential background and should they have been paired with one person each from Pair 2? How do we determine who rates together?

Next is an issue related to the rating scales. Although the prompt described to the test takers was content-specific and the test takers were instructed to role-play an argument concerning professional issues related to EFL teaching, the rubric and the rating scales did not explicitly address how content should be integrated into the different categories for scoring. For example, we saw that Fatima's lack of ability to construct a complex argument using a wide content-related lexicon seems to have affected only her topic control score. Should content-specific language produced by the test taker be integrated into the scoring rubric, and if so, should a separate category be created to address the issue of content?

Finally, we conclude that there is a very real need for more studies focusing on raters, including background and training, the features in the discourse they attend to, and the thought processes they employ. We have seen in this study that OPT scores and the test takers' performances are not necessarily related. If raters attend to different features in the discourse and apply the rubric and rating scales differently, we need to raise the critical issue of the validity and the reliability of the OPT scores. We recommend that future research studies include the use of verbal protocols to attempt to provide insight into both the features in the discourse attended to and the thought processes used when raters make their scoring judgements.

Notes

We would like to acknowledge the following people who worked with us on the initial stages of the study: Yutaka Kawamoto for his help in the research and contribution to the statistical analysis section and Mary Erin Crook for her participation in the research and editorial suggestions. We would especially like to thank Carmen Velasco-Martin for her valuable contributions to the background and methods sections as well as her work on the research. We would also like thank Antony J. Kunnan, without whom this study would not have been possible, and our anonymous reviewer(s) whose comments helped us place this study in a broader perspective.

Because our raters were not blind as to whether they were scoring pre- or post-tests, we used the quantitative results primarily to identify performances to be evaluated qualitatively, and we take our qualitative analyses as preliminary results to be used as indicators of areas for further study.

Suggested further reading

Chalhoub-Deville, M. (1996) Performance assessment and the components of the oral construct across different tests and rater groups. In Milanovic and Saville, (Eds.)The author asks what the dimensions are that underlie second language oral ratings across test techniques and what the relative weights are of these dimensions for different raters.

The author tested six learners of Arabic as a Foreign Language (AFL) using three test methods:

1 an oral interview;
2 a narration based on a sequence of six cartoon drawings; and
3 a read-aloud test of a short news-like printed passage.

The tests were subsequently rated by three groups of raters:

1 15 native speakers of Arabic who were teachers of AFL in the US;
2 31 non-teaching native speakers of Arabic who were college students in the US;
3 36 non-teaching native speakers who were college students in Lebanon.

The author found that the three prominent rating dimensions were:

1 grammar and pronunciation;
2 creativity in presenting information; and
3 amount of detail.

She also found that the three rating groups concentrated on different dimensions. Group (1) relied most on creativity; Group (2) on amount of detail; Group (3) on grammar and pronunciation.

Douglas, D. (1994) Quantity and quality in speaking test performance. *Language Testing.*

The author investigates the hypothesis that quantitatively similar scores may represent qualitatively different performances on a semi-direct speaking test. The field specific AGSPEAK test was administered to six subjects and scored by two raters who evaluated test takers on (1) grammar, (2) vocabulary, (3) fluency, and (4) content and rhetoric. The author used both quantitative and qualitative analyses to disambiguate scoring and found that there was little relationship between quantitative scores and the actual language produced by test takers. He concludes that further studies of the rating process should use subject protocol analyses and think-aloud protocols in order to better understand the bases upon which raters make their judgements.

Swales, J. (1990) *Genre analysis: English in Academic and Research Settings.* Cambridge: Cambridge University Press.

The author discusses the importance of genre analysis in academic and research settings in order to study spoken and written discourse. The three major concepts addressed are: (1) discourse community, (2) genre, and (3) language-learning task. Swales reviews past studies of genre and rhetoric, examines primarily written examples of academic genres, and offers new interpretations of old concepts. For example, he refines Hymes' (1974) culture-oriented concept of speech community to propose the professional-oriented concept of discourse community.

van Lier, L. (1989) Reeling, writhing, drawling, stretching, and fainting in coils: Oral proficiency interviews as conversation. *TESOL Quarterly* 23: 489–508.

The author asks how well the oral proficiency interview (OPI) tests oral proficiency as communicative competence and hypothesizes that there are major problems with testing oral proficiency using an interview format due to the differences between interviews and natural conversation. Van Lier uses a triangulated method of analysis based on:

1   the author's own experience of OPIs as an interviewee;
2   the study of transcripts and tapes of a variety of OPIs;
3   the author's past experience as an interviewer in diagnostic OPIs of children in bilingual education contexts.

He concludes that natural conversation and OPIs are different, especially from the point of view of social interaction in discourse, and recommends more research be done to clarify what constitutes natural conversation in order to better evaluate oral proficiency and construct oral proficiency tests.

References

Barnwell, D. (1989) 'Naive' native speakers and judgements of oral proficiency in Spanish. *Language Testing* 6: 152–163.

Brown, A. (1995) The effect of rater variables in the development of an occupation-specific language performance test. *Language Testing* 12: 1–15.

Chalhoub-Deville, M. (1995) A contextualized approach to describing oral language proficiency. *Language Learning* 45: 251–281.

Chalhoub-Deville, M. (1996) Performance assessment and the components of the oral construct across different tests and rater groups. In Milanovic and Saville, (Eds.): 55–73.

Douglas, D. (1994) Quantity and quality in speaking test performance. *Language Testing* 11: 125–144.

Douglas, D. and Selinker, L. (1992) Analysing oral proficiency test performance in general and specific purpose contexts. *System* 20: 317–328.

Douglas, D. and Selinker, L. (1993) Performance on a general versus a field-specific test of speaking proficiency by international teaching assistants. In *A New Decade of Language Testing Research: Selected Papers from the 1990 Language Testing Research Colloquium*. Alexandria, VA: TESOL.

Elder, C. (1993) How do subject specialists construe classroom language proficiency? *Language Testing* 10: 235–54.

Galloway, V. (1980) Perceptions of the communicative efforts of American students of Spanish. *Modern Language Journal* 64: 428–33.

Goodwin, C. (1984) Notes on story structure and the organization of participation. In Atkinson, M. and Heritage, J. (Eds.) *Structure of Social Action*. Cambridge: Cambridge University Press: 225–46.

Hadden, B. (1991) Teacher and non-teacher perceptions of second-language communication. *Language Learning* 41: 1–24.

Huot, B. (1993) The influence of holistic scoring procedures on reading and rating student essays. In Williamson, M. and Huot, B. (Eds.) *Validating Holistic Scoring for Writing Assessment: Theoretical and Empercial Foundations*. Cresskill, NJ: Hampton Press: 206–36.

Hymes, D. (1974) *Foundations in Sociolinguistics: An Ethnographic Approach*. Philadelphia, PA: University of Pennsylvania Press.

Lazaraton, A. (1996) Interlocutor support in oral proficiency interviews: The case of CASE. *Language Testing* 13: 151–172.

Milanovic, M. and Saville, N. (1994) An investigation of marker strategies using verbal protocols. Paper presented at the 16th annual conference of the Language Testing Research Colloquium, Washington, DC March 1994.

Milanovic, M. and Saville, N. (Eds.) (1996) *Studies in Language Testing 3: Performance Testing Cognition and Assessment: Selected Papers from the 15ᵗʰ Language Testing Research Colloquium (LTRC)*. Cambridge: Cambridge University Press and University of Cambridge Local Examination Syndicate.

Milanovic, M., Saville, N. and Shen, S. (1996) A study of the decision-making behaviour of composition markers. In Milanovic and Saville, (Eds.): 92–114.

Ross, S. and Berwick, R. (1992) The discourse of accommodation in oral proficiency interviews. *Studies in Second Language Acquisition* 14: 159–76.

Sacks, H., Schegloff, E. A. and Jefferson, G. (1978) A simplest systematics for the organization of turn-taking for conversation. In Schenkein, J. (Ed.) *Studies in the Organization of Conversational Interaction*. New York, NY: Academic Press: 7–56.

Schegloff, E. A. and Sacks, H. (1973) Opening up closings. *Semiotica* 8: 289–327.

Shohamy, E., Gordon, C. M. and Kraemer, R. (1992) The effect of raters' background and training on the reliability of direct writing tests. *The Modern Language Journal* 176: 27–33.

SPSS Graduate Package, Advanced Macintosh Version 6.1. Microsoft Corporation.

Swales, J. (1990) *Genre Analysis: English in Academic and Research Settings*. Cambridge: Cambridge University Press.

van Lier, L. (1989) Reeling, writhing, drawling, stretching, and fainting in coils: Oral proficiency interviews as conversation. *TESOL Quarterly* 23: 489–508.

Vaughan, C. (1991) Holistic assessment: What goes on in the rater's mind? In Hamp-Lyons, L. (Ed.) *Second Language Writing in Academic Contexts.* Norwood, NJ: Ablex Publishing Corporation.

Young, R. (1995) Conversational styles in language proficiency interviews. *Language Learning* 45: 3–42.

Young, R. and Milanovic, M. (1992) Discourse variation in oral proficiency interviews. *Studies in Second Language Acquisition* 14: 403–424.

Appendix A: Rating Scale Samples

Lexical control

Section	Score of 3	Score of 4
1	Shows *good* ability to use vocabulart accurately and appropriatly;	Shows *extensive* ability to use vocabulary accurately and appropriatly;
2	shows a *wide* range of lexicon;	shows *extensive* range of lexicon;
3	has the vocabulary to address the topic *adequately*;	has the vocabulary to address the topic *fully*;
4	*usually has* the vocabulary to communicate formally and informally;	*has* the vocabulary to communicate formally and informally;
5	may use innacurate words to make up for gaps in vocabulary.	may show gaps in vocabulary with certain aspects of the topic.

Grammatical control

Section	Score of 2	Score of 3
1	Shows limited ability to use grammar;	Shows good ability to use grammar;
2	often uses circumlocution;	may occaisionally use circumlocution;
3	*shows limited range of sytactic structures*;	shows good control of a limited number of syntactic structures
4	*shows frequent and systematic errors in syntactic structures which may cause misinterpretation of message*	may show inaccurate or inappropriate use of certain syntactic structures

Conversational control

Section	Score of 3	Score of 4
1	Shows *good* ability to structure converstaion <u>logically</u> and <u>appropriately</u>;	Shows *extensive*, but not shophisticated ability to <u>structure</u> converstaions <u>logically</u> and <u>appropriately</u>;
2		able to open and close discussions;
3	shows *some control* in using *different kinds* of language functions to agree, disagree, state problems, propose, solutions to problems, hypothesize, argue counterargue, appologize, criticize *but may do so with difficulty.*	shows *good control* in using *reletively wide* range of language functions to agree, disagree, state problems, propose solutions to problems, hypothesizs, argue, counterargue, apologize, criticize etc.

Appendix B

Transcription Key

CAPITAL LETTERS		Stress
colon	:	elongated phonemes
period	.	pause
equal sign	=	latching
parentheses	( )	unclear speech
dash	-	cut off
apostrophe	'	slight rising tone
slash	/	overlap
arrow	===>	points for discussion

13 A job-relevant listening summary translation exam in Minnan

Charles W. Stansfield
Weiping M. Wu
Second Language Testing, Inc.
Marijke van der Heide
Federal Bureau of Investigation

Abstract

This chapter describes the methodology followed to develop a performance-based language test that is used for the selection and placement of employees of the US Government and individuals supplied by private contractors. Two forms of a Listening Summary Translation Exam (LSTE) in Minnan were developed following rigorous procedures designed to ensure the relevancy of the test to the work that is performed on the job. Subsequently, they were field-tested and revised. Based on the analysis of examinee data collected on the tests and on self-assessment instruments developed for this project, the tests appear to be highly reliable and valid. The results suggest that the job analysis and test development procedures employed helped to produce a high quality instrument.

The need for a test

One of the tasks carried out by the Federal Bureau of Investigation (FBI) and other United States law enforcement agencies is the monitoring of telephone conversations involving persons under criminal investigation. These conversations are monitored after a co-operating individual has consented to monitoring, or after a magistrate has inspected the evidence of criminal activity and determined that a specific person's calls should be monitored.

Normally monitoring involves listening to tape recordings of phone conversations after they have taken place. The task of initially listening to conversations may be performed by freelance individuals contracted to do so by the government or by employees of companies that have contracted with the Government to perform this service. When a conversation is monitored, the first task of the listener is to determine if the conversation is relevant to the investigation. If it is determined to be relevant, then the listener writes a summary of the information that is conveyed in the conversation. The summary normally includes the names of the parties conversing, the purpose of the call, any factual information related, such as times, dates, places, and other persons mentioned. It may also include more details as appropriate. The summary is written in a journal which is inspected frequently by law enforcement officers. If necessary, the entire conversation can be transcribed. This is normally following an arrest, and prior to trial, with the transcription serving as evidence that may be introduced in the trial. The summary of the conversation may also serve as evidence. In the case of conversations that take place in a language other than English, the summary must be written in English. Thus, the person writing the summary must be able to understand the conversation in the foreign language and write an accurate and clear summary of it in English. This involves listening skills in the non-English language, writing skills in English, and summary translation skills across the two languages. Information presented in the summary must not be misrepresented or misconstrued, and all potentially important information must be included. This is particularly important in conversations involving languages other than English, since the law enforcement officer may not speak the language, and therefore is unable to actually listen to the tape even if so desired. The summary must also be written in clear and grammatically correct English. A summary containing bad grammar and orthography may cause a judge or juror to question the competency of the person preparing the summary.

Because it is important to the public welfare that summaries be written accurately and clearly, there is a need for a test that will determine if a prospective independent contractor or employee has the ability to do so. A listening summary translation exam (LSTE) in Minnan was developed by Second Language Testing, Inc. (SLTI) for the FBI for this purpose.

The test prototype

The first LSTE was developed in Spanish by Stansfield *et al.* (1990) under a contract with the FBI. The test consists of two sections, multiple-choice and summary writing. The multiple-choice section is based on a series of quasi-authentic recorded telephone conversations involving criminal activity. These conversations simulate exchanges regarding a variety of types of crime; in particular, the kinds of crime most often encountered in conversations involving speakers of the non-English language in question. Because they are unscripted, the conversations manifest all of the characteristics of natural speech, including hesitations, false starts, repetitions, interruptions, overlapping of speakers, misunderstandings, requests for clarification, etc.

Although the stimulus conversations are in the non-English language, the test questions are written in English in a test booklet. Each multiple-choice question is followed by four options, only one of which is the correct answer. The test items vary in purpose: some of them assess comprehension of specific details such as dates, times, locations, etc., while others require the examinee to infer the relationship of the speakers, their emotional reactions to the messages conveyed, and possible actions to follow from the conversations. The multiple-choice section is used as a screening test for the summary translation section that follows it.

The summary translation section of the LSTE requires the examinee to summarize in English three conversations spoken in the non-English language. The conversations vary in length (from approximately one to three minutes) and in sophistication of vocabulary. In the summary translation section, the examinee hears each conversation twice, and is permitted to take notes on it. Then, the examinee is given an appropriate amount of time to write a summary of the conversation in English. The first part of the summary translation section contains a module that is designed to teach the examinee the informational and linguistic characteristics of a good summary. The examinee combines the knowledge imparted in this portion of the test with his or her target language listening comprehension and English language writing skills to produce the three summaries that follow. Previous research (Stansfield *et al.* 1990) has shown that examinees believe the instructional module gives them a clear idea of the kind of summary they are to write.

Scoring of the LSTE

Examinees receive two scores for the summary translation section: one for Accuracy and the other for written Expression. Both are assessed by a trained rater.

Accuracy is scored by the rater through the use of a checklist that identifies the callers, the main topic, and key and supporting points in the conversation. As the rater reads a summary, he or she checks off those items on the list which the examinee has reported accurately; one point is awarded for each key and supporting point. Although the wording of the summary does not have to match exactly that of the checklist, it is important that the information be provided in the appropriate context. Because the content of the conversation is broken down into items of information on the checklist, an examinee can receive credit for each item that is accurately reported, even if other items are omitted or misunderstood. The Accuracy score is the sum of the points awarded for each of the three conversations.

Expression is scored by the rater through an evaluation of the written summary for correct grammar, spelling, punctuation, and syntax, precision of vocabulary, and organization. The principal criterion is communicative effectiveness of the English employed. An inability to communicate the intended information generates the lowest rating on the Expression scale. This written summary is rated holistically using the Expression Scoring Guide. For each of the three summaries, the examinee is awarded either a 'Deficient' (= 1 point), 'Functional' (= 2 points), 'Competent' (= 3 points), or 'Native' (= 4 points).[1] The total Expression score is the average of the Expression scores on the three summaries.[2] Once the average is computed, a final rating is awarded as follows:

Figure 13.1

Average Expression Score				Final Rating
1.0	1.33			Deficient
1.50	1.67	2.00	2.33	Functional
2.50	2.67	3.00	3.33	Competent
3.50	3.67	4.00		Native

The Accuracy and Expression scores on the summary section are always kept separate. However, a total score for Accuracy (TOTACC) on the LSTE is awarded by adding the raw score on the multiple-choice section and the Accuracy score on the summary translation section together.

Development of the LSTE-Minnan[3]

Development of conversations

Because the LSTE-Minnan is designed to be used in occupational settings, project staff felt that it was important that the conversations used on the test be as authentic as possible. For this reason, staff obtained information that influenced the nature of authentic conversations from a variety of sources. These include taped conversations provided by the FBI, interviews with private contractors who listen to and transcribe tapes provided by the FBI and other law enforcement agencies on a daily basis, and interviews (telephonic and face-to-face) with FBI staff that listen to such conversations. This approach to creating authentic conversations was used in the development of the LSTE-Spanish and is analyzed and validated in Scott *et al.* (1996).

Summary of linguistic features

In preparation for the creation of conversations, we conducted an informal analysis of the DEA tapes in order to identify the general characteristics of the conversations that might be monitored by law enforcement agencies. The analysis included identification of frequent topics, tone, and use of nicknames, colloquial expressions, and code words. We then prepared a summary of the general characteristics we discovered. We also interviewed a manager of an FBI contractor in New York City who is engaged in this type of translation activity. In addition, we developed a number of brief scenarios outlining the gist of conversations to be used for the LSTE-Minnan.

Telephone questionnaire

In order to gain information systematically from staff listening to tapes at FBI field offices, SLTI staff prepared a questionnaire that guided telephonic interviews. A draft questionnaire was sent to the FBI for review in December 1994 and, following revisions, the final version was completed in January 1995. The questionnaire dealt with the language background of the linguist, the age, sex, and background of participants in audited conversations, the nature of the conversations in terms of topics, type, and tone of language used in the conversations, the sources, types, and frequencies of conversations that they listen to, the general content areas, and the topics within each area. This questionnaire was used when interviewing FBI staff and contract linguists at different field offices. Sometimes the interviews were conducted in English, sometimes in Mandarin, sometimes in Minnan, and sometimes in a combination of the three languages. The SLTI staff member who conducted the interview made notes on each.

Because of security concerns as well as internal FBI policy and practice, those interviewed were not always able to respond fully to our questions. However, excellent co-operation was received from the language supervisor at one large field office, where contract linguists working with Minnan provided extensive information and examples, and subsequently reviewed and commented on a draft version of the entire test. For security reasons, the names of interviewees were generally not provided to SLTI.

Revised summary of linguistic features

SLTI staff and consultants met with FBI staff to discuss the general characteristics of monitored conversations, the scenarios which had been developed to that point, and the exam format and scoring. As a result of this meeting, the original summary of linguistic features was revised and expanded with information obtained from FBI staff.

Consultants

Because of the need to gather more explicit information on FCI topics and language, and the inability of FBI staff to discuss these matters with the test development team, SLTI contracted as consultants two Sinologists who are political science professors with considerable knowledge of sensitive issues. Based on the information they provided, we were able to construct scenarios in the FCI area, which were judged by FBI staff to be realistic.

Taxonomy and scenarios

Based on all of the information gathered, a taxonomy containing 37 topics and tasks (speech functions) was developed. This taxonomy was also reviewed by the FBI and refined on the basis of comments. Subsequently, draft scenarios of conversations were developed to match each topic and task. In this way, it became possible to inspect the content objectives (the topics and tasks in the taxonomy) and the way it was proposed that each objective would be tested. The taxonomy and draft tasks were submitted to FBI Headquarters. There they were reviewed by staff in the Language Services Unit, and forwarded to field offices with Minnan-speaking staff. Staff were asked to rate each objective and proposed conversation on a five-point scale in terms of its frequency of occurrence and difficulty. The written evaluations of individual reviewers were returned to and tallied by SLTI.

The analysis indicated that most proposed conversations were viewed as frequently occurring, thereby indicating their validity for inclusion on this occupational test. The conversations rated as frequently occurring were also rated as easy to work with. However, a few were viewed as rarely occurring and not easy to work with. These rarely occurring, more difficult conversations dealt with matters related to foreign counter-intelligence (FCI) work. Still, SLTI and the FBI felt it important to include a number of FCI conversations on the test. Such conversations increase the range of proficiency assessed by the instrument, and they make the test useful in the selection of a wider number of occupational specialities within the FBI and the US Government at large.

Selection and training of actors

Following further revisions and the writing of some additional FCI scenarios, SLTI staff interviewed 13 native speakers of Minnan who were willing to serve as actors in the recording of the conversations. Of these, we determined that nine individuals (seven of those interviewed plus two SLTI staff members) had the language proficiency and personal skills necessary to improvise the conversations based on the scenarios. The actors varied in age; six were male and three were female. SLTI staff trained the actors used in each taping session. Training involved a review of the general characteristics of monitored conversations followed by practice tapings. The actors were encouraged to speak naturally and to use slang, regionalisms, or even vulgarities that would be appropriate in a given situation.

Recording conversations

After reviewing the scenario for a given conversation, the actors agreed on code words and basic content, and rehearsed the conversation briefly several times face-to-face. One called the other on a phone (both phones were different extensions located at different desks at an office but were located in the same work area) and carried out the conversation by phone. The conversations were taped using a recording device attached to one of the phones, thus simulating as closely as possible conditions under which conversations are often recorded by the Bureau. A conversation was re-taped as many times as needed until it was determined to be wholly authentic by SLTI and FBI staff. An FBI linguist of the Washington, DC Field Office, was present at the initial recording sessions in order to provide feedback to the actors on the authenticity and acceptability of the conversations as they were being taped.

A total of 36 different conversations were taped over a number of recording sessions. Each test tape contains all of the speakers, with the result that a variety of voices are represented on each test form.

Review of preliminary conversations

A tape was constructed based on the conversations recorded and sent to the co-operating FBI field office. There, two Minnan-speaking independent contractors listened to each conversation and evaluated it using a questionnaire prepared for that purpose by SLTI. The questionnaire dealt with the authenticity of the language used in the conversations as well as the clarity, rate of speech, etc. Most conversations received high marks in this review. Still, some conversations were eliminated, which reduced the total number of speakers used on the final forms to seven, four males and three females.

Development of test forms

SLTI staff and consultants wrote multiple-choice items based on a number of the recorded conversations. The items were designed to assess the understanding of specific information and the ability to make inferences based on the information presented in the conversations.

Parallel forms of the LSTE-Minnan were constructed so as to ensure a similar distribution of the number of conversations (for each form 12 in the multiple-choice section and three in the summary section), length of conversations, the sex of the speakers, and the number of multiple-choice items which had been developed (57 items for the pretest versions, which became 50 items in the final versions). After developing the answer key for the multiple-choice portion of each form, we made changes in the ordering of the options to ensure equal distribution of correct answers across the four choices A, B, C, and D. More conversations and items than would be needed on the final versions were prepared, so that only those that functioned most effectively could be retained. SLTI worked with a professional recording studio, Lion and Fox, Inc., to edit and assemble the conversations from individually recorded cassette tapes into the two test forms. We also prepared test booklets and other ancillary materials.

Development of materials used to score the summary translations

Scoring procedures for the LSTE-Minnan are modelled on the LSTE-Spanish. The scoring of the multiple-choice section of the test was objective and straightforward, since there was only one correct answer to each question. For the summary translation section, however, we wanted the scoring procedures to focus on the examinee's ability to record important information that the conversation contained. Consequently, we devised a plan to identify the important points in the summary translation section conversations.

In order to do this, we wrote a summary of each of the conversations by listening to the conversation several times, stopping and re-playing the tape as often as needed in order to capture as much detail as possible. We also transcribed the conversation using traditional Mandarin Chinese characters and we then translated the transcription into English. Referring to the tape, the transcription, and the translation, we constructed a checklist of important points mentioned in a good summary for each conversation. FBI language specialists and three external consultants then read these sample good summaries and the checklists to verify that the checklists included all important and appropriate information. Once the checklists were validated by the FBI, they were considered ready for use in the field test administration.

Field test administration

The tests were administered at three sites: the University of Maryland, the University of California at Berkeley and the University of California at Davis. These sites were selected because we knew that substantial numbers of Minnan speakers were located there, and because we were able to enlist our colleagues at these universities for co-operation and assistance in recruiting field test examinees. All field test data were gathered between late February and early May 1996.

At each site, we contracted with a test administrator to recruit the examinees, to obtain space, and to administer the test on two different occasions approximately one week apart. Examinees were paid an honourarium for taking the test, and were paid again for taking the second form of the test, if they so desired. Over half of the examinees returned to take the second form of the test.

The order of administration of the forms was counter-balanced, so that approximately half of the examinees took Form A first and half took Form B first.

All summaries were scored twice by two native speakers of English. Since there were three summaries per test form and over 50 examinees took each form, over 300 summaries were scored twice resulting in over 600 Expression ratings. These ratings were then entered into a Paradox database and the database was used to identify summaries on which there was complete agreement across the two ratings. These summaries were then used as a pool from which benchmarks could be drawn. Subsequently, benchmarks were selected for training and testing raters using the self-instructional rater training kit that accompanies the test.

Following the field test administration, the test data were analyzed using both classical and IRT-based item and test analysis. The results showed the field test version of both forms to have excellent reliability. Therefore, we eliminated several of the less efficient items from both sections of the test. As a result, the multiple-choice section of both forms was left with 50 items, while the summary translation was left with 50 items on Form A and 56 items on Form B. An equating procedure was used to relate Form B scores to Form A equivalent scores.

Development of self-assessment questionnaires

Because no other measures of Minnan were available with which to correlate scores on the LSTE-Minnan, it was decided to develop and use self-assessment questionnaires. A review of the literature on self-assessment shows that such measures can be both valid and reliable. In this case, three measures were developed: a Self-Assessment of English Writing Ability (SA-EW), a Listening Comprehension Global Self-Assessment Questionnaire (SA-LC), and a Self-Assessment of Summary Translation Ability (SA-ST).

The Self-Assessment of English Writing ability (SA-EW)

The SA-EW was constructed to imitate the ILR writing scale, but in a format suitable for self-assessment by untrained raters. It was designed to be administered without any accompanying explanation of terms. Therefore, technical jargon for language teachers and references to government work in the ILR skill level descriptions were avoided in constructing each point on the scale. The format involves a condensed description of only the baseline points on the ILR writing scale. Thus, there is no description of the 'plus' levels. This format was chosen because the LSTE-Minnan is essentially a test of listening comprehension in Minnan. English writing ability plays only a minor role in the examinee's performance. In the LSTE-Minnan, the Expression score is considered less important than the Accuracy score. This is reflected in the scoring scale for Expression, which has only four levels, Deficient, Functional, Competent and Native.

It was decided to have the SA-EW serve as a criterion measure for evaluating the validity of the Expression score. That is, it was assumed that the SA-EW would be an adequately valid measure of English writing skills, and therefore, if the Expression score correlated with it, then that correlation would provide evidence of the validity of the Expression score.

The Listening Comprehension global Self-Assessment questionnaire (SA-LC)

The SA-LC was constructed based on a review of the ILR skill level descriptions for listening and of the ACTFL Proficiency Guidelines for listening.[4]

This particular version of the skill level descriptions for listening has several unique characteristics. The SA-LC was tailored to some degree to the subjects that would participate in the pretesting. Because the subjects would not be government linguists, technical jargon was avoided to the degree possible. In addition, revisions were made in an effort to keep the English employed in the descriptions at a fairly low level (level 2+ or below). In order to reduce the reading load on the examinee, unnecessary repetitions were also deleted. References to memorized utterances and learned material in the lower-level descriptions were deleted because they do not apply to native speakers.

The Self-Assessment of Summary Translation ability (SA-ST)

The SA-ST was based on a similar instrument that was used in the validation of the LSTE-Spanish. This type of self-assessment was found to correlate highly (.79) with the Total Accuracy score on the LSTE-Spanish. It also correlated highly (.78 for one form and .80 for the other) with the Accuracy score on the Spanish summary writing tasks when the tasks were evaluated by human raters. Thus, it was felt that, since the validity of this self-assessment questionnaire had previously been established, it would be appropriate to employ the SA-ST in the context of the Minnan test as well.

Pretest examinees were asked to complete the SA-ST after taking the LSTE-Minnan. At this point, they would have some experience on which to base their self-rating. However, their experience would be limited to only the three summary writing tasks on the test. The LSTE-Spanish was validated using a large number of examinees who were FBI agents and language specialists who did this kind of work. Thus, they were in a position to make a more accurate self-assessment of their summary writing ability. Therefore, it was felt that it would be unlikely that the SA-ST would correlate as highly with the examinee's Total Accuracy score for Minnan as it had for Spanish. Still, it was felt that even a moderate correlation between the SA-ST and the LSTE-Minnan would provide evidence of the validity of the latter. Such evidence is useful, since the SA-ST requires that the examinee rate his or her ability to perform the kinds of listening tasks that are often required of law enforcement personnel. Thus, it was felt that a moderate correlation would provide evidence of the relationship between the score on the test and the ability to do the job.

A basic difference between the SA-ST used for Spanish and that used with the Minnan examinees was the addition of a fourth type of conversation to the scale. This was type 4, which involves the ability to understand conversations dealing with scientific, military, or political matters. Although the description of this type of conversation has more to do with topic than with type of speech, it was felt that the addition would be useful in the context of the type of work that actual successful examinees might be asked to perform.

It should be understood that the SA-ST was to address issues of validity within an occupational context. The SA-EW and the SA-LC address the issue of the validity of the Accuracy and Expression scores as indicators of the relevant prerequisite language skills.

Reliability

Reliability of the multiple-choice section

The data on the final version of the multiple-choice section of Forms A and B are depicted in Table 13.1. These data are based on a reanalysis of the data following the deletion of the less effective items.

Table 13.1

Descriptive statistics for final versions: Multiple-choice

Form	Mean	Std. Dev.	Range	Mean Dif	KR-20
A	36.4	7.5	16-47	.73	.87
B	34.6	9.7	10-48	.69	.92

Table 13.1 indicates that Form B is slightly more difficult than Form A. The larger standard deviation for Form B suggests that (prior to equating) less competent examinees may have tended to score slightly lower and more competent examinees slightly higher on Form B than on Form A. Still the differences are not great.

The mean of Form A represents approximately 73% correct while the mean of Form B represents approximately 69% correct. Thus, for the group as a whole, the multiple-choice tests tended to be slightly easy, since we would expect a mean around 62.5% on a multiple-choice test of optimal difficulty if the sample fully and equally represented the total range of abilities.

It should be noted that while a good range of abilities was found in the sample, the sample contained more high ability students that low ability students as measured by the multiple-choice section of the tests. It should be remembered that the multiple-choice portion was intended to be used as a screen; i.e. to identify candidates who would not do well on the summary writing section of the test. Thus, good performance on the multiple-choice section would be a prerequisite to taking the rest of the test. If the total test (MC and summary) is appropriate for the total sample, then it is not surprising that the multiple-choice section would be slightly easy for the total sample. Thus, the sample does not seem atypical and their high scores on the multiple-choice section are consistent with its intended use.

The internal consistency reliability of the multiple-choice section of both forms of the LSTE is quite good. The reliabilities for the corresponding forms of the LSTE-Spanish were .86 and .88.

The parallel form reliability, the correlation between the score on the two forms, was .87 for a subsample of 29 examinees who took both forms of the LSTE-Minnan.

Accuracy score: Summaries

The reliability of the Accuracy score on the summaries is depicted in Table 13.2 through a classical test analysis.

Table 13.2

Descriptive statistics for final versions: Summary Writing Accuracy

Form	N items	Mean	Std. Dev.	Range	Mean Dif	KR-20
A	50	23.6	9.6	0-39	.46	.93
B	56	16.5	13.0	0-49	.29	.96

As can be seen, the data again suggest that Form B is harder than Form A, at least that is the way it turned out for the two samples that took each form on this classical analysis. Both summary writing test forms were quite difficult for these examinees. Optimal difficulty on this test would be 50% correct, yet the means here represent 47% correct on Form A and 29% correct on Form B. Thus, both tests were harder than is psychometrically optimal for this sample. This was especially true of Form B. Nonetheless, it is noteworthy that two examinees scored very high on Form B. These examinees scored 48 and 49 correctly reported points out of a possible 56, which represents 86% and 88% correct. The highest score on Form A was 39 correct out of 50, which represents only 78% correct. Thus, for the able candidate, Form B is not unrealistically hard.

The KR-20 internal consistency reliability coefficients for the summary writing section are high (.93 and .96).

The interrater reliability, as calculated on a subsample of half the papers that were scored by the second rater, is extremely high (.99) for both forms. For the LSTE-Spanish, the interrater reliability for the checklists was also very good, ranging from .85 to .93 on the six summaries. However, the almost perfect agreement between raters on the LSTE-Minnan demonstrates that the Scoring Guide for Accuracy makes determining if the answer is right or wrong a highly objective process. This means that only a single rater is needed to score the summaries for Accuracy.

The parallel form reliability for a subsample of 29 examinees who took both forms is also quite satisfactory (.87), although not as high as one might expect given the high internal consistency reliability.[5] For the Total Accuracy Score, which is the combined multiple-choice and summary writing section scores, the correlation between Form A and Form B for this same subsample of 29 examinees was .92.

Reliability of the Expression score

Summaries are also scored for Expression. The Expression score consists of the average of the Expression ratings on the three summary translations. All of the summaries were scored by two raters. The descriptive statistics and correlation between raters are depicted in Table 13.3 for each summary and rater, for the global rating, and for each form.

In Table 13.3, Variable refers to the score obtained when a summary is scored by a rater. Thus, Sum1,R1 refers to the scores on Form A summary 1 assigned by rater 1. N Cases refers to the number of ratings assigned by the rater on that summary. Thus, rater 1 provided 46 scores on summary 1.[6] Mean refers to the mean rating for the variable. Thus, the mean of the scores assigned by rater 1 on summary 1 was 2.66. The reliability (in this case inter-rater) is the correlation between the ratings assigned by raters 1 and 2. The reliability coefficients are based only on those cases where both raters assigned ratings.

The total score is the average of the ratings on the summaries. To obtain the total, the ratings were summed and divided by the number of ratings. However, if only one summary was rated, or if no summary was rated, no total score was calculated. The reliability of the total Expression score for a particular form is the correlation between the total Expression scores provided by each rater.

Table 13.3

Descriptive statistics for final version: Summary Writing – Expression

Form	Variable	N Cases	Mean	Reliability
A	Sum1, R1	46	2.66	
	Sum1, R2	47	2.68	0.85
	Sum2, R1	49	2.35	
	Sum2, R2	49	2.53	0.86
	Sum3, R1	49	2.27	
	Sum3, R2	49	2.37	0.83
	TotalA, R1	46	2.4	
	TotalA, R2	47	2.52	0.90
B	Sum1, R1	54	2.69	
	Sum1, R2	53	2.75	0.70
	Sum2, R1	53	2.35	
	Sum2, R2	49	2.45	0.89
	Sum3, R1	47	2.42	
	Sum3, R2	53	2.42	0.81
	TotalB, R1	49	2.48	
	TotalB, R2	45	2.47	0.87

The reliabilities of these short writing samples, usually less than one page in length, is impressive. Only one coefficient, .70 for Summary 1 in Form B, is unimpressive. This coefficient is in fact typical of the interrater reliability one finds on standardized formal writing assessments. For example, the Test of Written English (TWE), of which the Educational Testing Service is justifiably proud, has attained an average interrater reliability of .78 after 10 years of operation (ETS 1996:10). Five of the six summaries by themselves produced interrater reliabilities that easily exceeded that attained in the TWE program.

The interrater reliability of the global Expression rating is high for both forms (.90 and .87). Such consistency in rating is high enough so that the FBI may feel comfortable relying on only a single rating of Expression. The TWE program, for example, attains reliabilities of this magnitude for the composite rating provided by the averaging the ratings of two raters. For the LSTE-Minnan, only a single rating should be necessary to attain this degree of precision in measurement.[7]

Validity

In an effort to provide evidence for the construct validity of the LSTE-Minnan, data from the self-assessments were correlated with scores on the test, and subscores and sections of the test were correlated with each other. The resulting obtained correlations are depicted and discussed below. For purposes of understanding the variables being discussed, we begin by identifying and defining them below. These variables and correlations are based on the final versions of the test.

SA-LC

Self-Assessment of Minnan listening comprehension on an ILR type scale converted to a numerical value. Maximum score is 10 since 0+ was the lowest point on the scale.

SA-ST

Self-Assessment of summary translation ability total score based on the total of four self-ratings using a four-point scale for each rating. Maximum possible score is 16.

SA-EW

Self-Assessment of English writing ability on an ILR type scale converted to a numerical value. Maximum score is 10 since 0+ is the lowest point on the scale.

MCA

Score on Form A, multiple-choice section. Maximum score is 50.

MCB

Score on Form B, multiple-choice section. Maximum score is 50.

ACCA

Accuracy checklist total, Form A, Rater 1. This is the sum of all points earned for messages conveyed on the three summaries on Form A when they are rated by rater 1. (Rater 2 rated only half the summaries as a check for interrater reliability.)

ACCB

Accuracy checklist total, Form B, Rater 1.

TOTACCA

Accuracy Total (MC+checklist) Form A. The Accuracy Total is the sum of correct answers on the multiple-choice and summary translation sections, scored by rater 1.

TOTACCB

Accuracy total (MC + checklist) Form B.

EXAVALLA

Expression average (composite of ratings by two raters), Form A.

EXAVALLB

Expression average (composite of ratings by two raters), Form B.

Interrelationships between test scores

Table 13.4 displays the correlations between the multiple-choice section and the checklists. Both are considered to be measures of Accuracy. The numbers in parentheses to the right of the coefficients represent the number of cases (N) that were used to calculate each correlation.

Table 13.4

Correlations between MC Accuracy, Checklist Accuracy and Total Accuracy

	MCA	MCB
ACCA	0.85 (49)	0.90 (29)
ACCB	0.80 (29)	0.82 (55)
TOTACCA	0.95 (49)	0.92 (29)
TOTACCB	0.94 (49)	0.92 (29)

Table 13.4 shows is a high correlation between the multiple-choice section and the checklists for Forms A and B. The strength of this relationship supports the use of the multiple-choice section as a predictor of informational accuracy in the writing of summary translations. Thus, its use as a screening test is validated.

MCA and MCB correlate very highly with their corresponding Total Accuracy score TOTACCA (.95) and TOTACCB (.94), of which they form a part. This demonstrates that the MCA and MCB are efficient screening tests for the Total Accuracy score. It also suggests that MCA and MCB could substitute for their corresponding Total Accuracy score; i.e. the scoring of the checklists in order to determine the Total Accuracy score may not even be necessary.

The magnitude of the above relationships also supports combining the multiple-choice section and the summary translation to provide a Total Accuracy score. Further justification for this policy is found by referring to the reliabilities previously presented. It was noted that the correlation between the two MC forms was .87, and the correlation between the two checklist forms was also .87. The magnitude of these parallel form correlations falls within the range depicted above for cross-section correlations. Thus, it can be observed that correlations across Accuracy sections using different response modalities (MC and checklist) are of about the same magnitude as correlations between sections using the same response modality. Given these data, it is fair to conclude that the two sections tap the same construct with the same efficiency.

Relationships between the LSTE-Minnan Accuracy Scores and the Self-Assessments

Table 13.5 below shows the relationships between the multiple-choice sections and the self-assessment measures. These data permit us to evaluate the validity of the MC sections as a test of summary translation ability. For most examinees (i.e. those that don't pass this test) this will be the only section of the test on which they will be scored. Thus, it is appropriate to evaluate the convergent and divergent validity of this section alone.

Table 13.5

Correlations between Self-Assessments and Multiple-Choice section of the LSTE-Minnan

	SA-ST	SA-EW	SA-LC	MCA
SA-EW	-0.148 (70) P=0221			
SA-LC	0.745 (70) P=0.000	-0.258 (70) P=0.028		
MCA	0.745 (44) P=0.000	-0.276 (46) P=0.063	0.779 (46) P=0.000	
MCB	0.764 (53) P=0.000	-.0117 (53) P=0.404	0.775 (53) P=0.000	0.869 (29) P=0.000

Table 13.5 shows that the MC sections (MCA and MCB) correlate nicely with self-rated listening comprehension skills in Minnan (SA-LC). The correlations are identical when rounded to the nearest hundredth (.78),

indicating excellent consistency of measurement for both the MC section and the self-assessment of listening proficiency in Minnan. This fairly high correlation is quite good, since SA-LC is an indirect, rather than a direct measure of listening proficiency. This magnitude of correlation is as good as a test developer could reasonably hope to obtain.

The MC sections also correlate nicely (.75 and .76) with the examinee's mean self-rated summary translation ability (SA-ST) on four types of job-related summary translation tasks involving different types of language and information. The similarity in the correlations indicates excellent consistency of measurement for both the MC section and the self-assessment of summary translation ability. Again, this fairly high correlation is quite good, since SA-ST is an indirect, rather than a direct measure of summary translation ability. This magnitude of correlation is as good as a test developer could reasonably hope to obtain. The strength of the relationship with summary translation ability demonstrates the predictive validity of the MC screening test for predicting performance of a different nature. Although listening and summary translation are two different skills, the LSTE-Minnan MC screening test does an excellent job of predicting summary translation skills.

It is interesting to note that the self-assessments of listening and summary translation skills also correlated highly, indicating that the examinees correctly perceived the strength of the relationship between Minnan listening skills and summary translation of the overheard messages into English.

It is interesting to note the low negative correlations between self-assessed English writing ability and the MC section of the LSTE-Minnan. For neither form is the correlation significantly different from zero. This suggests a zero-to-low negative correlation between these tests and English writing proficiency. The correlations indicate that the MC section of the test is of no utility in predicting English writing proficiency. Thus, the Accuracy and Expression scores represent different constructs and the two should not be combined.

Finally, as would be expected based on the data seen thus far, the correlation between the self-assessments of listening and writing is low and negative (-.26). Again, this indicates that all measures (direct and indirect) used in this study functioned consistently in terms of precision of measurement and the construct being measured.

Table 13.6 below shows the same relationships for the Total Accuracy score. This score is the combined total obtained by adding the MC score and the sum of points earned on the checklists.

The table demonstrates the validity of the Total Accuracy score. The correlations are very similar to those discussed in Table 13.5 above, so there is no need to discuss the interrelationships here. All are as one would hope to find them given everything we know about the sample, the constructs, and the instruments.

Table 13.6

Correlations between Total Accuracy Scores (MC+Checklists) and Self-Assessments

	SA-ST	SA-EW	SA-LC	MCA
SA-EW	-0.148 (70) P=0221			
SA-LC	0.745 (70) P=0.000	-0.258 (70) P=0.028		
TOTACCA	0.746 (46) P=0.000	-0.277 (46) P=0.000	0.767 (46) P=0.069	
TOTACCB	0.758 (53) P=0.000	-.0172 (53) P=0.218	0.810 (53) P=0.000	0.923 (29) P=0.000

It is particularly noteworthy that the correlations are so similar to those involving the MC sections. Indeed, of the seven correlations involving TOTACCA and TOTACCB none differs from the MC relationships by more than .05. Two are identical to the nearest hundredth, and two differ by only .01. The average correlation with the self-assessments is about .01 higher for Total Accuracy than it is for the MC sections. None of these differences in correlation is significant. This indicates that for the LSTE-Minnan the Total Accuracy score has no greater validity than the MC Accuracy score alone.

Summary of evidence for the validity of the Accuracy Scores

The evidence produced in the above section shows that all three measures, the MC section, the summary writing section, and the Total Accuracy score, are valid measures of summary writing ability. In fact, they seem to be about equally valid. Because of this, for purposes of efficiency, the use of only the MC section could be justified.

Relationships between the LSTE-Minnan Expression score and the Self-Assessments

Table 13.7 below shows the correlations between the averaged Expression ratings for each form (three ratings by two raters) and the examinees' self-assessments of Minnan listening, English writing, and summary translation ability.

Table 13.7

Correlations between the LSTE-Minnan Expression score and Self-Assessments

	SA-ST	SA-EW	SA-LC
EXAVALLA	-0.520	0.632	-0.542
	(44)	(46)	(46)
	P=0.001	P=0.000	P=0,000
EXAVALLB	-0.181	0.416	-0.221
	(52)	(52)	(52)
	P=0.196	P=0.002	P=0.115

The relationships are moderate and positive for English writing ability; they are low to moderate and negative for Minnan listening and summary translation ability. Again, these directions are of the magnitude and in the directions that one would expect. That is, since Expression is a rating of English writing ability only in the very limited text type of a summary translation, one would not expect a high overall correlation with a more global measure of English writing, such as the self-assessment of English writing on the ILR-like scale that was used in this study. Thus, instead of expecting a high correlation, we expect a moderate correlation, which is what was obtained.

We would expect English writing ability in the restricted context of a summary translation to have some negative relationship with Minnan listening and summary translation ability (both of which we have seen are similar measures of Minnan language proficiency). Indeed, that is what was found here. The moderate correlations were highly significant while the low correlations were nearly significant.

It is noteworthy that the correlations for Form B were of less magnitude that those for Form A. This is because the first summary on Form B produced a lower interrater reliability that any of the others, thereby lowering the reliability of Form B overall. The lower reliability reduced the magnitude of these validity coefficients.

In summary, the Expression score was found to be valid as a measure of English writing ability in the context of summary translation. However, it should be remembered that Expression is best considered as a diagnostic score to be used only with examinees who meet or surpass the pass/fail criterion on the Accuracy score. Examinees who do not meet or surpass this criterion need not be evaluated for Expression.

Conclusions

This study was based on only a modest sample of examinees and the analyses performed involved only correlational approaches to validity. In addition, criterion measures used in the validation study were self-assessments, rather than other direct measures. However, based on the analyses of the data collected, we believe that the LSTE-Minnan is valid and reliable. We can also make the following additional observations about the relationship between the summary writing constructs measured on the LSTE-Minnan.

1 The multiple-choice and summary Accuracy section scores are highly interrelated.
2 The Expression score which represents English writing ability is negatively related to Accuracy on both the multiple-choice and summary translation sections.
3 The Accuracy score is related to listening comprehension skills in Minnan, but not to English writing ability.
4 English writing ability is negatively related to listening comprehension in Minnan and perceived summary writing ability.

Perhaps more important than the above is the methodology used to develop this job-relevant test. The methodology was designed to ensure that the test would be valid. The analysis of test results suggest that the methodology did help ensure the validity of the measures developed.

Notes

1   The original LSTE in Spanish scores Expression on a three-point scale. However, beginning with the LSTE-Minnan a fourth point, 'Native', was added to the scale.
2   If one of the summaries is so short (e.g. a few words or a single sentence) that it cannot be rated for English Expression, it is designated 'Unratable', and is not counted in the final Expression score. In this case, the other two summaries are averaged and the average becomes the final Expression score. At least two summaries must be ratable in order for an Expression score to be obtained.
3   Minnan is spoken by some 50 million speakers worldwide. Approximately one half of the speakers are located in the People's Republic of China (PRC), and most of these are located in the province of Fujian, which is located directly across from Taiwan. There are about 15 million speakers in Taiwan, and half a million or more speakers in Malaysia, Singapore, Thailand, Indonesia, Hong Kong, the Philippines, and the United States. It is the second most frequently spoken home language (after Cantonese) of

American-born Chinese. Although there are several dialects of Minnan, the widely spoken Amoy dialect was used on this test.

4   It should be remembered that the ILR listening scale does not specifically identify the overheard conversations tested on the LSTE as a type of listening. Thus, the LSTE focuses on a specific type of listening, while the ILR scale focuses on general listening skills. None the less, the general listening skills associated with the ILR scale appear to be highly relevant to successful execution of the type of listening tasks tested on the LSTE.

5   In theory, the parallel form reliability should be equivalent to the internal consistency reliability. However, in test development projects where examinees have no stake in their score, it is common for them to lose interest to some extent when taking the test the second time. It is probably the case that that happened here and that the true parallel form reliability is considerably higher than that obtained here. Indeed, when we did a Rasch analysis using BIGSTEPS, the analysis identified two misfitting examinees. When we removed those examinees from the sample the correlation between the two forms increased to .95.

6   The lack of complete data is due to the fact that not all examinees provided an adequate sample for rating their English writing skills. If an examinee did not write a summary or the examinee wrote a very short summary (e.g. 'I couldn't understand.' or 'Lin called Wu.'), the rater may not have felt that he or she had an adequate sample with which to make a judgement. In this case, the rater has the option of not assigning a rating. In such cases, it is better not to assign a rating than to assign an incorrect rating. If the lowest rating were assigned it would indicate that the examinee writes poorly in English, when this may not be the case. Rather, it could easily be that the examinee did not comprehend the conversation. Thus, only when a summary of minimal length is produced is it possible to assign a rating. It is up to the rater to determine if he or she feels confident to provide a rating. If the rater does not provide a rating for one of the summaries, then the global rating for Expression is based on the average of the ratings on the two scored summaries. If a rating is provided on only one summary, then no global rating for Expression is assigned at all.

7   While the high attained interrater reliabilities are encouraging, it should be noted that they describe only the raters used in this study. Raters in the operational program must be trained using the self-instructional rater training kit for Expression. Individuals vary in the extent to which they can learn to rate reliably. Thus, these reliability coefficients do not apply to any specific future rater. However, these ratings were assigned without the benefit of being trained with the training kit (although the raters subsequently developed the kit). Consequently, we believe that this degree of interrater reliability is generally replicable.

Suggested further reading

Scott, M. L., Stansfield, C. W. and Kenyon, D. M. (1996) Examining validity in a performance test: The Listening Summary Translation Exam (LSTE)-Spanish version. *Language Testing* 13 (1): 83–110.

This article applies the framework for analyzing validity outlined by Bachman (1990) in *Fundamental Considerations in Language Testing* to examining the validity of the LSTE-Spanish. Because of the careful attention to analyzing and then simulating key characteristics of actual job tasks when creating test procedures, the LSTE-Spanish was found to have a high degree of situational and interactional authenticity, including the use of appropriate metacognitive strategies.

Stansfield, C. W., Scott, M. L. and Kenyon, D. M. (1990) *Listening Summary Translation Exam (LSTE)-Spanish*. Final project report. Washington DC: Centre for Applied Linguistics. ERIC Document Reproduction Service, ED 323 786.

This research monograph discusses the two forms of the LSTE-Spanish in depth. Its six chapters deal with the format of the LSTE-Spanish, its development, trialing and pilot testing. A lengthy chapter on the validation study also analyzes the test's reliability, using both FACETS and classical approaches. The final chapter discusses the development of the ILR-like Summary Accuracy Scale and associated score conversion tables.

Nineteen appendices include selected pages from the test booklets, sample checklists for scoring summary accuracy, pilot and revised versions of the scoring guide, all questionnaires, test administration instructions and report forms, and score conversion tables.

Stansfield, C. W., Wu, W. and Liu, C. C. (1997) *Listening Summary Translation Exam (LSTE) in Taiwanese, aka Minnan*. Final project report. N. Bethesda, MD: Second Language Testing, Inc. ERIC Document Reproduction Service, ED 413 788.

This research monograph discusses the two forms of the LSTE-Minnan in depth. Its nine chapters deal with the Minnan language, the format of the LSTE-Minnan, its development, the development of self-assessment measures, a detailed description of the field testing, reliability, validity, and equating. Fourteen appendices include selected pages from the test booklets, the scoring guide, all questionnaires, instructions for test administrators, score conversion tables, and selected scatterplots.

References

Bachman, L.F. (1990) *Fundamental Considerations in Language Testing.* Oxford: Oxford University Press.

Scott, M. L., Stansfield, C. W. and Kenyon, D. M. (1996) Examining validity in a performance test: The Listening Summary Translation Exam (LSTE)-Spanish version. *Language Testing* 13 1: 83–110.

Stansfield, C. W., Scott, M. L. and Kenyon, D. M. (1990) *Listening Summary Translation Exam (LSTE)-Spanish.* Final project report. Washington, DC: Centre for Applied Linguistics. ERIC Document Reproduction Service, ED 323 786.

Stansfield, C. W., Wu, W. and Liu, C. C. (1997) *Listening Summary Translation Exam (LSTE) in Taiwanese, aka Minnan.* Final project report. N. Bethesda, MD: Second Language Testing, Inc. ERIC Document Reproduction Service, ED 413 788.

14 Schema theory and selected response item tests: From theory to practice

Ebrahim Khodadady
Kurdistan University
Michael Herriman
Nagoya University of Commerce and Business

Abstract

Selected response item tests, as well as being popular methods of measurement, are thought to be reliable and objective. They also meet the two cardinal requirements regarding efficiency and practicality. None the less, traditional selected response item tests lack a sound basis in terms of item writing theory. This chapter details the application of schema theory to the construction of selected response item tests in order to provide such a basis. The findings demonstrate that schema-based selected response items constructed on authentic texts are reliable and correlate significantly with the grammar, vocabulary and reading sections of TOEFL. Furthermore, the results indicate that while native and non-native English speakers perform differently on schema-based items, they both regard the tests as a good measure of English proficiency. Thus, in addition to having criterion and face validity, schema-based selected response item tests are reliable, enjoy theoretical advantage over their traditional counterparts, help item writers dispense with constructing reading passages for the sake of testing rather than reading, provide the item writers with a rich source of item options, and take less time to be answered than tests deemed equivalents, such as the reading section of TOEFL.

Introduction

Mehrens and Lehman (1991) stated that among various testing methods such as open-ended questions and essay writing, selected response or multiple-choice item tests (MCITs) are the most highly regarded types. Although MCITs are the most popular, reliable, time- and cost-effective testing methods, they suffer from one major shortcoming, i.e. they lack a solid basis in item writing theory. The underlying rationale for constructing MCITs has been questioned by many scholars (e.g. Bennett 1993; Haladyna 1994; Mislevy 1993; Resnick and Resnick 1990; Shepard 1991a, 1991b).

Since MCITs lack a sound theory, multiple-choice item writers are often uncertain as to how to generate plausible and attractive distracters. As Tindal and Marston (1990) stated 'the most difficult problem in writing multiple-choice items is creating effective options among which to include the correct answer' (p. 55). The purpose of this study was to apply schema theory to the selection of effective options for MCITs through utilising authentic reading materials and to compare them with a number of alternative forms.

Schema theory

Schema theory provides explanations as to how linguistic and cognitive processes are executed and how they interact with each other in reading comprehension (Rumelhart 1980). The theory can be applied to the task of reading comprehension and its measurement in terms of two processes: macrostructure and microstructure. According to Stanovich (1980), the former refers to processes that integrate information from different sentences and the text as a whole and the latter designates processes 'operating on the words and syntax within a sentence' (p. 51).

On the basis of a macrostructure approach researchers such as Clapham (1996), Moy (1975) and Shoham *et al.* (1987) investigated the question whether test takers' academic fields would affect their performance on subject-specific reading comprehension tests. They hypothesised that the test takers' scores on subject-specific reading comprehension tests would be significantly higher than those obtained on reading comprehension tests developed on general topics. Contrary to researchers' expectations they could not find a conclusive answer. For example, Shoham *et al.* investigated the relevance of subject-specific reading passages to performance on reading comprehension tests for 185 advanced students of English as a foreign language (EFL) majoring in science and technology (107), biology (29) and humanities and social sciences (49) at Ben Gurion University of The Negev. In agreement with the findings of Moy, Shoham *et al.* found that students of science and technology obtained the highest mean on the entire test as well as the highest mean on the individual test passages. The results showed that:

> ... *while there was a statistically significant difference in performance on subject-related test passages for students of science and technology and for students of biology, the humanities and social science students did not do significantly better on the test passage that was considered to be more closely related to their academic discipline. (Shoham et al.1987: 86)*

This suggests that macrostructure approach does not show the test taker's background knowledge as it should. In this study, therefore, a microstructure approach has been adopted and schema has been viewed as an abstract or idealised entity like lexis (Taylor *et al.* 1988). Accordingly, each schema or lexeme has a semantic network, or a set of interrelationships among different schemata, which is organised hierarchically (Collins and Quillian 1969). Within the organisation it has semantic interrelationships with different schemata on its higher end and certain attributes on its lower end. The realisation or otherwise of a certain schema depends on the presence of its attributes.

Taylor *et al.* (1988: 13) offered the schema of *chair* as an example. The example is illustrated in Figure 14.1.

Figure 14.1

The hierarchical organisation of the schema *chair* and its higher order schemata

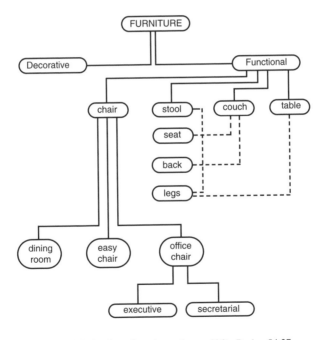

Source: P.D. Pearson (1982) A primer for schema theory. *Volta Review* 84:27

As shown in the figure, the schema of *chair* belongs to *functional furniture* as its higher schemata or macroschemata. The macroschemata of functional furniture include not only *chair* but also other schemata such as *stool, couch* and *table* as their lower schemata or microschemata. The recognition of the microschema *chair* and its differentiation from microschemata such as *stool*, *couch* and *table* depends on having a seat, a back and a set of legs as its attributes. Within an oral text, these attributes can be easily identified. They are 'influenced and constrained by text structure and the social circumstances surrounding the production of the text' (Gee *et al.* 1992: 232).

Within a written text, however, there are no physical text structures, i.e. immediate environment or social circumstances, to help the readers and test takers alike to understand or interpret the text. It is argued here that the meaning of any schema is determined and should therefore be understood in interrelationships with the other schemata immediately surrounding it. In fact, these environmental schemata act as the attributes of the schema under comprehension. Ideally, perfect reading comprehension will occur if, and only if, each and all of the schemata presented by the author are comprehended as the author does.

If reading comprehension accrues as a result of understanding each and all of the schemata present in an authentic text, then testing reading comprehension should depend on understanding each and all of the schemata brought up by the author in the text. Thus, the exact number of test items will rest on the number of schemata used in the texts. The more schemata there are in a text, the more test items should and can be constructed on the text. Among various testing methods, rationally constructed cloze tests (CTs) are the only measures which are capable of addressing and realising this function, i.e. testing as many of the author's schemata as possible. Testing the comprehension of any schema within a text depends on and should in fact be determined by the way it is understood.

Research findings show that schemata are understood in three possible manners: orthographically, semantically or both. These three microstructural approaches to reading are classified in schema literature as bottom-up, top-down and interactive models, respectively (e.g. Harris and Sipay 1990; Stanovich 1980; Taylor *et al.* 1988). They will be discussed briefly and applied to testing reading comprehension ability.

Bottom-up model of schemata theory

According to bottom-up models, reading comprehension starts with the recognition of letters, words, phrases and sentences and proceeds to grammar and discourse. Comprehension is, therefore, viewed as a process consisting of discrete stages requiring processing lower units before processing the higher units in a serial or one-way manner (Sperling 1967; Sternberg 1969; Theios 1973). In bottom-up models readers play a relatively passive role in reading and texts provide more information than the reader does.

Thus it is our view that CTs are bottom-up measures of test takers' comprehension if, and only if, the author's schemata are presented among multiple distracters which bear no relationship with those of the author's. The test takers are primarily passive in the process of answering traditional cloze MCITs because their distracters can easily be identified and discarded by focusing on the schemata surrounding the schema under question. These schemata reveal the irrelevance of the distracters and thus render the traditional cloze MCITs text driven.

Top-down models of schemata theory

In top-down models cognitive structure and linguistic competence assume the primary role of constructing meaning. Before or shortly after receiving any graphic inputs, readers generate hypotheses on the basis of their background knowledge and engage themselves in hypothesis testing as they proceed through texts. Although most top-down theories describe skilled readers rather than unskilled ones, Goodman and Goodman (1979, 1982) differentiated skilled readers from less skilled ones on the basis of mastery over strategies needed to extract meaning from print rather than background knowledge. Whether it is the background knowledge or the adopted strategy that distinguishes skilled readers from unskilled ones, it is unanimously held that readers are active in the top-down processing of reading.

Cloze tests in this study are treated as top-down measures of reading comprehension ability. In the process of answering the CTs, the test takers have to generate hypotheses regarding what schemata have been deleted, i.e. author's schemata. The very necessity of producing the missing schemata on the part of the test takers requires writing ability and thus undermines the validity of the CTs as measures of reading comprehension ability. The CTs are therefore test-taker driven measures which draw heavily on what hypotheses the test takers formulate rather than what the author says.

Interactive models of schemata theory

According to interactive models, text comprehension is the outcome of generating hypotheses and confirming or disconfirming these hypotheses by resorting to what exists in the texts which in turn determines what hypotheses readers should formulate in order to proceed with reading. While there are no findings substantiating the equal influence of top-down and bottom-up processing on each other, there is general consensus that reading involves what the readers know and what the texts present. It is assumed that in the process of reading, depending on the accuracy and the strength of formulated hypotheses, the readers take either an active or a passive role (Pearson and Kamil 1978).

Interactive models differ from top-down models in terms of the relative independence of processes at different levels (Mosenthal *et al.* 1978). In top-down models, higher-level or semantic processes determine lower-level processes through confirming hypotheses formulated upon processing minimum input, i.e. reading the title of the text. In interactive models, higher-level processes determine the lower-level processes through confirming reformulated hypotheses and are in turn constrained by lower-level processes through providing further information to develop informed hypotheses regarding the upcoming data.

In this chapter it is maintained that any form of CTs which involves the schemata of the author and challenges those of test takers is interactive. These two requirements can be operationalised in first-letter-given CTs and cloze MCITs which present the author's schemata along with the schemata having semantic interrelationships with those of the author's. In answering first-letter-given CTs, the test takers should comprehend the text and produce the author's schemata through generating hypotheses which are confirmed or disconfirmed by using minimum orthographic clues, i.e. the first letters of the deleted schemata, whereas in answering the schemata-based cloze MCITs they have to draw upon their experiences and background knowledge to distinguish the author's schemata from among the competitives which share some semantic features with those of the author.

The term competitives is specifically used for the options of schema-based cloze MCITs in order to differentiate them from the distracters of traditional cloze MCITs. Since there is a limited rationale behind the constructions of traditional cloze MCIT items, they are basically chosen to distract the less knowledgeable test takers from the keyed response. However, in schema-based cloze MCITs all options share some semantic features with the keyed response and thus compete with it in terms of the test takers' background knowledge.

The basic assumption underlying this study is that there is a difference between native speakers (NSs) and non-native speakers (NNSs) in terms of their background knowledge with the schemata expressed in the reading materials. Based on this assumption, the following hypotheses can be formulated:

1 Schema-based cloze MCITs will be reliable tests.
2 The number of schema-based cloze multiple-choice items which correlate significantly with the variable of language will be higher than the other alternative forms.
3 The scores of NSs on reading tests developed on the basis of bottom-up, top-down and interactive models of schema theory will be significantly higher than those of NNSs.
4 NNSs' scores on schemata-based cloze MCITs will correlate with the structure, vocabulary and reading comprehension sections of the ELPT.
5 Schemata-based cloze MCITs will have face validity.

Method

Participants

The participants in this study were 135 first-year undergraduate students. They majored in agriculture (2%), arts (3%), commerce (25%), engineering (6%), human movement (4%), law (7%), science (51%), and economics (3%) at the University of Western Australia. Ninety-two students were native speakers (NSs) of English and 43 were non-native speakers (NNSs) who spoke Chinese (54%), Persian (12%), Czech (5%), Polish (5%), Arabic (2%), Azary (2%), Danish (2%), German (2%), Hindi (2%), Indonesian (2%), Italian (2%), Samoan (2%), Sinhale (2%), and Japanese (2%) as their mother language.

Ninety per cent of the participants were 15 to 20 (mostly 19) years old and the ages of the rest ranged between 21 and 45 years. The highest percentage of NNSs (42%) had stayed in an English-speaking country from six to ten years or more. The second highest percentage of NNSs (21%) had stayed from two to three years and the length of stay for the rest ranged between six months and nine years. All of the participants were paid (Aus$20) for their time and inconvenience in accordance with the guidelines provided by the Human Rights committee of the University of Western Australia.

Materials

Materials for the study comprised one authentic and unmodified article, Fear Over Access to Medical Records, which was adopted from *New Scientist* magazine (18 November 1995, No 2004, p. 7). Some of the articles in *New Scientist* have been used in the construction of the International English Language Testing System (IELTS) and are 'thought to be more academic than … articles in quality newspapers' (Clapham 1996: 145). The articles of *New Scientist* provide standard scientific texts for public readership. The Readability Ease Score of Flesch (39) indicated that the text was suitable for undergraduate students.

Instruments

English language proficiency test

Following Yano *et al.* (1994) who used the Structure Subtest of the Comprehensive English Language Test (CELT) as a criterion of language proficiency, the disclosed structure, vocabulary and reading comprehension subtests of the TOEFL published in 1991 (TOEFL91) by the Educational Testing Service (ETS) were utilised in order to control the English language proficiency of test takers and validate the tests constructed in this study. They consisted of 15, 30 and 30 multiple-choice items each.

Cloze test

Research results show that neither NSs nor NNSs have difficulty in reading and understanding function words used in the composition of authentic materials (Khodadady and Herriman 1996). Based on these results, a CT was developed on the lexemes, i.e. author's schemata, of the text. Since the number of lexemes used in a passage is almost always fewer than the number of function words (Khodadady 1995), gapping lexemes will lead to omission of fewer words in constructing reading comprehension tests as suggested by Gillet and Temple (1990).

The text consisted of 271 lexemes from which 38 words were deleted to construct the CT (seven adjectives, two adverbs, 13 nouns, and 16 verbs). However, due to discourse constraints, e.g. having few lexemes between the gapped items to provide the necessary context, two function words were also deleted (one possessive adjective, one pronoun). Thus the test consisted of 40 items.

In scoring the CT two methods were followed: the exact word scoring method (EWSM) and acceptable word scoring method (AWSM). In EWSM, only the author's exact words are allowed whereas in the AWSM any given answer viewed as acceptable by NSs is scored correct. These acceptable answers are generally collected in consultation with some educated native speakers of English prior to marking (Kobayashi 1995)

In the present study, since the educated NSs were going to take the CT, the answers of both NSs and NNSs were collected, alphabetically ordered and given to four native English teachers to be marked. The words which had been marked as appropriate by at least three teachers were accepted as correct. Thus each participant had two scores on the CT, one on exact word CT and one on acceptable word CT.

First-letter-given cloze test

The cloze test developed on the authentic and unmodified text was changed into a first-letter-given CT. As the name of the method indicates, the first letter of each deleted word was kept intact in order to provide minimum orthographic clues to the author's schemata, i.e. deleted lexemes. Similar to the CT, the first-letter-given CT consisted of 40 items.

Traditional cloze multiple-choice item test

In addition to the first-letter-given CT, a traditional cloze MCIT was also constructed on the CT. According to Hale *et al.* (1988) three approaches have been adopted in constructing traditional cloze MCITs: computerised, empirical, and rational. As explained below, in this study a combination of the three approaches was used to construct the traditional cloze MCIT.

For the computerised approach the list of lexemes prepared by Matthiesen (1993), Sharpe (1986) and Khodadady (1995) used. While Matthiesen's and

Sharpe's lists consisted of the most frequent content words used in the construction of TOEFL tests, Khodadady's list consisted of the lexemes used in twelve recent English newspaper and magazine articles, disclosed vocabulary and reading comprehension of the TOEFL (ETS 1987) and Stanford Diagnostic Reading Test Level III. Based on these lists, on erroneous responses given to the CT, as well as on rational arguments, the alternative of the traditional cloze MCIT was constructed. The first item of the traditional cloze MCIT is presented as an example in which the three approaches have been combined.

Example 1
Fears over access to medical records
   Privacy campaigners in the US have launched a fierce ... (1) on a bill
   that they believe will expose medical records to too many ... (2) eyes.

   a. *campaign*   empirical distracter (erroneous response)
   b. *discussion*   random distracter (based on the lists)
   c. *attack*   author's schema or key response
   d. *protest*   rational distracter

   Distractor a is designed on the basis of the answers given to the CT. Based on the list prepared by Khodadady (1995), Matthiesen (1993), and Sharpe (1986) distractor b was randomly selected. For constructing the rational distracter d, it was argued that since the privacy campaigners believed that the bill would expose medical records to many prying eyes, the readers might infer that the campaigners protested against it.

Schemata-based cloze multiple-choice item test
Based on the deleted words of the CT, a schema-based cloze MCIT was constructed. (The schema-based cloze MCIT is reproduced in Appendix 1.) For developing the schema-based cloze MCIT each deleted schema was given as the key response among semantically related schemata. The semantic relationship between the deleted schema and the competitives was decided on the basis of their common and distinctive semantic features or traits. In contrast to traditional cloze MCITs whose distractors are the products of probability or the test designer's interpretation of the text, the competitives of the schema-based cloze MCITs are lexemes which are interrelated with the keyed schema.

   In this study, semantic features are used synonymously with semantic traits as defined and employed by Cruse (1986). In order to avoid the theoretical controversy shrouding the concept of *semantic features,* Cruse (1986) employed the term *semantic traits* to designate 'a particular word-meaning which participates ... in the meaning of another word' (p.16). The schema-based competitives of item 1 and item 2 given in Example 1 illustrate these features. These two items were used in the schema-based cloze MCIT.

Figure 14.2 presents the semantic features of four schemata used in item 1: *raid, slander, attack* and *ambush*. As presented, the keyed response, i.e. *attack*, and its competitives, i.e. *raid, slander* and *ambush,* have some semantic features in common. The author schema of *attack* shares the semantic feature of physical assault with *raid* and *ambush* and verbal assault with *slander*. However, the schemata of *raid, ambush* and attack share more semantic features with each other than with *slander.* It is argued that the schemata preceding and following the deleted schema determine the author's choice of a certain schema and should act in the same manner for the readers.

Figure 14.2

Semantic features of the microschemata of
raid, slander, attack* and *ambush

Microschemata	Semantic Features		
	physical assult	verbal assult	hindering
a. raid	+	-	-
b. slander	-	+	-
c. attack	+	+	+
d. ambush	+	-	-

The semantic features of schemata used in item 2 are given in Figure 14.3. As shown, the author's schema *prying* has the semantic feature of making a search which is shared by the schemata *inquiring* and *probing*. However, the schema *prying* also has the semantic feature of acting uninvitedly which is not shared by the schemata *inquiring* and *probing*. Instead the schema *interfering* shares the semantic feature of acting uninvitedly with the schema *prying* but differs from it in terms of having its own semantic feature of hindering.

Figure 14.3

Semantic features of the microschemata of
inquiring, prying, interfering* and *probing

Microschemata	Semantic Features		
	making a search	acting uninvitedly (searching)	hindering
a. inquiring	+	-	-
b. prying	+	+	-
c. interfering	-	+	+
d. probing	+	-	-

The provision of competitives which share some semantic features with the author's schema involves the test takers' background knowledge and provides them with enough context to decide which is the best option. The competitives of the schema-based cloze MCITs can easily be found in thesauri such as *Roget's Thesaurus of English words and phrases* (Chapman 1992) and the *New Collins Thesaurus* (McLeod 1984).

Questionnaire

The opinions of the participants towards CTs, first-letter-given CTs and schema-based cloze MCITs were gathered through a questionnaire adapted from Jaffarpur (1995). The questionnaire was printed at the end of the booklets and all the participants were asked to answer the questions after completing the tests. The same questions were asked in all booklets save those dealing with CTs, first-letter-given CTs and schema-based cloze MCITs. The participants who had answered the CT gave their opinion on CTs and those who had taken the first-letter-given CT opined about first-letter-given CTs.

Procedure

The English language proficiency test (ELPT) consisting of the structure, vocabulary and reading comprehension subtests of TOEFL 91 was administered under standard conditions in April 1996. After scoring the ELPT, native speakers and NNSs were ranked separately from the highest score on the ELPT to the lowest score. Since four formats of the same test were going to be explored, i.e. the CT, first-letter-given CT, traditional cloze MCIT and schema-based cloze MCIT, the participants were blocked into four groups using the ELPT as the matching variable. This blocking enabled comparisons among the tests even though four different samples took the four tests. The tests were administered two weeks after the administration of the ELPT.

Data analyses

The completed cloze test was scored for exact and acceptable replacements. The internal consistency reliability of the tests was assessed via Cronbach's μ by using SPSS Release 6.1, standard version. The responses to individual items were correlated with the total test scores (biserial) and their p-values were estimated in order to identify misfitting items whose response pattern was unusual (Reynolds *et al.* 1994). Items having p-value of less than 0.33 or greater than 0.67 were considered to be misfitting.

The data from the CT, first-letter-given CT, traditional cloze MCIT and schema-based cloze MCIT were subjected to an analysis of variance with repeated measures to find out whether constructing reading comprehension tests on the basis of the three models of schemata theory produces different tests for NNSs and NSs in terms of their difficulty.

Results and discussion

The descriptive statistics for the scores of the participants on the five tests are presented in Table 14.1. Exact word CT was the least reliable test for both NNSs and NSs (0.60 and 0.53, respectively), and the first-letter-given CT was the most reliable test (0.90 and 0.73, respectively). Furthermore, the traditional cloze MCIT proved to be a more reliable test for NNSs (0.74) but of low reliability for NSs (0.54). The schema-based cloze MCIT had the second highest reliability for both NNSs and NSs (0.83 and 0.66, respectively). These results confirm the first hypothesis that schema-based cloze MCITs are reliable measures of reading comprehension ability.

Table 14.1

Descriptive statistics for the scores of the participants on the exact word cloze test (EWCT), acceptable word cloze test (AWCT), first-letter-given cloze test (FLGCT), traditional cloze multiple-choice item test (TCMCIT), and schema-based cloze multiple-choice item test (SBCMCIT)

Participants Cronbach's	Test		Mean*	Standard	Skew
				deviation	∞
	EWCT (n=11)	8.73	3.56	0.73	.60
	AWCT (n=11)	16.36	5.97	0.01	.78
NNSs	FLGCT (n=11)	20.73	7.94	0.52	.90
	TCMCIT (n=11)	36.10	3.20	-1.99	.74
	SBCMCIT (n=11)	29.90	5.70	-0.52	.83
	EWCT (n=21)	10.67	3.28	0.32	.53
	AWCT (n=21)	19.67	4.32	-0.58	.62
NSs	FLGCT (n=24)	24.25	4.60	1.58	.73
	TCMCIT (n=24)	38.40	1.70	-2.61	.54
	SBCMCIT (n=22)	36.30	2.70	-0.98	.66

As shown in Table 14.1, the means indicated the exact word CT was as difficult for NNSs (8.7) and NSs (10.7) as the traditional cloze MCIT was easy for them (36.1 and 38.4, respectively). The means of the first-letter-given CT fell between these two extremes for NNSs (20.7) and NSs (24.3) and yielded the highest standard deviation for both NNSs (7.9) and NSs (4.6). The mean of NNSs on the acceptable word CT (16.4) showed that it was as difficult as the schema-based cloze MCIT (29.9) was easy. However, the standard deviation for NNSs on the acceptable word CT (5.97) and the schema-based cloze MCIT (5.7) was approximately the same, indicating that in spite of being easy the schema-based cloze MCIT discriminates among NNSs as well as the acceptable word CT.

These results indicate that reading comprehension tests designed on the basis of top-down model of schema theory, i.e. CTs, are difficult not only for NNSs but also for NSs, i.e. both groups achieved the lowest scores on CTs. Even scoring the CT on the basis of the acceptable word scoring method does not make it as easy as the first-letter-given CT. Since CTs depend on the test takers' ability to produce the deleted schemata, they fail to provide a fair picture of the test takers' reading comprehension ability.

The results also suggest that reading comprehension tests designed on the basis of a bottom-up model of schema theory, i.e. traditional cloze MCITs, are the easiest methods of testing for both NNSs and NSs. Since in the traditional cloze MCIT the author's schemata had been given without resorting to the test takers' schemata, i.e. competitives which have semantic interrelationships with the author's schemata, the test takers could score the highest. Because the traditional cloze MCIT was too easy, its standard deviation was the lowest, indicating that it could not discriminate among the high-ability and low-ability test takers as well as the other test methods could.

In contrast to the top-down and bottom-up models of schema theory, the interactive model provides the best reading comprehension measures for NNSs, i.e. first-letter-given CTs and schema-based cloze MCITs. The results presented in Table 14.1 indicate that first-letter-given CTs and schema-based cloze MCITs are neither as difficult as CTs nor as easy as traditional cloze MCITs. Compared with the first-letter-given CT, the scores of test takers are higher on the schema-based cloze MCIT, but the standard deviation of the first-letter-given CT is much larger than the schema-based cloze MCIT. This difference stems from the fact that on first-letter-given CTs the test takers should produce the author's schemata with minimum orthographic input whereas on schema-based cloze MCITs they are required to recognise the author's schemata. In other words, first-letter-given CTs measure both writing and reading ability whereas schema-based cloze MCITs probably assess reading ability only.

The percentage of p-value and the alternative test items that correlate significantly with the participants' total test scores and language are presented in Table 14.2. The percentage of p-value and point biserial coefficients indicated that the first-letter-given CT had the highest percentage of fitting items for NNSs (54% and 35%, respectively). However, for NSs the percentage of p-values (40%) indicated acceptable word CT as the best measure, whereas the point biserial coefficients (25%) designated the schema-based cloze MCIT and first-letter-given CT.

Since first-letter-given CTs and acceptable word CTs require the production of deleted schemata on the part of test takers, it seems that writing ability affects the performance of students on these items as an intervening variable. When the individual items of the alternative tests were correlated with the language of test takers as a controlled variable, the percentage of point biserial correlation coefficients demonstrated that the schema-based cloze MCIT (23%) is the only test method that discriminates NNSs from NSs.

Table 14.2

Percentage of p-value and the exact word cloze test (EWCT), acceptable word cloze test (AWCT), first-letter-given cloze test (FLGCT), traditional cloze multiple-choice item test (TCMCIT), and schema-based cloze multiple-choice item test (SBCMCIT) items correlating with the total test scores and language of the participants

Tests	P-value (%)		Point biserial correlation (%)		Language (%)
	NNSs	NSs	NNSs	NSs	
EWCT	25	23	20	20	3
AWCT	50	40	10	15	5
FLGCT	54	23	35	25	13
TCMCIT	13	3	25	2	5
SBCMCIT	20	20	28	25	23

These results support the second hypothesis that the number of schema-based cloze multiple-choice items which correlate significantly with the variable of language will be higher than the other alternative forms.

Table 14.3 presents the results of a one-way ANOVA with repeated measures for the scores of participants on the alternative tests. As can be seen, there are significant differences between the means obtained by NNSs and by NSs ($p < 0.0001$). These results support the third hypothesis that the scores of NSs on reading tests developed on the basis of bottom-up, top-down and interactive models of schema theory will be significantly higher than those of NNSs.

Table 14.3

One-way ANOVA with repeated measures for the scores of participants on the exact word close test (EWCT), acceptable word cloze test (AWCT), first-letter-given cloze test (FLGCT), traditional cloze multiple-choice item test (TCMCIT), and schema-based cloze multiple-choice item test (SBCMCIT)

Participants P value	Source of variance	DF	MS		F-test
	Between subjects	9	55.413	.393	
NNSs	Within subjects	40	140.96		
(n=10)*	Tests	4	1190.33	48.857	< .0001
	residual	36	24.363		
	Total	49			
	Between subjects	20	10.7	.073	
NSs	Within subjects	84	145.843		
(n=21)*	Tests	4	2856.367	276.869	< .0001
	residual	80	10.317		
	Total	104			

Note: * in blocks of 5

Follow-up Scheffe tests are presented in Table 14.4. While scoring the cloze test on the basis of the EWSM and AWSM yielded a marginally significant difference for NNSs (p < 0.05), it produced substantially different means for NSs (p < 0.001), indicating that acceptable word CTs favour NSs. Moreover, allowing for the acceptable words in scoring the CT for NNSs did not render it different from providing orthographic clues to the author's schemata. By contrast, these two approaches resulted in fairly significant performances on the part of NSs (p < .01).

The Scheffe *post hoc* test, however, indicated that the first-letter-given CT as an interactive test is substantially different not only from the traditional cloze MCIT as a bottom-up test but also from the schema-based cloze MCIT as another interactive test for both NNSs and NSs. Furthermore, the means of neither NNSs nor NSs on the traditional cloze MCIT are significantly different from the schema-based cloze MCIT, indicating that supplying the test takers with the author's schemata leads to higher scores on both tests on the part of the participants.

Table 14.4

Scheffe F-tests of NNSs and NSs' performance on the exact word close test (EWCT), acceptable word cloze test (AWCT), first-letter-given cloze test (FLGCT), traditional cloze multiple-choice item test (TCMCIT), and schema-based cloze multiple-choice item test (SBCMCIT)

Participants	Test	AWCT	FLGCT	TCMCIT	SBCMCIT
	EWCT (n=11)	3.366*	6.668**	37.68****	37.68****
	AWCT (n=11)		0.559	18.522****	10.2****
NNSs	FLGCT (n=11)			12.647****	5.984**
	TCMCIT (n=11)				1.23
	EWCT (n=21)	20.61***	43.633***	195.433****	170.12****
	AWCT (n=21)		4.267**	89.112****	72.303****
NSs	FLGCT (n=24)		.379****	41.44****	
	TCMCIT (n=24)				0.878

Note   * p<.05, **p<.01, ***p<.001, ****p<.0001

Concurrent validity

Table 5 provides the correlation coefficients of the alternative tests with the ELPT subtests. As a reading comprehension test, the schema-based cloze MCIT is the only test which correlated positively and significantly with the reading comprehension subtest of the ELPT (0.85) only for NNSs. The schema-based cloze MCIT also correlated with the vocabulary subtest (0.82) and structure subtest (0.72) of the ELPT. These results support the fourth hypothesis that NNSs' scores on schema-based cloze MCITs will correlate with the structure, vocabulary and reading comprehension sections of the ELPT.

Table 14.5

Correlation coefficients of the exact word close test (EWCT), acceptable word cloze test (AWCT), first-letter-given cloze test (FLGCT), traditional cloze multiple-choice item test (TCMCIT), and schema-based cloze multiple-choice item test (SBCMCIT) with the subtests of the ELPT

Participants	Test	Structure	Vocabulary	Reading Comprehension
	EWCT	.41	.47	.46
	AWCT	.54	.53	.53
NNSs	FLGCT	-.03	-.31	-.61*
	TCMCIT	.80	.90****	.39
	SBCMCIT	.72	.82***	.85****
	EWCT	.70	.68***	.21
	AWCT	.44	.51*	.61***
NSs	FLGCT	.17	-.08	-.06
	TCMCIT	-.29	.26	-.09
	SBCMCIT	.53	.28	-.10

Note: *p<.05, **p<.01, ***p<.001, ****p<.0001

The scores of NSs on the acceptable word CT correlated significantly with the ELPT (0.72), and its subtests of structure (0.44), vocabulary (0.51), and reading comprehension (0.61), indicating that the acceptable word CT is an externally valid test of NSs' reading comprehension ability, structure and vocabulary knowledge (see Table 14.5). These results provide further support for the claim that NNSs and NSs perform differently on different test methods. While the schema-based cloze MCIT had concurrent validity for NNSs, the acceptable word CT proved to be a valid test for only NSs.

Face validity

Summary views of the participants on how CTs, first-letter-given CTs and schema-based cloze MCITs look appear in Table 14.6. Compared with the CTs, the percentage of participants who have expressed positive attitudes towards the schema-based cloze MCITs (87%) is greater than the CTs (56%). In contrast, the majority of participants view the first-letter-given CTs negatively (70%). In response to the question: Do you think CTs/first-letter-given CTs/ schema-based cloze MCITs are a fair test of English, the majority of participants (52%), however, selected only the schema-based cloze MCITs. Similarly, most of the participants (56%) specified the schema-based cloze MCITs to be used as the preferred criterion for acceptance at universities.

In response to the question: Why do you think that CTs/first-letter-given CTs/schema-based cloze MCITs are fair tests of English, most of the participants who had selected CTs and first-letter-given CTs as fair tests opined that the element of chance does not play any role in answering CTs and first-letter-given CTs. In contrast, the participants who had chosen the schema-based cloze MCITs as fair tests explained that they require not only using English in context, but also reading and understanding the passages and competitives. According to the participants, schema-based cloze MCITs measure both comprehension and proficiency at various levels and allow them the chance to demonstrate their competence through challenging competitives.

Table 14.6

Participants' responses to three questions dealing with cloze tests (CTs), first-letter-given cloze tests (FLGCTs), and schema-based cloze multiple-choice item tests (SBCMCITs)

Question		Response (%)	
		Positive	Negative
What do you think of	CTs	56	44
	FLGCTs	30	70
	SBCMCITs	87	23
Do you think ... are a fair	CTs	29	71
test of English	FLGCTs	19	81
	SBCMCITs	52	48
Would you want your	CTs	9	91
acceptance at universities	FLGCTs	34	66
to depend on	SBCMCITs	56	44

As Bachman (1990) and Jafarpur (1995) emphasised, the appearance of a test plays a very important role in its application. The results of this study indicate that the CTs and first-letter-given CTs do not fulfil the exigency of this requirement. When face validity is flimsy, test takers do not take the test seriously enough to try their best (Bachman 1990: 288). In contrast, the schema-based cloze MCITs have strong face validity and thus provide the test takers with the opportunity to 'demonstrate that they understand' with 'limited time and resources'.

Practicality

The allotted time for taking the vocabulary and reading comprehension subtests of TOEFL is 45 minutes (ETS 1991). These two subtests require 15 and 30 minutes to be taken, respectively. In contrast to the reading subtest of the TOEFL which requires one minute per item, the schema-based cloze MCIT administered in this study consisted of 40 items and was answered in ten minutes on average, i.e. the required time is reduced to one-fourth of a traditional reading comprehension multiple-choice item. Given the high correlations between the performance of NNSs on the schema-based cloze MCIT and the vocabulary and reading subtests of the TOEFL, utilising schema-based cloze MCITs renders measuring the vocabulary knowledge and reading ability of test takers more time effective than the TOEFL.

The construction of schema-based cloze MCITs does not require a special knowledge of the psychometrics of test development nor does it demand the talent or speciality of the multiple-choice item writers as the TOEFL, for example, does. Nor does it require preparing and utilising computerised lists of lexemes, erroneous responses of the test takers, and the multiple-choice item writers' rational interpretations of the text as the traditional cloze MCITs do. Moreover, the results of the schema-based cloze MCITs do not depend on the scoring methods adopted in correcting cloze tests. Whereas exact word CTs fail to provide a fair picture of the participants' reading comprehension ability, acceptable word CTs require seeking the response of educated NSs who often disagree as to what the acceptable answer is. These advantages highlight the superiority of the schema-based cloze MCITs as the most time- and cost-effective measures of structure knowledge, vocabulary knowledge and reading comprehension ability for NNSs.

Summary and conclusion

In this study, on the basis of bottom-up, top-down and interactive models of schema theory, four tests, i.e. a CT, first-letter-given CT, traditional cloze MCIT and schema-based cloze MCIT, were constructed on identical text and items and were administered to first-year undergraduate native speakers (NSs) and non-native speakers (NNSs). The findings indicated that:

1 The performance of NNSs and NSs is significantly different on these tests.
2 Scoring CTs as top-down measures of reading comprehension on the basis of exact word method and acceptable word method produces marginally different tests for NNSs and substantially different tests for NSs.
3 Exact word CTs and acceptable word CTs lack concurrent validity for NNSs. Since exact word CTs and acceptable word CTs depend on the test takers' ability to restore the deleted words representing author's schemata, they are as difficult for NNSs as the schema-based cloze MCITs are easy.
4 Acceptable word CTs are valid tests of reading comprehension ability, vocabulary and structure knowledge for NSs. However, given the small size of the sample and the fact that the ELPT used in this study was specifically designed for NNSs, this concurrent validity seems to be in need of further analysis.

5 Although first-letter-given CTs as interactive measures of reading are reliable tests, they lack concurrent and face validity as attested by both NNSs and NSs.

6 Traditional cloze MCITs as bottom-up measures of reading comprehension ability are the easiest test methods and consequently fail to discriminate between high-ability and low-ability test takers. This deficit can only be compensated for by performing elaborate item difficulty measures, in most cases a task beyond the capability of most language teachers. While traditional cloze MCITs are valid tests of vocabulary and structure knowledge for NNSs, they are not valid tests of reading comprehension ability for either NNSs or NSs.

7 As interactive measures of reading comprehension, schema-based cloze MCITs are reliable and valid tests of structure knowledge, vocabulary knowledge and reading comprehension for NNSs. In addition to concurrent validity and reliability, schema-based cloze MCITs enjoy face validity and meet the requirements of time and cost effectiveness.

The researchers acknowledge the fact that the number of NNSs in particular and NSs in general who took part in the project had very low proficiency in English. Furthermore, all of the NNSs were using English as a second language and most of them had stayed in an English-speaking country (mainly Australia) for ten or more years. None the less, the probe has demonstrated that schema-based cloze MCITs are the best measures of English language proficiency, reading comprehension ability, vocabulary and structure knowledge among the other testing methods. Considering the internal, external and face validity as well as the practicality of schema-based MCITs, further research is needed to answer the question of whether similar results will be obtained if they are administered to larger populations and learners of English as a foreign language.

References

Bachman, L. F. (1990) *Fundamental Considerations in Language Testing.* New York, NY: Oxford University Press.

Bennett, R. E. (1993) On the meaning of constructed response. In Bennett, R. E. and Ward, W. C. (Eds.) *Construction Versus Choice in Cognitive Measurement: Issues in Constructed Response, Performance Testing and Portfolio Assessment.* Hillsdale, NJ: Lawrence Erlbaum Associates, Publishers: 1–28.

Chapman, R. L. (Ed.) (1992) *Roget's International Thesaurus* (5th ed.). New York, NY: Harper Perennial.

Clapham, C. (1996) *The Development of IELTS: A Study of the Effect of Background Knowledge on Reading Comprehension.* Cambridge: Cambridge University Press.

Collins, A. M. and Quillian, M. R. (1969) Retrieval time from semantic memory. *Journal of Verbal Learning and Verbal Behaviour* 8: 240–7.

Educational Testing Service (1987) *Reading for TOEFL.* Princeton, NJ: ETS.

Educational Testing Service (1991) *Reading for TOEFL.* Princeton, NJ: ETS.

Gee, J. P., Michaels, S. and O'Connor, M. C. (1992) Discourse analysis. In LeCompte, M. D., Millroy, W. L. and Preissle, J. (Eds.) *The Handbook of Qualitative Research in Education.* San Diego, CA: Academic Press: 227–92.

Gillet, J. W. and Temple, C. (1990) *Understanding Reading Problems: Assessment and Instruction* (3rd ed.). Glenview, IL: Scott, Foresman/Little, Brown Higher Education.

Goodman, K. S. and Goodman, Y. M. (1979) Learning to read is natural. In Resnick, L. and Weaver, P. (Eds.) *Theory and Practice of Early Reading*, Vol. 1. Hillsdale, NJ: Lawrence Erlbaum Associates, Publishers.

Goodman, K. S. and Goodman, Y. M. (1982) A whole-language comprehension-cantered view of reading development. In Reed, L. and Ward, S. (Eds.) *Basic Skills Issues and Choices: Approaches to Basic Skills Instruction* 2. St. Louis, MO: CEMREL.

Haladyna, T. M. (1994) *Developing and Validating Multiple-choice Test Items.* Hillsdale, NJ: Lawrence Erlbaum Associates, Publishers.

Hale, G. A., Stansfield, C. W., Rock, D. A., Hicks, M. M., Butler, F. A. and Oller Jr., J. W. (1988) *Multiple-choice Cloze Items and the Test of English as a Foreign Language (TOEFL Research Report No. 26).* Princeton, NJ: Educational Testing Service.

Harris, A. J. and Sipay, E. R. (1990) *How to Increase Reading Ability: A Guide to Developmental and Remedial Methods* (9th ed.). New York NY: Longman.

Jaffarpur, A. (1995) Is C-testing superior to cloze? *Language Testing* 12 (2): 194–216.

Khodadady, E. (1995) T*extual analysis of testing materials: Validity readdressed.* Paper presented at the 8th Educational conference of the ELICOS Association of Australia. Fremantle, Western Australia.

Khodadady, E. and Herriman, M. (1996) *Contextual lexical knowledge and reading comprehension: Relationship and assessment.* Paper presented at the 9th Educational conference of the ELICOS Association of Australia. Sydney, New South Wales.

Kobayashi, M. (1995) *Effects of text organisation and test format on reading comprehension test performance.* Unpublished PhD dissertation. Thames Valley University, London.

Matthiesen, S. J. (1993) *Essential Words for the TOEFL.* New York, NY: Baron's Educational Series, Inc.

McLeod, W. T. (Ed.) (1984) *The New Collins Thesaurus.* London: Collins.

Mehrens, W. A. and Lehman, I. J. (1991) *Measurement and Evaluation in Education and Psychology* (4th ed.). Fort Worth, TX: Holt, Rinehart and Winston, Inc.

Mislevy, R. J. (1993) Foundations of a new test theory. In Fredriksen, N., Mislevy, R. J. and Bejar, I. I. (Eds.) *Test Theory for a New Generation of Tests.* Hillsdale, NJ: Lawrence Erlbaum Associates Inc.

Mosenthal, P., Walmsley, S. and Allington, R. (1978) Word recognition reconsidered: Toward a multi-context model. *Visible Language* 12: 448–68.

Moy, R. H. (1975) *The effect of vocabulary clues, content familiarity and English proficiency on cloze scores.* Unpublished M. A. thesis, UCLA.

Pearson, P. D. (1982) A primer for schema theory. *Volta Review* 84.: 27.

Pearson, P. D. and Kamil, M. L. (1978) Basic processes and instructional practices in teaching reading. *Reading Education Report No. 7.* Champaign, IL: Centre for the Study of Reading, University of Illinois.

Resnick, L. B. and Resnick, D. P. (1990) Tests as standards of achievement in schools. In Pfleiderer, J. (Ed.) *Proceedings of the 1989 ETS Invitational Conference: The uses of standardised tests in American education.* Princeton, NJ: Educational Testing Service: 63–80.

Reynolds, T., Perkins, K. and Brutten, S. (1994) A comparative item analysis study of a language testing instrument. *Language Testing* 11 (1): 1–13.

Rumelhart, D. E. (1980) Schemata: The building blocks of cognition. In Spiro, R., Bruce, B. and Brewer, W. (Eds.) *Theoretical Issues in Reading Comprehension.* Hillsdale, NJ: Lawrence Erlbaum Associates, Publishing.

Sharpe, P. J. (1986) *Baron's how to prepare for the TOEFL Test of English as a Foreign Language* (5th ed.). New York, NY: Baron's Educational Series, Inc.

Shepard, L. (1991a) Interview on assessment issues with Lorrie Shepard. *Educational Researcher* 20 (2): 21–3, 27.

Shepard, L. (1991b). Psychometricians' beliefs about learning. *Educational Researcher* 20 (6): 2–16.

Shoham, M., Peretz, A. S. and Vorhau, R. (1987) Reading comprehension tests: General or subject specific? *System* 15: 81–8.

Sperling, G. (1967) Successive approximations to a model for short-term memory. *Acta Psychologica* 27: 285–92.

Stanovich, K. (1980) Toward an interactive-compensatory model of individual differences in the development of reading fluency. *Reading Research Quarterly* XVI (1): 32–72.

Sternberg, S. (1969) The discovery of processing stages: Extensions of Donder's method. In Koster, W. G. (Ed.) *Attention and Performance II.* Amsterdam: North-Holland Publishing Co.

Taylor, B., Harris, L. A. and Pearson, P. D. (1988) *Reading Difficulties: Instruction and Assessment.* New York, NY: McGraw-Hill Publishing Company.

Theios, J. (1973) Reacting time measurements in the study of memory processes: Theory and data. In Bower, G. (Ed.) *The Psychology of Learning and Motivation: Advances in Research and Theory* (Vol. 7). New York, NY: Academic Press.

Tindal, G. A. and Marston, D. B. (1990) *Classroom-based Assessment: Evaluating Instructional Outcomes.* Columbus, OH: Merrill Publishing Company.

Tuckman, B. W. (1978) *Conducting Educational Research* (2nd ed.). New York, NY: Harcourt Brace Jovanovich.

Yano, Y., Long, M. H. and Ross, S. (1994) The effects of simplified and elaborated texts on foreign language reading comprehension. *Language Learning*, 44 (2): 189–219.

Appendix 1

Schema-based cloze multiple-choice item test

Directions
40 words from the following passageshave been deleted and replaced with a numbered
blank space. For each deleted word four choices marked **a, b, c** and **d** have been
offered. Choose the **word** which you think is the most appropriate to fill the blank.
Your choice should be based on what comes before and after the blank and the text as
a whole. Indicate your choice by **circling** one of the four letters.

Time allotted: **20** minutes

Fears over access to medical records

Privacy campaigners in the US have launched a fierce ... (1) on a bill that they believe will expose medical
records to many ... (2) eyes. The bill aims to set uniform privacy standards for medical ... (3), making it easier
to set up national databases of medical records. But the ... (4) agrue that it would allow people such as medical
researchers and the police to ... (5) at the records without patient's permission.

1.	a. raid	b. slander	c. attack*	d. ambush
2.	a. inquiring	b. prying*	c. interfering	d. probing
3.	a. news	b. message	c. knowledge	d. information
4.	a. critics*	b. arbiters	c. umpires	d. judges
5.	a. gaze	b. observe	c. look*	d. view

"People are ... (6) concerned about this bill" says Marc Rotenberg of the Electronic Privacy Information Center
in Washington DC. "Medical privacy really is one of those cases in which you have the ... (7) right of privacy."

6.	a. learnedly	b. profoundly*	c. movingly	d. severely
7.	a. frank	b. neet	c. authentic	d. absolute*

In the US, a person's medical records are often ... (8), with different parts held in different places. Doctors in
private ...(9) have details of treatments they have ...(10), hospitals have their records and health insurers keep
... (11) of treatments for which they have paid.

8.	a. fragmented*	b. shattered	c. smashed	d. demolished
9.	a. exercise	b. practice*	c. drill	d. discipline
10.	a. managed	b. governed	c. conducted	d. administered*
11.	a. articles	b. components	c. details*	d. pieces

Growing numbersof Amenrican are also ... (12) away from individual medical practices in favour of managed
care organisations, ... (13) clinics in which patients may not see the same doctor twice. In such settings,
computerised records would reduce paperwork and cut health ... (14). They would also makeit possible for
doctors to ... (15) up a person's full medical history at the touch of a ... (16).

12.	a. rolling	b. turning*	c. spinning	d. twisting
13.	a. bulky	b. broad	c. huge*	d. ample
14.	a. prices	b. funds	c. fines	d. costs*
15.	a. recall	b. bring	c. call*	d. look
16.	a. disc	b. button*	c. plate	d. circuit

The Medical Records Confdentiality Act would make it ... (17) for companies to bring the tragnebts of a person's records ... (18). Companies that keep details of people's credit ratings and ... (19) records for insurers are eager to move into the medical ... (20).

17.	a. easier*	b. calmer	c. quieter	d. milder
18.	a. jointly	b. mutually	c. together*	d. at one
19.	a. directing	b. driving*	c. goading	d. pushing
20.	a. status	b. rank	c. globe	d. sphere*

The bill, which was being ... (21) by the Senate Committee on Labour and Human Resources this week, would ... (22) existing confidentiallity laws, clearing the way for these companies to begin ... (23). At present, states have their own confidentiallity laws. Companies which are to ... (24) up databases of medical records say they need national ... (25) to cut through the tangle of different state laws. Without ... (26) they would have to set up 50 different systems governed by 50 different sets of ... (27).

21.	a. interrogated	b. tested	c. examined*	d. questioned
22.	a. discard	b. supersede*	c. abandon	d. usurp
23.	a. performing	b. behaving	c. conducting	d. operating*
24.	a. set*	b. take	c. pick	d. call
25.	a. regulation	b. prescription	c. instruction	d. legislation*
26.	a. them	b. her	c. it*	d. him
27.	a. guides	b. orders	c. princeples	d. rules*

But privacy pressure groups are worried that the bill ... (28) too many people to see the records without the patient's permission. In its present form, it ... (29) no restraint on who woul;d be permitted to ... (30) the records within, for example, insurance companies or colleges that ... (31) their own clinics. The bill would also allow medical researchers and ... (32) health agencies, such as the health department, to ... (33) through the records.

28.	a. allows*	b. grants	c. admits	d. provides
29	a. locates	b. places*	c. rests	d. settles
30.	a. recognise	b. know	c. see*	d. notice
31.	a. place	b. recieve	c. experiance	d. have*
32.	a. civil	b. common	c. public*	d. general
33	a. inspect	b. search*	c. ransack	d. explore

Police officers would still need a ... (34) or subpoena to examine medical records. Investigators working for insurance companies looking for evidence of ... (35) would be able to see people's records without ... (36) permission.

34.	a. warrant*	b. guarentee	c. license	d. bond
35.	a. craft	b. sham	c. fraud*	d. deceit
36.	a. its	b. their*	c. this	d. those

"A medical information system of the kind will radically ... (37) the character of the paitient medical records, " says the American Civil Liberties Union of Massachusetts, which ... (38) the bill. "Every medical record will become a source that can be ... (39) by corporate and governmental enterties for business purposes, governmental investigations and ... (40) of many kinds (*New Scientist*, 18 November 1995, No 2004, p.7)

37.	a. turn	b. revise	c. transform*	d. vary
38.	a. contradicts	b. opposes*	c. defies	d. counters
39.	a. mined*	b. burrowed	c. tunnelled	d. hoed
40.	a. watch	b. vigilance	c. notice	d. surveillance

Section Four
Dilemmas and Post-modern Test Design

The two chapters in this section present different perspectives. William Grabe presents in this survey article a more current and comprehensive view of the construct of reading and ways in which such interpretation of reading might influence the assessment of reading. He also outlines several potential dilemmas for second language reading assessment. Henry Braun in a written version of his plenary address presents an ecological approach to test design. This includes consultations with various constituencies like clients, customers, academy and industry. He argues that these will provide three essential building blocks: the constructs of the measurement process, the kinds of information to be conveyed based on test results, and the constraints or the unchanging features of the setting in which tests are to be designed, developed and delivered.

15 Reading research and its implications for reading assessment[1]

William Grabe
Northern Arizona University

Abstract

In the course of the past ten years, there have been many advances in reading theory. These advances have come mostly in the field of English L1 reading research, carried out by comprehension researchers and educational psychologists. From the fields of second language reading and bilingual processing, research has contributed additional insights to the English L1 reading perspectives. In this chapter, these developments (both L1 and L2) will be examined with two goals in mind:

1   to provide a more current and more comprehensive view of the construct of reading, and
2   to indicate ways in which such a current interpretation of reading might influence testing practices.

The chapter will first outline briefly a view of reading abilities based primarily on research in first language contexts and note briefly social and affective influences on reading comprehension. Contexts for second language reading will then be introduced so that the general construct of reading abilities can be reconceptualized with respect to second language reading abilities. Implications of this research for assessment will then be briefly noted as will also the relative lack of application of reading research to assessment approaches.

Introduction

Before developing the main arguments of this chapter, five preliminary points need to be made about reading at the outset so that my perspective is clearly recognized. The points stated here, as a foundation for this chapter, have considerable empirical support and, for the most part, widespread acceptance among cognitive and educational psychologists. These five initial points will orient the reader to interpret the following overview appropriately:

1 The 'psycholinguistic guessing-game' model of reading is clearly wrong and is not considered seriously by current researchers. We do not sample texts and hypothesize meaning as the basic reading comprehension process.

2 Reading is best understood by looking at the research on the skilled L1 reader, since that is the end point of expertise that an L2 reader is aiming towards. This perspective also reveals ways in which L2 reading may be different, and what L2 readers need to be able to do in order to read well.

3 Learning to read involves reading a lot, and there is no way around this point. There are no magic short cuts for the development of reading abilities.

4 Reading comprehension is most likely a simple multiplication of word recognition abilities and general language comprehension abilities (the 'simple view of reading'). The word recognition 'reading' part is strongly bottom-up driven; the comprehension part is strongly interactive, or, in certain cases, top-down driven.

5 Any comprehensive theory of reading will eventually need to develop and integrate the following five components:
   a A theory of language
   b A theory of processing
   c A theory of learning (not restricted to language learning)
   d A theory of social context influences
   e A theory of affective and motivation factors

Points one, four, and five deserve further elaboration. The first of these five points emphasizes the fact that there is no strong evidence supporting the 'psycholinguistic guessing game' model of reading (nor the 'socio-psycholinguistic' model of reading, nor 'transactional' models of reading, nor 'constructive' models of reading). Moreover, there is considerable, probably overwhelming, evidence that contradicts the guessing-game model of reading, and all other predominantly 'top-down' models of reading. For example, there is no evidence that we sample texts and then generate hypotheses (as controlled processing) about what words are likely to come next as part of the basic process of on-line reading. There is no evidence that we actually direct our eyes to where we might sample texts, but much evidence demonstrates that eye movements are highly constrained and relatively automatic. There is no evidence that using context heavily to get the meaning of the text is a hallmark of good reading; rather, this practice consistently identifies weaker readers who are over-compensating because they have inadequate word recognition skills and lack automaticity in comprehension processing. There is no evidence that reading and writing abilities are naturally developing processes just like speaking and listening – otherwise, one fifth of the world's population must be labelled as unnatural since they are illiterate. In fact, the guessing-game model of reading, along with other transactional and constructive models of reading, presupposes many of the skills and abilities that it is supposed to be explaining.

Research which explains these points, and others, in detail can be found in a large number of resources (Adams 1990, 1994; R. C. Anderson 1993; Biemiller 1994; Juel 1995; Liberman and Liberman, 1992; Nicholson, 1991; Perfetti 1991, 1994; Pressley 1994; Stanovich 1986, 1992; Stanovich and Stanovich 1995; Vellutino 1991; Wong and Underwood 1996). The interested reader willing to explore and review the wide range of reading research will have no difficulty finding the evidence and arguments I refer to. The key point is that many applied linguists and second language teachers have been accepting a view of reading which has little to offer by way of theoretical explanations, instructional practices, or assessment purposes (see also Bernhardt 1991; Paran 1996). These comments will remove any ambiguities of reader interpretation with respect to my position on the various top-down so-called models of reading.

Point four (the simple view of reading) brings out a central claim of many reading researchers, regardless of the actual model adopted. Reading comprehension is most often described as a combination of identification and interpretation abilities, or, more specifically, word recognition abilities and comprehension abilities (Gough and Juel 1991; Tunmer and 1992; Vellutino and Scanlon 1991). The key point for many researchers is that comprehension abilities are not specific to reading – they also operate in spoken language processing and in visual processing. So what is unique to reading is word recognition abilities (Perfetti 1992). Moreover, general comprehension abilities among learners are typically well developed already by the time learners start reading instruction (except for strategy use and executive control processing with difficult comprehension tasks). This view does not say that reading comprehension is word recognition, though detractors try to argue as much. Rather, word recognition abilities are the part of the overall set of abilities that needs to be developed most thoroughly for reading comprehension to operate. One version of this argument that has been argued quite forcefully is the simple view of reading (see pages 241–242). In this model, reading is most likely a simple multiplication of word recognition abilities and general language comprehension abilities.

Point five addresses not only reading but any language-based construct. Any comprehensive theory of reading must, in principle, try to account for the range of factors which will influence (and perhaps explain) learning and assessment outcomes. Such a framework will need to address and integrate a theory of language, a theory of processing, a theory of learning, a theory of social-context influences, and a theory of attitude/motivation factors.

The present chapter presupposes a minimally theoretical descriptive approach to language (within language processing constraints as indicated in Chapelle *et al.* 1997; Gernsbacher 1990, 1997; Kintsch 1995), and it outlines a processing orientation to reading. The chapter assumes a theory of learning that would be informed by some combination of associative learning (J. R. Anderson 1983, 1993, 1996; Anderson *et al.* 1996; Ellis 1994, 1996; Landauer and Dumais 1997; Shanks 1995), guided instruction (Brown *et al.* 1996; Lantolf and Pavlenko 1995; McGilly 1994; Pressley 1995; Slavin 1995), and expertise development (Bereiter and Scardamalia 1993; Ericsson 1996; Stanovich *et al.* 1996; Wagner and Stanovich 1996). It also assumes a theory of social-context influences which will need to account for L1 learning contexts, L1 language and culture factors, L1 learning socialization factors, home environment factors, school and institutional factors, L2 learning contexts, teacher and peer factors, and instructional/task factors (Bowey 1995; Bus *et al.* 1995; Dunning *et al.* 1994; Elliott and Hewison 1994; Guthrie and McCann 1997; Heath 1986; Leseman 1994; Mason 1992; Mikulecky 1996; Rowe 1991; Scarborough and Dobrich 1994; Snow *et al.* 1991; Weinberg 1996; Whitehurst *et al.* 1994). Finally, the chapter assumes the need to account for attitude and motivation factors as central to the reading acquisition process (see e.g. Borkowski *et al.* 1990; Chapman and Tunmer 1995; Czikszentmihalyi 1991; Mathewson 1994; McKenna 1994; Schiefele 1992).

It should be readily apparent that any full specification of the construct of reading is beyond our current capabilities. Nevertheless, it is important to keep in mind that accounts of reading will be necessarily partial until the wider range of factors in this general framework are explored more systematically. Having said this, I would now like to propose a more modest overview of reading as a set of processes that are central to our understanding of reading, even if incomplete, and then explore the additional issues raised by L2 reading.

The nature of reading

A definition

While one can safely say that reading involves understanding a printed text, this notion does not provide any indication of what specifically must be done in reading, nor how it is to be done. A more useful extended definition of reading would describe the reading process and outline the critical features of this process. Fluent reading includes the following defining features:

- Reading is a rapid process.
- Reading requires processing efficiency.
- Reading requires strategic processing.
- Reading is interactive.
- Reading is purposeful.
- Reading requires sufficient knowledge of language.

- Reading requires sufficient knowledge of the world and of a given topic.
- Reading requires extensive time on task.

Rapid reading can best be defined as reading most material at between 200 and 300 words per minute. Reading at much slower rates, particularly for L2 students, can cause comprehension problems because working memory capacity is used ineffectively (Carpenter *et al.* 1994; Gernsbacher 1990), and may indicate limited processing efficiencies (Biemiller 1994; Breznitz 1997; Breznitz and Share 1992; Carver 1997; Perfetti 1994). Good readers are efficient because they recognize words automatically, form meaning propositions quickly, integrate propositional information into a text model rapidly, and restructure the text model to reflect the main ideas of the text being read (van Dijk and Kintsch 1983; Perfetti 1994; Singer 1990).

It is also clear that fluent reading is purposeful and involves goal setting, incorporates interactions among various levels of cognitive processing, and requires combinations of appropriate reading strategies (adjusting reading rates, rethinking goals, previewing texts, predicting discourse organization, monitoring comprehension, etc.). Moreover, reading requires both sufficient knowledge of language and knowledge of the world as basic supporting foundations on which to build comprehension. The combination of these features of reading requires extensive amounts of reading practice. Finally, while not features of cognitive processing themselves, aspects of social contexts and individual motivation inform and support reading comprehension processes.

These points have been discussed in numerous contexts, so there is little need to review them at length in this overview (see Adams 1990; Barr *et al.* 1991; Carr and Levy 1990; Carver 1997; Gough, Ehri and Treiman 1992; Haenggi and Perfetti 1994; Just and Carpenter 1987; Perfetti 1989, 1991, 1992, 1994; Pressley and Woloshyn 1995: Rayner and Pollatsek 1989; Stanovich 1991a, 1992; Wagner and Stanovich 1996). In the description of the reading process to follow, these issues will also arise in discussions of the various components of reading comprehension abilities.

Components of the reading process

The study of reading components provides an important way to understand how fluent readers comprehend texts. The central components of reading processing include the following: orthographic processing, phonological coding, word recognition (lexical access), working memory activation, sentence parsing, propositional integration, propositional text-model formation, comprehension strategy use, inference making, text-model development, and the development of an appropriate situation model (or mental model). Throughout the study of these components, basic issues such as the role of a reader's prior knowledge, the relative importance of each subprocess, and the extent of interaction among various sub-processes are important concerns.

Lower-level processing

A central component in all current models of reading is the major role of low-level recognition processes. Low-level processing can be discussed in terms of three sub-component processes: The recognition of orthographic structure (recognizing line forms, letter shapes, letter group patterns), the recognition of morpheme structure, and the processing of phonemic information (Barker *et al.* 1992; Bjaalid *et al.* 1996; Foorman 1994; Stanovich 1991b; Stanovich *et al.* 1991). Perhaps the most important sub-component is the *phonemic coding* of visual input for assisting word recognition and for maintaining information in working memory. In its more reflective form, as phonemic awareness, it is also now considered the best early predictor of later reading development (Adams 1990; Brady and Shankweiler 1991; Gough *et al.* 1992; Stanovich 1992).

The three sub-word processes described above all work together as a part of *word recognition,* or *lexical access.* (Some researchers distinguish these terms, some do not. For second language learning, it is more useful to distinguish between the two.) The sub-word processes illustrate well the interactive nature of processing that occurs during reading. For the purposes of word recognition, all three sub-word processes begin simultaneously when visual information is perceived. Together, they assist word recognition, one of the key processing components for reading (Adams 1990; Biemiller 1994; Perfetti 1991, 1992; Seidenberg and McClelland 1989). While specific aspects of word recognition processes have been debated for over twenty years, virtually all researchers recognize the central role of word recognition in reading (van Dijk and Kintsch 1983; Juel 1991; Stanovich 1986, 1991b; Perfetti 1989, 1992, 1994; Rayner and Pollatsek 1989).

Word recognition fluency is critical for reading because readers need to see word forms and access the appropriate meanings both rapidly and accurately. The contributing information from the visual form and from phonological decoding allows readers to recognize words and access their lexical entries with minimal cognitive effort. Fluent word recognition provides the building blocks for comprehension of the text as a whole: to put it simply, it is the fuel for the engine. Slow word recognition, on the other hand, creates series difficulties for reading comprehension that are not easily overcome. Moreover, Perfetti (1992) argues that this fluent word recognition ability requires a large set of automatically recognizable vocabulary: words must be recognized both quickly and thoroughly. Fluent readers are great word recognizers – a point that is too often understated. (See also Ehri 1992; Stanovich 1991b; Zuckernick 1996.) One critical implication for reading instruction is that reading development will require a large automatically recognizable store of vocabulary. Of course, the question of how much vocabulary is needed, or how elaborate the knowledge of a word should be, is an issue that has yet to be resolved for either first language or second language contexts (cf. Anderson 1996; Anglin 1993; Arnaud and Savignon 1997; Goulden *et al.* 1990; Hazenberg and Hulstijn 1996; Nation and Newton 1997).

As words are accessed and information is activated, they are brought together in *working memory*, the metaphorical space in which comprehension processing is carried out. Working memory seems to have an activation capacity (rather than storage capacity), and when activation reaches its capacity, processing slows or stops and tasks are not carried out efficiently. Capacity can be reached due to proficiency limits, referential and lexical ambiguities, syntactic complexities, distance across referents or concepts, time constraints, or task interference (Carpenter *et al.* 1994).

Because of the many simultaneous processing operations in working memory (word recognition, syntactic parsing, word and structure storage, propositional integration, text model building, etc.), this processing environment is a major source of variation in reading abilities, and, in particular, a source of differences between better and less-skilled readers. Those readers who have less efficient (and perhaps smaller) working memory capacity are not able to store and use as much information as other readers, and at times this bottleneck interferes with text comprehension (Carpenter *et al.* 1994; Daneman 1991; Jonides 1995; Just and Carpenter 1987, 1992; Perfetti 1994; for L2, cf. Harrington and Sawyer 1992; MacWhinney 1997; Segalowitz 1997). Issues of processing efficiency in working memory also implicate speed of lexical access and speed of proposition integration. As a consequence, reading processes need to be carried out at a reasonably rapid rate to ensure fluent reading.

As lexical information begins to enter (or become activated in) working memory, the processes of *syntactic parsing and propositional integration* are also activated (Daneman 1991; Kintsch 1995; Perfetti and Britt 1995; Rayner and Pollatsek 1989). These two processes begin to act on lexical information immediately as the first one or two words are recognized (Perfetti and Britt 1995). While there are a number of unresolved issues in explaining exactly how these two processes operate, a general account would suggest that, as words are activated, syntactic-category information, word-order information, morphological information, and phrase and clause structure information all help generate partial syntactic structures. From these parts, the structure of the clause is constructed and the meanings of individual words are integrated into a larger meaning unit, the proposition. The end-product of this processing in working memory is the meaning proposition, or what the sentence means.

The structure building framework of Gernsbacher (1990, 1997) provides one way to see the contribution of syntactic parsing and propositional integration as central components of reading comprehension. She suggests that sentence processing, as part of discourse processing, is a matter of:

1 laying a foundation structure,
2 mapping new information onto an existing structure, or
3 shifting to open a new structure.

Syntactic and semantic information provide the basic resources to accomplish these three processes.

Up to this point in the discussion, most reading researchers would be willing to accept the general outlines of the processes discussed, recognizing that many of these component processes generate various specific disagreements. These specific sources of difference are seen in competing theories which examine evidence from experiments and computer simulations (Balota 1994; Carpenter *et al.* 1994; Garnham 1994; Gough *et al.* 1992a; Henderson *et al.* 1995; Perfetti 1994). Nevertheless, current research perspectives would all recognize the role of orthographic processing, phonemic coding, word recognition, syntactic parsing, propositional integration, and working memory in reading comprehension.

Higher-level processing

As one moves from explanations describing lower-level processing to those describing higher-level processing (that is, working with larger units of information and information contributed by the reader), the issues become less clear and more controversial. Up until recently, many researchers disagreed strongly on the processes that may be involved in higher-level comprehension, and others suggested that there was not enough evidence to make confident assertions about the full range of processing that takes place (van Dijk and Kintsch 1983; Rayner and Pollatsek 1989; Singer 1990). However, more recently, research on discourse processing has converged on a number of central ideas, while still disagreeing on a number of specifics. The central notions now provide a reasonable general account for discourse processes, and the ways that they support text comprehension.

Most researchers now agree that some form of text-comprehension network, a text model which reflects the textual information closely, is generated by the reader. A second network, a situation model, includes much more reader background knowledge, affective responses, and individual interpretations of the text information (Britton and Graesser 1996; Gernsbacher 1994; Lorch and O'Brien 1995; Zwaan 1994; Zwaan and Brown 1996). In addition, most researchers believe that some types of inferencing are necessary while reading, that syntactic and discourse signalling in texts is used to strengthen or restructure the text network, and that the textual context contributes to text interpretation. At the same time higher-level processing also generates considerable disagreement over the specific processing mechanisms involved in text comprehension. In particular, the roles of inferencing, contextual information, reader background knowledge, discourse structuring knowledge, and reading strategies (executive processing) have generated a range of alternative positions. The discussion which follows is somewhat more speculative than that presented in the previous section and involves interpretations of arguments from several sources; nevertheless, the explanation given below for text comprehension processing at the discourse level offers a plausible account.

Important general descriptions of higher-level comprehension processing are proposed by Gernsbacher (1990, 1997), Kintsch (1988, 1994), van Dijk and Kintsch (1983), and Singer (1990). (See also various chapters in Gernsbacher 1994.) In each explanation, text comprehension extends beyond sentence-level propositional integration by incorporating each newly formed propositional unit in working memory into a textual propositional network, *a text model of comprehension*. Such a text model creates a close mental representation of the information given (or intended) by the text up to that point in the reading. The text model has hierarchical structure, with a network of important (e.g., thematic, repeated), and widely connected locally-linked propositional ideas being gradually restructured to generate higher-level macropropositions that capture the main ideas of the text. (See also Gernsbacher 1990.) As each proposition is entered into the text-model network, the network restructuring makes certain propositions more central, strengthens the connections among main themes, sorts thematic information from supporting information, consolidates information in a more summary-like form, and adjusts the highest-level proposition, or the macro-proposition (Kintsch 1994, 1995; Singer 1990).

At the same time that the text model is being created as a close representation of text information, a second model is constructed that represents the reader's interpretation of text information, referred to as a *situation model*. This interpretation of the text is not closely limited to the information provided in the text. Rather, the situation model calls on information that is supplied by reader background knowledge, goals for reading, reader motivation, reader attitudes, and reader evaluations of the information given (Kintsch 1988, 1995).

Situation models are created as a reader begins to read a text. The reader will call up, based on whatever minimal initial clues are available, a framework that anticipates the information in a text, accounts for the attitudes and expectations of the reader, and interprets the attitudes and assumptions of the writer, to the extent possible. Situation models provide the initial world knowledge frame for interpreting and evaluating the text as it is read. In many instances the situation model and the developing text model may differ, particularly at the beginning of a reading, and a good reader is able to adjust the situation model to the text comprehension model.

Often, however, weaker readers will overwhelm the text comprehension model and force it to fit the situation model. In these cases, poor comprehension abilities may be 'compensated for' by a coherent (though inaccurate) situation model. This problem commonly arises with difficult and counter-intuitive texts, such as with the case of science textbooks. (See also discussions concerning incompatible and inconsiderate texts: Gardner 1991; Grabe and Gardner 1995; Guzzetti *et al.* 1993). The imposition of a faulty situation model is also a likely outcome when L2 students are asked to read texts that are too difficult, given the students' limited L2 proficiencies.

The information activated by a situation model could include information from the many related texts that have been read before (intertextuality), the level of topic-specific knowledge available to the reader in long-term memory (background knowledge), personal feelings and attitudes towards texts and tasks of a given type (affect and motivation), goals for reading and anticipated outcomes (planning), and the on-going evaluations of the text as it is processed (text model being developed). Some of this information called up for the situational model may also be visual in nature (Fletcher 1994; Garnham and Oakhill 1996; Kintsch 1994; Mannes and St George 1996; McNamara *et al.* 1996).

By posing two models of comprehension, it is possible for the reader both to recognize and understand the information in the text, and also to create an interpretation that is unique to the particular reader. Thus, different readers are able to provide similar summaries of texts but also interpret them quite distinctly in terms of their own background knowledge and interests (and also depending on the text genre). This approach to text understanding on two levels allows researchers to argue for both the uniformity of text comprehension and the potential variability of interpretation (cf. Oakhill and Garnham 1988; Singer 1990; Zwaan 1994; Zwaan and Brown 1996). In this way, the situation model also offers a means to incorporate notions of reader response and constructive interpretation of text meaning within a processing explanation of reading comprehension.

The ability of a reader to make appropriate *inferences* is also seen as critical for reading comprehension. However, many current theories differ on when inferencing is likely to be used, what types of inferences are made while comprehending a text, and how inferences contribute to various levels of processing, particularly at the levels of text-model and situation-model construction. Most researchers agree that sentence-level propositional integration (forming the proposition) may be the first process component which calls on coherence-building inferences. At lower levels of processing, for word recognition processes or for first efforts to parse the incoming information in working memory, inferencing is seldom likely to play a major role in fluent reading, though inferencing may assist lexical disambiguation and help confirm appropriate parsing (cf. Perfetti 1994).

It should be noted that efforts to establish inferencing abilities as a source of difference between good and poor readers have yet to be very successful. There is evidence that inferencing skills are important for reading comprehension, that good readers are, generally speaking, better at making inferences, and that inferencing abilities can be taught to some extent. However, the ways in which inferencing skills assist comprehension are not entirely clear, nor is there a well established set of inferencing skills that are readily identifiable for the improvement of comprehension (or for testing purposes). These limitations have been raised for L2 contexts in articles by Alderson (1990a, 1990b) and Alderson and Lukmani (1989). At present, we know that reasoning about the text is important, but it is not clear what types of inferencing are critical.

Aside from inferencing, *discourse structuring principles* also appear to be important processes both for text-model construction and for situation-model building, though there is much less research on this topic than on inferencing. These principles include:

1 presenting given information before new information;
2 foregrounding main information and backgrounding supporting information;
3 placing important information in first-mention position;
4 marking thematic information by repetition, pronoun forms, or unusual structures; and
5 signalling relations between local propositions as well as their relations to the macroproposition.

Discourse processing researchers argue that these discourse structuring principles contribute to the coherence of a text, giving the reader sufficient textual resources to construct a comprehensible text model and an interpretable situation model (Beck *et al.* 1991; van Dijk and Kintsch 1983; Lorch and O'Brien 1995; Singer 1990). It is also important to recognize that the notion of grammatical structure as signalling mechanisms for discourse processing is gaining greater influence. This perspective is most convincingly presented by Gernsbacher's (1990, 1997) Structure Building Framework. (See also Britton 1994; Givon 1995; Kintsch 1995).

The role of *strategies* in reading comprehension processes has been a source of much discussion in the past ten years, though more so among educational psychologists than cognitive psychologists (cf. Brown *et al.* 1996; Oakhill 1994; Pressley and Woloshyn 1995). On a general level, strategies implicate an executive processing mechanism guided in some way by purposes for reading, goals being set while reading, and the evolving situation and text models. As a theoretical concept, then, the notion of reading strategies is protean, and thus not very appealing as a specific component for a theory of reading comprehension processes (cf. Block 1986, 1992). Nevertheless, the role of reading strategies in reading comprehension is well recognized, and training studies have demonstrated both that strategy instruction can improve reading abilities and that strategic efficiency in reading distinguishes good readers from poor readers (Brown *et al.* 1996; Lysynchuk *et al.* 1990; Pressley and Woloshyn 1995; Slavin 1995). The notion of reading strategies, however, is not a simple issue.

The notion of reading strategies may be applicable at many levels of comprehension processing and its functioning in cognitive processing accounts of reading is not entirely clear. Nevertheless, the idea that fluent readers are strategic readers is well established. There needs to be a greater effort to incorporate these issues into the cognitive processing research on reading comprehension. On the level of theoretical research, perhaps the best characterization of strategic processing is found in recent discussion of working memory, particularly the work of Gathercole and Baddeley (1993; see also Baddeley 1992; Jonides 1995). Their discussion of the roles of central executive processing may provide a locus for strategic processing. Similarly, van Dijk and Kintsch (1983) argue that their situation model includes control processes and goal setting as influences on working memory. There are, however, few explicit cognitive theories of goal setting, cognitive monitoring, and executive processing (cf. Plaut *et al.* 1996). This may be due partly to limitations in current research methodologies, and partly due to the protean nature of the issues raised – many strategies may be of a more general nature than language processing itself (see, e.g. Gernsbacher 1990). Having said all this, it is nevertheless true that the good reader is a strategic reader.

Further issues in reading comprehension processing

There has been much written about the impact of context on reading, as well as the roles of schema theory and content knowledge. These topics raise a number of complex issues for theories of reading, and detailed discussion goes beyond the scope of the present chapter. However, this section will briefly note positions which are reasonably well supported by empirical evidence (as opposed to primarily logical arguments that have little empirical support).

With respect to *the role of context effects* in reading, there are a number of issues that should be noted. First, context does not usually influence fluent word recognition processes except with unknown words that readers notice and attend to (Perfetti 1992, 1994; Stanovich 1986, 1992). Moreover, context use does not distinguish good readers from poor readers as they are engaged in real-time reading processes, except in cases when poor readers overuse context resources (Adams 1990; Daneman 1991, Stanovich and Stanovich 1995). (Testing contexts, which may not typically reflect on-line reading processing constraints, can demonstrate better context use by good readers.) Second, there are indeed some context effects which play a role in word recognition, but these typically involve automatic priming of words due to the previous activation of related words in a network. This spreading activation process certainly produces context effects, though not of the sort discussed by Frank Smith (1982), for example. Third, context effects are important for confirming appropriate meanings of words already active in working memory and for the development of text models and situation models of reading comprehension. Thus, context effects will consistently contribute to proposition formation, propositional integration, inferencing, and text interpretation.

The concept of *schema theory* has been discussed widely in the past fifteen years, and it has served a useful role in arguing for the importance of content knowledge or world knowledge in the interpretation of texts. At the same time, schema theory has been the subject of many serious critiques which require that the term be used cautiously. It has taken on many different interpretations and it often generates as much ambiguity as it does clarity. While it is a useful metaphor for the role of background knowledge in reading, it should perhaps be used far less than it is when referring to reading comprehension. In fact, there is relatively little specific empirical theory attached to schema theory, and the concept of a schema may be too vague to help research specify the nature and specific contribution of content knowledge. (Criticisms of schema theory may be found in Alexander *et al.* 1991; Carver 1992; Daneman 1991; Dansereau 1995; Rayner and Pollatsek 1989: Sadoski *et al.* 1991; Shanks 1996.)

The importance of *world knowledge or content knowledge* on reading abilities has been widely discussed and debated for the past 20 years (Alexander *et al.* 1994): In one respect, it is simply the most general of these three similar concepts being reviewed in this section, and, once again, there are a number of issues that need to be disentangled (Willson and Rupley 1997). The first issue is the distinction between the role played by general background knowledge – or knowledge of the world – and the role of specific and often detailed knowledge of topical domains (such as engineering knowledge or English literature knowledge). Specific domain (or topical) knowledge does seem to play an important role in reading comprehension (Alexander *et al.* 1994). Readers with more detailed or even specialist knowledge of a topic will generally comprehend texts better and offer more detailed interpretations of texts. In contrast, when reading material does not make strong demands on specialist topical knowledge, the supportive effects of topical knowledge on comprehension decrease. A number of studies have shown that background knowledge has a minimal influence on individual differences in L1 reading comprehension more generally, assuming a non-specialist text (Baldwin *et al.* 1985; Long *et al.* 1996; Schiefele 1992; Willson and Rupley 1997). Similarly, Bernhardt (1991) found no supportive effects for background knowledge in second language German students on reading texts that were not strongly biased to a student's major.

Second, background knowledge is widely recognized as essential to the development of an elaborated situation model for interpreting texts. In this respect, a well elaborated and appropriate situation model can greatly assist a reader's comprehension, especially a good reader who is able to adapt the situation model to the new information that develops in the text model of comprehension. The integration of the two models in these cases is very powerful for learning. The danger with the role of background knowledge in the form of a situation model occurs when language proficiencies, processing efficiencies, or text integration abilities are limited; then the situation model (or background knowledge in this case) may overwhelm the effort to comprehend the text, imposing a coherent but wrong interpretation.

Third, background knowledge has been shown to have a minimal impact in general language proficiency testing contexts. Hale (1988) has demonstrated that students' majors had a minimal impact on TOEFL reading scores even when they read texts completely in line with their major fields or completely aside from their major fields. These readings were not heavily specialized and the effect of domain knowledge in these cases was minimal. Waters (1996), in a more recent review of research, arrived at essentially the same conclusion.

Despite a general observation about learning that students learn best when new information fits with prior knowledge, there is sufficient evidence in the reading research literature to treat this generalization with some caution (e.g., Willson and Rupley 1997). The role of prior knowledge on learning is known to be generally supportive, but its impact may not be very robust in certain circumstances, one of which may involve the context of standardized reading comprehension tests using general interest texts without specialist knowledge assumptions. In other cases, background knowledge may overrule text comprehension completely.

The review of context effects, schema theory, and content knowledge illustrates the more general issue facing reading researchers. Once efforts go beyond well established components of reading comprehension processing, the nature of comprehension mechanisms becomes less clear. Aside from the vague, though still real contributions of background knowledge, there are also ambiguous results with research on inferencing, strategy use, and metacognitive processing. In almost all cases, training studies indicate some role for these factors, but research results to date do not converge on a clear set of processes or principles that promote comprehension.

Finally, any effort to account for reading processes needs to consider *social context factors and motivation and affective factors* which influence reading comprehension and the development of reading abilities. In the case of social context effects, there are many studies but few efforts to integrate the information in a more comprehensive theory. There are a number of recent efforts to develop the role of *affective factors* in reading comprehension (e.g. the roles of interest, involvement, attitude, goal-setting, attributions of success, self-regulation). Both Mathewson (1994) and McKenna (1994) have developed recent models of affective influences on reading. In addition, a number of reviews and research studies have demonstrated the importance of affective factors for reading development (Borkowski *et al.* 1990; Schiefele 1992; Turner 1993; Wade 1992). Further exploration of specific issues related to motivation and affective factors would require a separate chapter, however.

Models of reading

Having reviewed in the previous section the many real and possible components of reading ability, there remains the issue of their assembly for on-line processing during reading. In order to make clearer sense of the operations and interrelationships among components of reading, models become very useful. Models must offer descriptive decisions about the processes involved, the relationships between processes, the possible sequencing of processes, and the competition for processing resources at any moment. As a result, it is possible to suggest constraints on reading processes, and hypothesize the relative contributions of various components in future reading contexts.

It needs to be noted, in passing, that certain proposed models provide little more than a basic metaphor for how reading comprehension might be carried out and offer very little potential for explaining how reading is actually carried out within reasonable time-constrained processing. Thus models designated as 'transactional', 'reader response', or 'constructivist' give no account for how, specifically, cognitive processes are to be used for reading purposes, or how these processes might develop. In fact, most discussions of these so-called models require that a learner already be a reader, though perhaps not a critical reader or a skilled interpreter of complex text. In the case of the 'guessing-game' model of reading, clear evidence has already falsified such an account.

There are a number of models of reading that are particularly useful for general descriptions of reading. For the most part, these models provide ways to integrate many of the component parts of reading that have been discussed in the previous section. Among the most accessible are those proposed by Bruer (1993), van Dijk and Kintsch (1983), Just and Carpenter (1987), and Rayner and Pollatsek (1989). These models are reviewed briefly in Grabe (1997), and they are also discussed in more extended reviews of reading models by Perfetti (1994) and Stanovich (1991b). Many of these more current models have as a central feature the notion that reading is some combination of word recognition abilities and general comprehension abilities. The most overt and perhaps the most controversial of these models is known as 'the simple view of reading', noted earlier in the introduction section.

In the 'simple view of reading' (Hoover and Gough 1990; Gough *et al.* 1996), equal emphasis is given to both word recognition processes and comprehension processes. This model, rather than describing the combinations of component processes, offers a general account of reading in that the model makes a statistical argument. The model simply states that reading comprehension is basically the product of word recognition abilities and comprehension abilities. Since comprehension skills are not specific to reading (e.g. Gernsbacher 1990), the only specifically reading-based abilities are the various lower-level visual word recognition skills. This view is most commonly captured as D x C = R (decoding times comprehension equals reading) (Chen andVellutino 1997; Gough, Juel and Griffith 1992; Hoover and Gough 1990; Juel 1992; Perfetti 1994; Tunmer and Hoover 1992; see also Carver 1997 for independent converging evidence).

The claims for this model rest primarily with English L1 student performance on measures of word recognition and measures of reading comprehension (cf. Hoover and Gough 1990). To give a hypothetical example, suppose a learner scores 90% on a combined word recognition battery and 90% on a grade-level comprehension measure (listening); that student's reading comprehension ability will be 81%. Of course, with younger learners, age-appropriate comprehension measures will be easier and the word recognition measures may be the greatest source of variation (since normal English L1 school-aged children can all comprehend a relatively simple story). With older fluent readers, word recognition abilities will rise to near 100%, and the comprehension measures, using more complex tasks and texts, will generate the greater range of variation. It should also be pointed out that proponents of this view expect reading abilities to be shaped by other factors as well. But the central argument remains that the two major components of reading comprehension are word recognition and comprehension. Whether or not this model will hold up well under further testing is an open question (e.g. Chen and Vellutino 1997), but it is certainly a falsifiable model. In second language contexts, moreover, it will need to be tested independently since L2 learners have a much wider range of variation in their L2 word recognition and comprehension abilities (cf. Geva *et al.* 1997).

Reading in a second language: Adapting a model of reading

For the most part, the component-processes analysis of reading which has been described for L1 reading is also applicable for L2 reading contexts. There are, of course, a number of further factors that define L2 reading contexts and which ague for adaptations of any model of reading that might inform instruction and assessment. Perhaps most importantly, L2 contexts place a number of processing constraints on reading that are unique. Many of these specific constraints, outlined below, are commonly discussed and do not require extensive rationales. They will, however, require a somewhat different understanding of reading comprehension, particularly at beginning levels of L2 proficiency (Durgunoglu 1997; Geva *et al.* 1997).

A first important difference for L2 reading, and one that typically takes many years to overcome, is the very different ranges of vocabulary knowledge. First language readers have a large recognition vocabulary, likely to run in the range of 40,000 words (Nagy 1988; cf. Goulden *et al.* 1990; Hazenberg and Hulstijn 1996; Zechmeister *et al.* 1993). In first language reading contexts, students are expected to know at least 95% of words encountered (Shany and Biemiller 1995; Stahl 1997). In fact, first language students at most grade levels read material in which they know 99% of the words on a given page (Carver 1994). Even when students are given reading material three grade levels beyond their school grade, they typically know 98% of the words on any page.

In L2 reading contexts, minimal word knowledge for fluent reading has been estimated at 95% coverage on a given page (Laufer 1989). However, most L2 readers are regularly asked to read L2 text material which includes many more unknown words than the minimal 95% criterion. (And this is a serious dilemma for the use of only authentic texts in the L2 classroom.) Second language readers will need years of reading practice to achieve the 95% criterion on a regular basis. Only the best second language readers will experience reading in the way that first language students do, reading texts with 98–99% vocabulary knowledge (and highly accurate word recognition). Certainly this criterion will mark the early years of second language reading as distinct from L1 reading contexts.

Related to issues of size of vocabulary is the role of the bilingual lexicon in reading processes, particularly in word recognition. There is now a reasonable amount of evidence to indicate that the bilingual lexicon may be organized differently from the monolingual's lexicon (Grosjean 1997; Kroll and de Groot 1997; Smith 1997). Little is known, however, about how the bilingual lexicon might lead to distinct processing of a text as a reading outcome. This issue may be most important in the first years of L2 reading. As the L2 grows stronger with years of reading, the processing issues clearly change.

A second major difference for the L2 reader is the type of response they may have to difficult 'authentic' text resources. There is no doubt that L2 readers often encounter difficult text materials and are asked to comprehend them. While the language classroom often provides scaffolding to support this reading activity, it is not clear what sorts of motivational and affective responses these activities generate. Nor is it clear whether such distinct tasks strongly influence attributions for success and failure with L2 reading. First language readers who move on to post-secondary education do not typically encounter authentic material that regularly passes beyond their comprehension *because of the language used*. We also know what happens to first language readers who regularly encounter very difficult material on a regular basis in primary and secondary education contexts. They typically quit!

A third distinction that L2 reading must account for is the role of the L2 language threshold for reading. While it is not possible to specify what level of language efficiency and language knowledge any reader needs to have in order to read fluently, there does appear to be a language threshold that readers must pass through in order to make full use of higher-level comprehension-processing strategies that are available in L1 reading (Bernhardt and Kamil 1995; Bossers 1992; Carrell 1991; Geva *et al*. 1997). This threshold will vary from individual to individual; it will be influenced by the difficulty of any given text; and it will vary even within the individual reader depending on task, topic, time available, goals, and attitudes.

A fourth major difference between L1 reading and L2 reading is the different levels of awareness of language. L2 readers experience a much more conscious awareness of how language works at both the syntactic and discourse levels. L2 readers at beginning levels, in particular, will need to develop syntactic knowledge as well as knowledge of discourse organizing principles and overt markers of organization (Bernhardt 1991). The distinguishing aspect of this need is that L2 learners will not be able to rely on intuitive knowledge, and they must spend much more time attending to formal aspects of the L2.

A fifth difference is the role of the Orthographic Depth Hypothesis (ODH) for L2 reading (Frost 1994; Frost and Katz 1992; Geva *et al*. 1997; Katz and Frost 1992; Segalowitz and Hebert 1990; Shimron and Sivan 1994). The ODH argues that different languages have relatively shallower or deeper orthographies with respect to their transparency with the phonology of the languages. For example, Finnish, Turkish, and Serbo-Croat are seen as the most shallow languages for phonological processing. Spanish, Portuguese and Italian are regular with a few minor irregularities. German, Dutch, and Swedish are much more consistent than English. French and Danish are somewhat opaque, but not as much as is English. English is much less transparent (thus deeper); Hebrew and Arabic would be deeper still; and Japanese and Chinese may be the deepest (Elley 1992; Oney *et al*. 1997). The central issue is whether differing degrees of orthographic depth in a language will lead learners to pursue different strategies for reading at various stages of their development (Durgunoglu 1997; Perfetti and Zhang 1996). Learners in English, for example, appear to make use of initial sight word reading until they learn to crack the phonological code. In contrast, learners of Serbo-Croat appear to make early and consistent use of phonological regularities in their early reading and do not need to spend as much time 'cracking the code'. At beginning stages of reading, this issue may have a significant impact on L2 processing. Many issues which are raised by the ODH have yet to be explored, and research over the next ten years should bring out the major implications of this hypothesis in greater detail. (See Chikamatsu 1996; Koda 1996.)

A sixth difference involves the patterns of actual and perceived distance for L1 readers who learn to read different L2s. That is, when a student from a given L1 learns to read in an L2, there are likely to be distinct paths of learning and reading development depending on the specific orthographic, morphemic, phonemic, lexical, and syntactic differences between the two languages. For example, Shimron and Sivan (1994) note the much greater morphological density of Hebrew for reading comprehension. Koda (1996, 1997) notes the differing morphological and syntactic structures that L2 learners of Japanese focus on when they engage in L2 Japanese reading. How this research will develop and what the implications will be, is unclear at the present time. There are also many semantic and syntactic differences between L1s and L2s that are now being recognized as potentially playing a role in L2 reading processing differences (Chikamatsu 1996; Geva *et al.* 1997: Kellerman 1995; Koda 1996, 1997; MacWhinney 1997; Yu 1996; Zuckernick 1996). An issue related to distance factors is the extent to which aspects of L1 reading processes, language knowledge, discourse knowledge, and world knowledge transfer to the L2 reading situation. There is evidence that word recognition, semantic information, and world knowledge can have important transfer effects, while morphological and syntactic knowledge does not seem to transfer as readily (Durgunoglu 1997; Geva *et al.* 1997; Verhoeven 1994). There are, however, many mediating and confounding variables which make broad generalization very difficult in this regard.

A seventh difference, one related to formal awareness of language, is the role of translation, cognates, bilingual dictionaries and glosses in second language reading. While much advice for second language readers has discouraged the use of mental translating for reading comprehension, this translating ability (as opposed to written translation practice) may represent an important strategic resource of both language awareness and reading comprehension. In fact, mental translation can be used to provide strong positive mechanisms for noticing formal aspects of the L2 and using this knowledge to comprehend texts. This role of translation in various stages of L2 reading does not match any comparable strategic resource which could be used by L1 readers (Kern 1994). The role of cognates in L2 reading has also received more attention in the past five years. The majority view is that for closely related languages the ability to use cognates effectively can significantly enhance reading performance. The role of bilingual dictionaries to improve reading has received mild research support, but more work is needed. A similar mild supporting view can be taken for the role of glosses in L2 reading. All of these features of, or resources for, L2 literacy are unique to L2 contexts, and are now receiving more attention as legitimate research questions (Durgunoglu 1997; Fischer 1994; Jacobs 1994; Nagy *et al.* 1993; Stewart and Cross 1993; Treville 1996).

An eighth major difference is the wide variability in reading rates and reading fluency for L2 students. Because students have restricted recognition vocabularies, greater 'attending to language' demands, limited practice with word recognition skills, and fewer opportunities to read extended texts on a regular basis (i.e. exposure to L2 print), they will typically have much lower reading rates and less automaticity (or efficiency) in their processing. This bottleneck for reading processing is not easily circumvented and may take many years to overcome, if it ever is overcome (Bernhardt 1991; Geva *et al.* 1997; Haynes and Carr 1990; Segalowitz 1997; Segalowitz *et al.* 1991). This issue also subsumes differing efficiencies in the use of working memory resources for L2 readers.

A ninth major difference applies at the level of cultural knowledge; it is represented by the different cultural knowledge of the L2 learner and the extent of these cultural differences from the target L2. This distinction can also apply to specific topical domains of knowledge relevant to one culture but not to a second. While there is considerable evidence that appropriate cultural assumptions and greater cultural knowledge of the L2 will assist language comprehension, it is not clear what such an issue means for reading comprehension processes except that knowing more of the appropriate types of cultural information will improve reading abilities. Again, this is an issue with no direct comparison to most L1 reading contexts (Durgunoglu 1997).

A tenth difference involves the greater awareness of conceptual categories and systems, which would be more typical of the L2 reader. This difference reflects the fact that most L2 readers are older when they are learning to read in an L2 and already have experiences with L1 reading that they can draw upon. This set of knowledge, as well as a greater level of metacognitive awareness and more efficient learning abilities, can improve L2 learning by assisting interpretations of vocabulary, syntactic complexities, patterns of discourse organization, and situation model resources. At the present time, there does not seem to be controlled empirical research on these specific issues as advantages for L2 learners.

An eleventh difference involves different motivations for reading and for learning to read. L2 students typically will have different motivations for reading as well as different long-term goals. These motivations will be shaped by the specific contexts in which students have learned to read in their L1s and their experiences in learning to read in the L2. Issues such as student attributions for success and failure, student self-concepts, student abilities for autonomous learning, student interest in topic and in learning, student involvement in specific text materials and tasks, student attitudes towards teachers and institutions, and the consistent difficulty levels of texts and tasks will all have an impact on L2 reading outcomes. It is very likely that factors which have strong influences on many L1 readers would vary from those factors which are most significant for many groups of L2 learners. There is not very much research on these issues as they apply to differences between L1 and L2 reading contexts.

A twelfth difference involves different social contexts for reading. Given the wide range of variability in social contexts for differing groups of L1 learners, it should be no surprise to recognize that the social contexts influencing L2 reading development are likely to be considerable. As with the factors listed as important social context variables for L1 readers, L2 learners will be affected by many L1 contextual factors as well as many L2 factors, including home literacy contexts, uses of L1 and L2 reading, contexts for L2 reading instruction, etc. There has not yet emerged any coherent effort to develop a comprehensive research agenda on this issue for L2 reading (cf. McKay 1993).

These twelve differences between L1 and L2 reading lead to two straightforward conclusions, though neither offers immediate implications for assessment practices. First, it is evident that there are a number of differences with respect to L2 learners which, together, must require distinct conceptualizations of reading assessment and instruction practices. Second, the array of factors influencing L2 reading abilities, and the wide range of L2 individual and group variation, make it difficult to develop a clear set of generalizable implications. If this section does nothing more, it certainly points out a large number of research agendas that can be developed to support L2 reading assessment and instruction practices and the great need to understand better the specific influences on learning to read in an L2 setting.

Issues/dilemmas for second language reading assessment (an outsider looking in)

Overall, the impact of reading research on reading assessment does not seem to be very prominent. Rather, it would appear that reading assessment has been, and commonly still is, driven either by language learning notions of communicative language performance or by assessment theory more generally, including the reasonably strong psychometric qualities of traditional reading comprehension tests. Simple and straightforward measures of main idea and detailed comprehension questions on passages, combined with sections on vocabulary, provide strong reliability and at least arguable validity for these testing approaches. These traditional approaches are also popular because they are easy to administer, to score, and to scale, and they are economical.

Given this historical foundation for reading assessment, it is not easy to see exactly how the recent advances in reading research will have an impact on assessment in the future. In the near term, innovations that could be adaptable for reading assessment will most likely still have to pass through traditional evaluations in terms of reliability and validity. At issue, however, is whether such evaluations can evolve to incorporate future reading assessment procedures. Revised views on validity and reliability may allow new concepts and findings from reading research to inform innovation in reading assessment. In particular, the use of the computer opens up many options for assessment that would be cumbersome via paper-and-pencil delivery. For example, a variety of measures of reading rate, word recognition, and vocabulary and reading fluency could be developed for computer delivery. In addition, computer delivery may allow for easy juxtaposition of a number of texts that could be used for integrated reading tasks across multiple texts.

In order to move beyond the perceived limitations of current reading assessment practices, issues which may have an impact on future assessment efforts need to be discussed and explored further. One way to suggest issues for discussion is to propose a set of dilemmas for reading assessment. These dilemmas potentially indicate areas to consider in alternative approaches to reading assessment. Below are seventeen potential dilemmas for second language reading assessment. The importance of each is perhaps debatable, and that is, in fact, the purpose for including them in the list.[2] At issue is the extent to which such dilemmas for reading assessment are being considered, and in certain cases, being addressed in interesting ways.

Dilemma 1

Can we assess some concept of 'stages of development' for L2 reading beyond a general proficiency concept? Or beyond some simple rate and accuracy combination? If this is not easy to do, then do we need to know more about various abilities of L2 readers? Is the notion of 'stages of reading development' useful for large-scale reading assessment practices? How does assessment change for beginning readers versus intermediate and advanced readers?

Dilemma 2

Will reading in different second languages require different types of reading assessment at different proficiency stages? What problems would this create in Modern Languages Departments?

Dilemma 3

Will students coming from different L1s need different types of reading tests, particularly at beginning levels?

Dilemma 4

How can the computer environment open up new assessment options that may tap into some of the criteria of good reading abilities noted above? Or are there good reasons to stay within typical bounds of current reading assessment item types?

Dilemma 5

Will Computer-Adaptive Testing (CAT) restrict the range of assessment item types that could be explored, and that should be explored?

Dilemma 6

Can we assess reading abilities as they interact with other language abilities, primarily writing? Do we want, in some cases (and to some extent), to measure some type of joint ability levels?

Dilemma 7

Do we want a straight power test or do we want some measure of reading rate and processing speed as well, in combination or separately? For example, in power tests of reading comprehension, students have a relatively large amount of time for problem-solving approaches to test questions, yet this emphasis on power may test study skills more than on-line reading comprehension skills, and offering large amounts of texts to read is, in itself, not necessarily a reliable way to determine rate and processing speed abilities.

Dilemma 8

Should some measure of extended reading become part of reading assessment? What can be gained by items based on extended readings? Can new item types be used with extended readings? If assessment items are more likely to be linked, how would interdependence of items be handled?

Dilemma 9

Can tests provide reliable measures of word recognition abilities and reading rate levels? What will be gained from such measures in assessment terms? Can these measures be done quickly and effectively? For which students would this information be most informative?

Dilemma 10

Do we want some measure of working memory efficiency? Should we try to create tasks that push processing capacities, whether by response times, text and sentence ambiguities, syntactic complexities, competing-referent density, text distance limits, or multiple on-line tasks? What might such indicators of working memory efficiency tell us?

Dilemma 11

Can a test provide, or account for, some useful measure of cultural/world knowledge from the L2 perspective? Do we want this?

Dilemma 12

How can a test measure the extent to which students are becoming strategic readers in the L2? What are the problems with pursuing this sort of assessment information? What is to be gained? How might this sort of information be at odds with other types of information sought in reading assessment? What would item types look like that could tap into strategic reading abilities? For example, how might items be designed that would measure predictions? Question-forming abilities? Paraphrase and summarizing? Comprehension monitoring? Imagery? Can a computer be useful in developing these types of measures?

Dilemma 13

How can a test measure students' abilities to recognize the structure of text organization? Should a test want to tap into this type of reading ability? If so, what would item types look like? Could computer item types be particularly useful for this issue?

Dilemma 14

How can we measure the extent to which students can extract, synthesize, and restructure information from texts? What are the advantages of pursuing this sort of information? What difficulties will be encountered? How will computer applications help or hinder this type of measure? What would item types look like?

Dilemma 15

Can L2 reading assessment work with interdependent items in a computer environment? If so, how will reliability be handled? Will sections with interdependent items be scored according to some overall performance assessment criterion or according to a specific task criterion?

Dilemma 16

How should assessment research move from construct knowledge (such as reading ability) to test design? What mediating analyses are needed?

Dilemma 17

Can we use empirical efforts, such as concurrent validity measures or factor analytic methods, to establish reading constructs for assessment purposes when the data used are typically based on traditional item types and formats of reading comprehension assessment?

Various dilemmas proposed here suggest a number of possible innovations for reading assessment or, perhaps in some cases, a return to more traditional notions of reading measurement. In this summary V, I will only note briefly some possibilities. Working memory efficiencies have become a major factor in individual-differences research in reading. Just and Carpenter (1992; Carpenter *et al.* 1994) provide strong arguments for various task complexities which could provide measures of working memory efficiencies. These task complexities could include introducing or using texts with many 'distractor' referents, reducing reading time systematically, increasing syntactic complexity systematically in the reading material, or increasing the textual distance between items to be related by a question. Both reading rate and word recognition measures, which are essential contributors to reading comprehension, could be measured more easily via computer delivery. Vocabulary measures could explore depth of word knowledge in addition to size of vocabulary knowledge. Strategy measures could be manipulated to some extent and might include clarification of misleading information, evaluation of larger discourse structures, summarizing, or evaluation of options that might represent specific text information, selection of main idea statements, or organizing sentences. Extensive reading and knowledge integration may both be assessed by reading multiple texts for a variety of purposes: such tasks may create reliability difficulties, but they represent task types that are commonly expected in academic settings. These suggestions only begin to scratch the surface of options that can be developed with the use of computers.

Conclusion

This chapter has presented a synthesis of research on the nature of reading. In so doing , it suggests a number of ways in which our understanding of reading has progressed in the past decade. It has also examined unique aspects of processing for second language reading. From this foundation of research, the chapter then explored issues that concern second language reading assessment. In particular, it suggests that reading assessment, for the most part, has not made significant efforts to stay abreast of current research in reading, or its implications for assessment (cf. the reading papers in the advanced examinations of the University of Cambridge Local Examinations Syndicate for certain more innovative assessment tasks). The dilemmas proposed in this last section are intended to raise issues for the assessment of reading, taking into consideration recent research. The issues raised may also suggest questions and research agendas for future work in reading assessment.

Notes

1   This overview is a companion piece to (Grabe 1999), an overview of reading presented at the Minnesota Conference of Computer-Adaptive Testing of Foreign Language reading. While both papers provide a general overview, each develops different ideas and introduces unique issues.

2   I do not claim expertise in assessment issues. These dilemmas are only intended to suggest, perhaps naively, linkages that may be developed further between reading research issues and assessment practices. It is also likely that certain testing programs and instruments carry out more innovative assessment practices which are not noted or recognized by these dilemmas.

References

Adams, M. (1990) *Beginning to Read: Thinking and Learning about Print.* Cambridge, MA: MIT Press.

Adams, M. (1994) The progress of the whole-language debate. *Educational Psychologist* 29: 217–22.

Alderson, J. C. (1990a) Testing reading comprehension skills (part 1). *Reading in a Foreign Language* 6(2): 425–37.

Alderson, J. C. (1990b) Testing reading comprehension skills (part 2). *Reading in a Foreign Language* 7(1): 465–503.

Alderson, J. C. and Lukmani, Y. (1989) Cognition and levels of comprehension as embodied in test questions. *Reading in a Foreign Language* 5(2): 253–70.

Alexander, P., Kulikowich, J. and Schulze, S. (1994) How subject matter knowledge affects recall and interest. *American Education Research Journal* 31: 313–37.

Alexander, P., Schallert, D. and Hare, V. (1991) Coming to terms: How researchers in learning and literacy talk about knowledge. *Review of Educational Research* 61: 315–43.

Anderson, J. R. (1983) *The Architecture of Cognition.* Cambridge, MA: Harvard University Press.

Anderson, J. R. (1993) Problem solving and learning. *American Psychologist* 38: 35–44.

Anderson, J. R. (1996) A simple theory of complex cognition. *American Psychologist* 51: 355–65.

Anderson, J. R., Reder, L. and Simon, H. (1996) Situated learning and education. *Educational Researcher* 25: 5–11.

Anderson, R. C. (1993) The future of reading research. In Sweet, A. and Anderson, R. C. (Ed.) *Reading Research into the Year 2000.* Hillsdale, NJ: Lawrence Erlbaum Associates, Publishers: 17–36.

Anderson, R. C. (1996) Research foundation to support wide reading. In Greaney, V. (Ed.) *Promoting Reading in Developing Countries*. Newark, DE: IRA: 55–77.

Anglin, J. (1993) *Vocabulary Development: A Morphological Analysis*. Chicago, IL: The University of Chicago Press. [Monographs of the Society for Research in Child Development]

Arnaud, P. and Savignon, S. (1997) Rare words, complex lexical units and the advanced learner. In Coady and Huckin (Eds.): 157–73.

Baddeley, A. (1992) Working memory. *Science* 255: 556–9.

Baldwin, R. S., Peleg-Bruckner, A. and McClintock, A. (1985) Effects of topic interest and prior knowledge on reading comprehension. *Reading Research Quarterly* 2: 497–504.

Balota, D. (1994) Visual word recognition: The journey from features to meaning. In Gernsbacher (Ed.): 303–58

Barker, T., Torgeson, J. and Wagner, R. (1992) The role of orthographic processing skills on five different reading tasks. *Reading Research Quarterly* 27: 334–45.

Barr, R., Kamil, M., Mosenthal, P. and Pearson, P. D. (1991) *Handbook of Reading Research. Volume II*. New York, NY: Longman.

Beck, I., McKeown, M., Sinatra, G. and Loxterman, J. (1991) Revising social studies text from a text-processing perspective: Evidence of improved comprehensibility. *Reading Research Quarterly* 26: 251–76.

Bereiter, C. and Scardamalia, M. (1993) *Surpassing Ourselves: An Inquiry into the Nature and Complications of Expertise*. Chicago, IL: Open Court Press.

Berent, I. and Perfetti, C. (1995) A rose is a REEZ: The two-cycles model of phonology assembly in reading English. *Psychological Review* 102: 146–84.

Bernhardt, E. (1991) *Reading Development in a Second Language*. Norwood, NJ: Ablex Publishing Corporation.

Bernhardt, E. and Kamil, M. (1995) Interpreting relationships between L1 and L2 reading: Consolidating the linguistic threshold and the linguistic interdependence hypothesis. *Applied Linguistics* 16: 15–34.

Biemiller, A. (1994) Some observations on beginning reading instruction. *Educational Psychologist* 29: 203–9.

Bjaalid, I.-K., Hoien, T. and Lundberg, I. (1996) The contribution of orthographic and phonological processes to word reading in young Norwegian readers. *Reading and Writing* 8: 189–98.

Block, E. (1986) The comprehension strategies of second language readers. *TESOL Quarterly* 20: 463–94.

Block, E. (1992) See how they read: Comprehension monitoring of L1 and L2 readers. *TESOL Quarterly* 26: 319–43.

Borkowski, J., Carr, M., Rellinger, E. and Pressley, M. (1990) Self-regulated cognition: Interdependence of metacognition, attributions, and self-esteem. In Idol, B. and Idol, L. (Eds.) *Dimensions of Thinking and Cognitive Instruction.* Hillsdale NJ: Lawrence Erlbaum Associates, Publishers: 53–92.

Bossers, B. (1992) *Reading in Two Languages: A Study of Reading Comprehension in Dutch as a Second Language and in Turkish as a First Language.* Rotterdam: Drukkerij Van Driel.

Bowey, J. (1995) Socioeconomic status differences in preschool phonological sensitivity and first grade reading achievement. *Journal of Educational Psychology* 87: 476–87.

Brady, S. and Shankweiler, D. (Eds) (1991) *Phonological Processes in Reading: A Tribute to Isabelle Y. Linenman.* Hillsdale, NJ. Lawrence Erlbaum Associates, Publishers.

Breznitz, Z. (1997) Effects of accelerated reading rate on memory for text among dyslexic readers. *Journal of Education Psychology* 84: 193–9.

Breznitz, Z. and Share, D. (1992) Effects of accelerated reading rate on memory for text. *Journal of Educational Psychology* 84: 193–9.

Britton, B. (1994) Understanding expository text: Building mental structures in induce insights. In Gernsbacher (Ed.): 641–74.

Britton, B. and Graesser, A. (Eds.) (1996) *Models of Understanding Text.* Mahwah, NJ: Lawrence ErlbaumAssociates, Publishers.

Brown, R., Pressley, M., Van Meter, P. and Schuder, T. (1996) A quasi-experimental validation of transactional strategy instruction with low-achieving second-grade readers. *Journal of Educational Psychology* 88: 18–37.

Bruer, J. (1993) *Schools for Thought.* Cambridge, MA: MIT Press.

Bus, A., Ijzendoorn, M. and Pelegrini, A. (1995) Joint book reading makes for success in learning to read: A meta-analysis on intergenerational transmission of literacy. *Review of Educational Research* 65: 1–21.

Carpenter, P., Miyake, A. and Just, M. (1994) Working memory constraints in comprehension: Evidence from individual differences, aphasia, and aging. In Gernsbacher (Ed.)

Carr, T. and Levy, B. (Eds.) (1990) *Reading and its Development: Component Skills Approaches.* New York, NY: Academic Press.

Carrell, P. (1991) Second language reading: Reading ability or language proficiency? *Applied Linguistics* 12: 159–79.

Carver, R. (1992) Effect of prediction activities, prior knowledge and text type on the amount of comprehension: Using rauding theory to critique schema theory research. *Reading Research Quarterly* 27: 164–74.

Carver, R. (1994) Percentage of unknown vocabulary words in text as a function of the relative difficulty of the text: Implications of reinstruction. *Journal of Reading Behaviour* 26: 413–37.

Carver, R. (1997) Reading for one second, one minute, or one year from the perspective of rauding theory. *Scientific Studies of Reading* 1: 3–43.

Chapelle, C., Grabe, W. and Berns, M. (1997) *Communicative Language Proficiency: Definitions and Implications for TOEFL 2000*. Princeton, NJ: ETS. [TOEFL Monograph Series, MS-10]

Chapman, J. and Tunmer, W. (1995) Development of young children's reading self concepts: An examination of emerging subcomponents and their relationship with reading achievement. *Journal of Educational Psychology* 87: 154–67.

Chen, R.-S. and Vellutino, F. (1997) Prediction of reading ability: A cross-validation study of the Simple View of Reading. *Journal of Literacy Research* 29: 1–24.

Chikamatsu, N. (1996) The effects of L1 orthography on L2 word recognition: A study of American Chinese learners of Japanese. *Studies in Second Language Acquisition* 18: 403–432.

Coady, J. and Huckin, T. (Eds) (1997) *Second Language Vocabulary Acquisition*. New York, NY: Cambridge University Press.

Cornoldi, C. and Oakhill, J. (Eds) (1996) *Reading Comprehension Difficulties*. Mahwah, NJ: Lawrence Erlbaum Associates, Publishers.

Czikszentmihalyi, M. (1991) Literacy and intrinsic motivation. In Graubard, S. (Ed.) *Literacy: An Overview by 14 Experts*. New York, NY: Noonday Press: 115–140.

Daneman, M. (1991) Individual differences in reading skills. In Barr *et al.* (Eds.): 512–538.

Dansereau, D. (1995) Derived structural schemas and the transfer of knowledge. In McKeough, Lupant and Marini (Eds.): 93–121.

van Dijk, T. and Kintsch, W. (1983) *Strategies of Discourse Comprehension*. San Diego, CA: Academic Press.

Dunning, D., Mason, J. and Stewart, J. (1994) Reading to preschoolers: A response to Scarborough and Dobrich (1994) and recommendations for future research. *Developmental Review* 14: 324–339.

Durgunoglu, A. (1997) Bilingual reading: Its components, development, and other issues. In de Groot and Kroll (Eds.): 255–276.

Ehri, L. (1992) Reconceptualizing the development of sight word reading and its relationship to recoding. In Gough, Ehri, and Treiman (Eds.): 107–143.

Elley, W. (1992) *How in the World do Students Read?* Hamburg: International Association for the Evaluation of Educational Achievement.

Elliott, J. and Hewison, J. (1994) Comprehension and interest in home reading. *British Journal of Educational Psychology* 64: 203–220.

Ellis, N. (Ed.) (1994) *Implicit and Explicit Learning of Language*. London: Academic Press.

Ellis, N. (1996) Sequencing in SLA. *Studies in Second Language Acquisition* 18: 91–126.

Ericsson, K. A. (Ed.) (1996) *The Road to Excellence*. Mahwah, NJ: Lawrence Erlbaum Associates, Publishers.

Fischer, U. (1994) Learning words from context and dictionaries: An experimental comparison. *Applied Psycholinguistics* 15: 551–74.

Fletcher, C. (1994) Levels of representation in memory for discourse. In Gernsbacher (Ed.): 589–607.

Foorman, B. (1994) Phonological and orthographic processing: Separate but equal? In Berninger, V. (Ed.) *The Varieties of Orthographic Knowledge: Vol 1. Theoretical and Developmental Issues*. Dordrecht, the Netherlands: Kluwer Academi Press: 319–55.

Frost, R. (1994) Prelexical and postlexical strategies in reading: Evidence from a deep and a shallow orthography. *Journal of Experimental Psychology: Learning, Memory, and Cognition* 20: 116–29.

Gardner, H. (1991) *The Unschooled Mind*. New York, NY: Basic Books.

Garnham, A. (1994) Future directions. In Gernsbacher (Ed.): 1123–44.

Garnham, A. and Oakhill, J. (1996) The mental models theory of language comprehension. In Britton and Graesser, (Eds.): 313–39.

Gathercole, S. and Baddeley, D. (1993) *Working Memory and Language*.

Gernsbacher, M. A. (1990) *Language Comprehension as Structure Building*. Hillsdale, NJ: Lawrence Erlbaum Associates, Publishers.

Gernsbacher, M. A. (Ed.). (1994) *Handbook of Psycholinguistics*. San Diego CA: Lawrence Erlbaum Associates, Publishers.

Gernsbacher, M. A. (1997) Two decades of structure building. *Discourse Processes* 25: 265–304.

Gernsbacher, M. and Givon, T. (Eds.) (1995) *Coherence in Spontaneous Text*, Philadelphia, PA: J. Benjamins.

Geva, E., Wade-Woolley, L. and Shany, M. (1997) Development of reading efficiency in first and second language. *Scientific Studies of Reading* 1: 119–44.

Givon, T. (1995) Coherence in text vs. coherence in mind. In Gernsbacher and Givon (Eds.): 59–115.

Gough, P., Ehri, L. and Treiman, R. (Eds.) (1992) *Reading Acquisition*. Hillsdale NJ: Lawrence Erlbaum Associates, Publishers.

Gough, P., Hoover, W. and Peterson, C. (1996) Some observations on a simple view of reading. In Cornoldi, Oakhill: 1–13.

Gough, P., Juel, C. and Griffith, P. (1992) Reading, spelling, and the orthographic cipher. In Gough, Ehri and Treiman (Eds.): 35-48.

Goulden, R., Nation, P. and Read, J. (1990) How large can a receptive vocabulary be? *Applied Linguistics* 11: 341–63.

Grabe, W. (1998) Developments in reading research and their implications for compute-padaptive reading assessment. In Chalhoub-Deville, M. (Ed.) *Issues in Computer-Adaptive Testing of Reading Proficiency*. Cambridge: Cambridge University Press. [Studies in Language Testing 10]

Grabe, W. and Gardner, D. (1995) Discourse analysis, coherence, and reading instruction. *Lenguas Modernas* 22: 69–88.

Grabe, W. *et al.* (Eds.) (1995) *Annual Review of Applied Lingustics.* Vol. 15. New York, NY: Cambridge University Press.

de Groot, A. and Kroll, J. (Eds.) (1997) *Tutorials in Lingualism: Psychological Perspectives.* Mahwah, NJ: Lawrence Erlbaum Associates, Publishers.

Grosjean, F. (1997) Processing mixed languages: Issues, finding, and models. In De Groot and Kroll (Eds.): 225–54.

Guthrie, J. and McCann, A. (1997) Characteristics of classrooms that promote motivations and strategies for learning. In Guthrie, J. and Wigfield, A. (Eds.) *Reading Engagement: Motivating Readers Through Integrated Instruction.* Newark, DE: IRA: 128–48.

Guzzetti, B., Snyder, T., Glass, G. and Gamas, W. (1993) Promoting conceptual change in science: A comparative meta-analysis of instructional interventions from reading education and science education. *Reading Research Quarterly* 28: 116–59.

Haenggi, D. and Perfetti, C. (1994) Processing components of college-level reading comprehension. *Discourse Processes* 17: 83–104.

Hale, G. (1988) The interaction of student major-field group and text content in TOEFL reading comprehension. *TOEFL Research Report* 25. Princeton, NJ: Educational Testing Services.

Harrington, M. and Sawyer, M. (1992) Second language working memory capacity and second language reading skill. *Studies in Second Language Acquisition* 14: 25–38.

Haynes, M. and Carr, T. (1990) Writing system background and second language reading: A components skills analysis of English reading by native speaker-readers of Chinese. In Carr and Levy, (Eds.): 375–421.

Hazenberg, S. and Hulstijn, J. (1996) Defining a minimal receptive second-language vocabulary for non-native university students: An empirical investigation. *Applied Linguistics* 17: 145–63.

Heath, S. B. (1986) Sociocultural contexts of language development. In California Office of Bilingual Education (Ed.) *Beyond Language: Social and Cultural Factors in Schooling Language Minority Children.* Los Angeles: Evaluation, dissemination and assessment Centre, California State University, Los Angeles, CA: 143–86.

Henderson, J., Singer, M. and Ferreira, F. (Eds.) (1995) *Reading and Language Processing.* Mahwah, NJ: Lawrence Erlbaum Associates, Publishing.

Hoover, W. and Gough, P. (1990) The simple view of reading. *Reading and Writing* 2: 127–60.

Jacobs, G. (1994) What lurks in the margins: Use of vocabulary glosses as a strategy in second language reading. *Issues in Applied Linguistics* 5: 115–57.

Jonides, J. (1995) Working memory and thinking. In Osherson, D. (Ed.) *An Invitation to Cognitive Science. Thinking. Volume 3* (2nd ed.). Cambridge, MA: MIT Press: 215–65.

Juel, C. (1991) Beginning reading. In Barr *et al.* (Eds.): 759–88.

Juel, C. (1992) Longitudinal research on learning to read and write with at-risk students. In Dreher, M. and Slater, W. (Eds.) *Elementary School Literacy: Critical Issues.* Norwood, MA: Christopher Gordon: 73–99.

Juel, C. (1995) The messenger may be wrong, but the message may be right, *Journal of Research in Reading* 18: 146–53.

Just, M. and Carpenter, P. (1987) *The Psychology of Reading and Language Comprehension.* Boston, MA: Allyn and Bacon.

Just, M. and Carpenter, P. (1992) A capacity theory of comprehension: Individual differences in working memory. *Psychological Review* 99: 122–149.

Katz, L. and Frost, R. (1992) Reading in different orthographies: The orthographic depth hypothesis. In Frost, R. and Katz, L. (Eds.) *Orthography, Phonology, Morphology, and Meaning.* Amsterdam: North Holland: 67–84.

Kellerman, E. (1995) Crosslinguistic influence: Transfer to nowhere? In Grabe *et al.* (Eds.): 125–150.

Kern, R. (1994) The role of mental translation in second language reading. *Studies in Second Language Acquisition* 16: 441–61.

Kintsch, W. (1988) The role of knowledge in discourse comprehension: A construction-integration model. *Psychological Review* 95: 163–82.

Kintsch, W. (1994) Psycholinguistics and reading ability. In Gernsbacher (Ed.): 849–894.

Kintsch, W. (1995) How readers construct situation models for stories: The role of syntactic cues and causal inferences. In Gernsbacher and Givon (Eds.): 139–60.

Knight, S. (1994) Dictionary use while reading: The effects on comprehension and vocabulary acquisition for students of different verbal abilities. *Modern Language Journal* 94: 285–99.

Koda, K. (1996) L2 words recognition research: A critical review. *Modern Language Journal* 80: 450–460.

Koda, K. (1997) Orthographic knowledge in L2 lexical processing. In Coady, and Huckin (Eds.): 35–52.

Kroll, J. and de Groot, A. (1997) Lexical and conceptual memory in the bilingual: Mapping form to meaning in two languages. In de Groot and Kroll (Eds.): 169–199.

Landauer, T. and Dumais, S. (1997) A solution to Plato's problem: The latent semantic analysis theory of acquisition, induction, and representation of knowledge. *Psychological Review* 104: 211–240.

Lantolf, J. and Pavlenko, A. (1995) Sociocultural theory and second language acquisition. In Grabe *et al.* (Eds.): 108–124.

Laufer, B. (1989) What percentage of text-lexis is essential for comprehension. In Lauren, C. and Nordman, M. (Eds) *Special Language: From Humans Thinking to Thinking Machines.* Philadelphia, PA: Multilingual Matters: 316–23.

Leseman, P. (1994) Socio-cultural determinants of literacy development. In Verhoeven, L. (Ed.) *Functional Literacy.* Philadelphia, PA: J. Benjamins: 163–84.

Liberman, I. and Liberman A. (1992) Whole language versus code emphasis: Underlying assumptions and their implications for reading instruction. In Gough, Ehri and Treiman (Eds.): 343–66.

Long, D., Seely, M., Oppy, B. and Golding, J. (1996) The role of inferential processing in reading ability. In Britton and Graesser (Eds.): 189–214.

Lorch, J. (1995) Integration of topic information during reading. In Lorch and O'Brien (Eds.): 279–94.

Lorsch, R. and O'Brien, E. (Eds.) (1995) *Sources of Coherence Reading.* Hillsdale, NJ: Lawrence Erlbaum Associates, Publishers

Lysynchuk, L., Pressley, M. and Vye, N. (1990) Reciprocal teaching improves standardized reading comprehension performance in poor comprehenders. *Elementary School Journal* 90, 469–84.

MacWhinney, B. (1997) Second language acquisition and the competition model. In de Groot and Kroll (Eds.): 113–42.

Mannes, S. and St. George, M. (1996) Effects of prior knowledge on text comprehension: A simple modeling approach. In Britton and Graesser (Eds.): 115–39.

Mason, J. (1992) Reading stories to preliterate children: A proposed connection to reading. In Gough, Ehri and Treiman (Eds.): 215–41.

Mathewson, G. (1994) Model of attitude influence upon reading and learning to read. In Ruddell, R., Ruddell, M. and Singer, H. (Eds.) *Theoretical Models and Processes of Reading* (4th ed.). Newark, DE: IRA: 1131–61.

McGilly, K. (Ed.) (1994) *Classroom Lessons: Integrating Cognitive Theory.* Cambridge, MA: MIT Press.

McKay, S. (1993) *Agendas for Second Language Literacy.* New York, NY: Cambridge University Press.

McKenna, M. (1994) Toward a model of reading attitude acquisition. In Cramer, E. and Castle, M. (Eds.) *Fostering the Love of Reading: The Affective Domain in Reading Education.* Newark, DE: IRA: 18–40.

McKeough, A., Lupant, J. and Marini, A. (Eds.) (1995) *Teaching for Transfer: Fostering Generalization in Learning.* Mahwah, NJ: Lawrence Erlbaum Associates, Publishers.

McNamara, D., Kintsch, E., Songer, N. and Kintsch, W. (1996) Are good texts always better? Interactions of text coherence, background knowledge, and levels of understanding in learning from text. *Cognition and Instruction* 14: 1–43.

Mikulecky, L. (1996) Family literacy: Parent and child interaction. In Benjamin, L. and Lord, J. (Eds.) *Family Literacy: Directions in Research and Implications for Practice*. Washington, DC: U.S. Department of Education: 55–63.

Nagy, W. (1988) *Teaching Vocabulary to Improve Reading Comprehension*. Urbana, IL: NCTE.

Nagy, W., Garcia, G., Durgunoglu, A. and Hancin-Bhatt, B. (1993) Spanish-English bilingual students' use of cognates in English reading. *Journal of Reading Behaviour* 25: 241–59.

Nation, P. and Newton, J. (1997) Teaching vocabulary. In Coady and Huckin (Eds.): 238–54.

Nicholson, T. (1991) Do children read words better in context or in lists? A classic study revisited. *Journal of Educational Psychology* 83: 444–50.

Oakhill, J. (1994) Individual differences in children's reading comprehension. In Gernsbacher (Ed.): 821–48.

Oakhill, J., and Garnham, A. (1988) *Becoming a Skilled Reader*. New York, NY: Basil Blackwell.

Oney, B., Peter, M. and Katz, L. (1997) Phonological processing in printed word recognition: Effects of age and writing system. *Scientific Studies of Reading* 1: 65–83.

Paran, A. (1996) Reading in EFL: Facts and fictions. *Enslish Language Teaching Journal* 50: 25–34.

Perfetti, C. (1989) There are generalized abilities and one of them is reading. In Resnick, L. (Ed.) *Knowing, Learning and Instruction: Essays in Honor of R. Glazer*. Hillsdale, NJ: Lawrence Erlbaum Associates, Publishers: 307–34.

Perfetti, C. (1991) Representations and awareness in the acquisition of reading competence. In Rieben and Perfetti (Eds.): 33–44.

Perfetti, C. (1992) The representation problem in reading acquisition. In Gough, Ehri and Treiman (Eds.).

Perfetti, C. (1994) Psycholinguistic and reading ability. In Gernsbacher (Ed.): 849–94.

Perfetti, C. and Britt, M. (1995) Where do propositions come from? In Weaver III, C., Mannes, S. and Fletcher, C. (Eds.) *Discourse Comprehension: Essays in Honor of Walter Kintsch*. Hillsdale, NJ: Lawrence Erlbaum Associates, Publishers: 11–34.

Perfetti, C. and Zhang, S. (1996) What it means to learn to read. In Graves, M., van den Broek, P. and Taylor, B. (Eds.) *The First R: Every Child's Right to Read*. New York, NY: Teachers College Press: 37–61.

Plaut, D., McClelland, J., Seidenberg, M. and Patterson, K. (1996) Understanding normal and impaired word reading: Computational principles in quasi-regular domains. *Psychological Review* 103: 56–115.

Pressley, M. (1994) State-of-the-science primary-grades reading instruction or whole language? *Educational Psychologist* 29: 211–215.

Pressley, M. (1995) A transactional strategies instruction christmas carol. In McKeough, Lupart, and Marini (Eds.): 177–213.

Pressley, M. and Woloshyn, V. (1995) *Cognitive Strategy Instruction that Really Improves Children's Academic Performance*. Cambridge, MA: Brookline Books.

Rayner, K. and Pollatsek, A. (1989) *The Psychology of Reading*. Englewood Cliffs, NJ: Prentice-Hall.

Renninger, K. Hidi, S. and Krapp, A. (Eds.) (1992) *The Role of Interest in Learning and Development*. Hillsdale, NJ: Lawrence Erlbaum Associates, Publishers.

Rieben, L. and Perfetti, C. (Eds.) (1991) *Learning to Read: Basic Research and its Implications*. Hillsdale, NJ: Lawrence Erlbaum Associates, Publishers.

Rowe, K. (1991) The influence of reading activity at home on students' attitudes towards reading, classroom attentiveness and reading achievement: An application of structural equation modeling. *British Journal of Educational Psychology* 61: 19–35.

Sadoski, M., Paivio, A. and Goetz, E. (1991) Commentary: A critique of schema theory in reading and a dual coding alternative. *Reading Research Quarterly* 26: 463–84.

Scarborough, H. and Dobrich, W. (1994) On the efficacy of reading to preschoolers. *Developmental Review* 14: 245–302.

Schiefele, U. (1992) Topic interest and levels of text comprehension. In Renninger, Hidi and Krapp (Eds.): 151–82.

Segalowitz, N. (1997) Individual differences in second language acquisition. In de Groot and Kroll (Eds.): 85–112.

Segalowitz, N. and Hebert, M. (1990) Phonological recoding in the first and second language reading of skilled bilinguals. *Language Learning* 40: 503–38.

Segalowitz, N., Poulson, C. and Komoda, M. (1991) Lower level components of reading skill in higher level bilinguals: Implications for reading instruction. In Hulstijn, J. (Ed.) *Reading in Two Languages. AILA Review* 8: 15–30.

Seidenberg, M. and McClelland, J. (1989) A distributed, developmental model of word recognition and naming. *Psychological Review* 96: 523–68.

Shanks, D. (1995) *The Psychology of Associative Learning*. New York, NY: Cambridge University Press.

Shany, M. and Bielmiller, A. (1995) Assisted reading practice: Effects on performance of poor in grades 3 and 4. *Reading Reaserch Quarterly* 30: 382–395.

Shimron, J. and Sivan, T. (1994) Reading proficiency and orthography: Evidence from Hebrew and English. *Language Learning* 44: 5–27.

Singer, M. (1990) *Psychology of Language*. Hillsdale, NJ: Lawrence Erlbaum Associates, Publishers.

Slavin, R. (1995) *Co-operative Learning: Theory, Research and Practice* (3rd ed.). Englewood Cliffs, NJ: Prentice Hall.

Smith, F. (1982) *Understanding Reading* (3rd ed.). New York, NY: Holt, Rinehart & Winston.

Smith, M. C. (1997) How do bilinguals access lexical information. In De Groot and Kroll (Eds.): 145–168.

Snow, C., Barnes, W., Chandler, J., Goodman, I. and Hemphill, L. (1991) *Unfulfilled Expectations: Home and School Influences on Literacy.* Cambridge, MA: Harvard University Press.

Stahl, S. (1997) Instructional models in reading: An introduction. In Tahl, S. and Hayes, D. (Eds.) *Instructional Models in Reading.* Mahwah, NJ: Lawrence Erlbaum Associates, Publishers: 1–29.

Stanovich, K (1986) Matthew effects in reading: Some consequences of individual differences in the acquisition of literacy. *Reading Research Quarterly* 21: 360–407.

Stanovich, K. (1991a) Changing models of reading and reading acquisition. In Rieben and Perfetti (Eds.): 19–31.

Stanovich, K. (1991b) Word recognition: Changing perspectives. In Barr *et al.* (Eds.): 418–52.

Stanovich, K. (1992) The psychology of reading: Evolutionary and revolutionary developments. In Grabe *et al.* (Eds.): 3–30.

Stanovich, K. and Stanovich, P. (1995) How research might inform the debate about early reading acquisition. *Journal of Research in Reading* 18: 87–105.

Stanovich, K., West, R. and Cunningham, A. (1991) Beyond phonological processes: Print exposure and orthographic processing. In Brady. and Shankweiler (Eds.): 219–35.

Stanovich, K., West, R., Cunningham, A., Cipielewski, J. and Siddiqui, S. (1996) The role of inadequate print exposure as a determinant of reading comprehension problems. In Cornoldi and Oakhill (Eds.): 15–32

Stewart, R. and Cross, T. (1993) A field test of five forms of marginal gloss study guide: An ecological study. *Reading Psychology* 14: 113–39.

Treville, M.-C. (1996) Lexical learning and reading in L2 at the beginning level: The advantage of cognates. *The Canadian Modern Language Review* 53: 173–90.

Tunmer, W. and Hoover, W. (1992) Cognitive and linguistic factors in learning to read. In Gough, Ehri, and Treiman (Eds): 175–214.

Turner, J. (1993) A motivational perspective on literacy instruction. In Leu, L. and Kinzer, C. (Eds.) *Examining Central Issues in Literacy Research, Theory and Practice*. Chicago, IL: National Reading Conference: 153–61.

Vellutino, F. (1991) Introduction to three studies on reading acquisition: Convergent findings on theoretical foundations of code-oriented versus whole-language approaches to reading instruction. *Journal of Educational Psychology* 83: 437–43.

Vellutino, F. and Scanlon, D. (1991) The preeminence of phonologically based skills in learning to read. In Brady and Shankweiler (Eds.): 237–52.

Verhoeven, L (1994) Transfer in bilingual development: The linguistic interdependence hypothesis revisited. *Language Learning* 44: 381–415.

Wade, S. (1992) How interest affects learning from text. In Renninger, Hidi and Krapp (Eds.): 255–77.

Wagner, R. and Stanovich, K. (1996) Expertise in reading. In Ericsson (Ed.): 189–225.

Waters, A. (1996) *A Review of Research into Needs in English for Academic Purposes of Relevance to the North American Higher Educational Context*. Princeton, NJ: [TOEFL Monograph Series MS-6].

Weinberg, J. (1996) A longitudinal study of children's early literacy experiences at home and later literacy development at home and school. *Journal of Research in Reading* 19: 14–24.

Whitehurst, G., Epstein, J, Angell, A., Payne, A., Crone, D. and Fischell, J. (1994) Outcomes of an emergent literacy intervention in head start. *Journal of Educational Psychology* 86: 542–55.

Willson, V. and Rupley, W. (1997) A structural equation model for reading comprehension based on background, phonemic, and strategy knowledge. *Scientific Studies of Reading* 1: 45–63.

Wong, M. and Underwoood, G. (1996) Do bilingual children read words better in lists or in context? *Journal of Research in Reading* 19: 61–76.

Yu, L. (1996) The role of L1 in the acquisition of motion verbs in English by Chinese and Japanese learners. *The Canadian Modern Language Review* 53: 191–218.

Zechmeister, E., D'Anna, C., Hall, J., Paus, C. and Smith, J. (1993) Metacognitive and other knowledge about the mental lexicon: Do we know how many words we know? *Applied Linguistics* 14: 188–206.

Zuckernick, H. (1996) Second language word decoding strategies. *The Canadian Modern Language Review* 53: 76–96.

Zwaan, R. (1994) Effect of genre expectations on text comprehension. *Journal of Experimental Psychology: Learning, Memory and Cognition* 20: 920–33.

Zwaan, R. and Brown, C. (1996) The influence of language proficiency and comprehension skill on situation-model construction. *Discourse Processes* 21: 289–32

16 A post-modern view of the problem of language assessment

Henry Braun
Educational Testing Service

In this chapter, I would like to address three questions: Why does good test construction seem to be an inclrasingly difficult activity? What are the forces shaping the proctice of the test construction? What lies ahead? I will also consider the impact fo validity on the test design and the impact of technology. I conclude by suggesting a more ecological approach to test design.

Certainly, I will not be able to fully respond to these questions to anyone's satisfaction. They are indeed difficult questions and do not admit simple answers.

Let me suggest, though, a short answer to the first question. It is that we are redefining 'good' so that there are greater demands on those who must develop tests. Indeed, it is not only that the demands are greater but that they are more likely to come into conflict. This brings to mind a book that I have just read, *In Over Our Heads: The Mental Demands of Modern Life*, by the noted psychologist Robert Kegan. He argues that many of us are living in a post-modern psychological state, in which the familiar anchors of family, tradition and religious or civil authority no longer hold sway as they once did. More of us, more of the time, are forced to rely on our own capacities to sort out complicated situations, to make complex judgements and to reach difficult decisions among options that are equally attractive – or equally unattractive.

Kegan makes a strong case that these demands confront us in our roles as spouses, as parents and as workers. So perhaps we who are developing tests are just experiencing the post-modern world firsthand in our own work.

One can think of building a test as a problem that falls under the rubric of 'optimal design under constraints'. In general, a realized design is a particular combination of design elements or an algorithm for generating such combinations that satisfies certain a prior constraints and can be evaluated against one or more orders of merit. Optimality may only mean achieving an acceptable balance among the different orders of merit.

From this perspective, test construction may have much in common with other design professions such as architecture. In my view, test designers have been rather insulated from other designers and perhaps we can learn something valuable from the struggles of other design professions to understand what they do and how to do it better. These thoughts have been stimulated by my long-standing involvement in building computer-based simulations of architectural practice as part of a major effort to computerize the entire battery of architectural registration examinations. The research and development during this nine-year period has forced my colleagues and me to grapple with issues in test design, but has also led to a greater appreciation of the practice of architecture itself, and how it has a great deal in common with assessment design.

Some of these similarities are indicated in Table 16.1 below. In both cases, design is shaped by purpose: what is to be accomplished and for whom. Lack of clarity in purpose or naive overambition often result in poor designs. For both sets of practitioners, critical questions are how to generate candidate designs and how to evaluate them once they are available. The latter question requires explicit criteria for optimality or what I referred to above as orders of merit.

Table 16.1

Similarities between architecture and testing

Architecture	Testing
Landscape Design Elements	Domain Items/Probes
Engineering Constraints	Modes of delivery Scoring Procedures Psychometric tools

Table 16.2a presents some of the criteria employed by architects while Table 16.2b presents some of the criteria employed by test designers. Obviously, the purpose of the design effort will influence the salience of the various criteria and the ranges of acceptable or desirable values. Except in the most trivial cases, each feasible design represents a tradeoff among the optimality criteria.

Table 16.2a

Architectural criteria

Fuctionality	Structural integrity Traffic Flow Space adjacency
Conformity to code	Zoning restrictions Safety considerations
Aesthetics	Appropriateness to site Visual attractivness
Cost	Time to build Material cost

Table 16.2b

Test design criteria

Measurement	Distribution of difficulty Reliability Comparability Generalizability
Business	Cost Time Efficiency
	Evidential Consequential

One reason the test developer's job has become more difficult is that the design criteria have become more demanding. For example, the modern conception of validity changes the scope of the design world by bringing into consideration a broader set of issues, as the following quote from Sam Messick indicates:

> *Validity is an integrated evaluative judgment of the degree to which empirical evidence and theoretical rationales support the adequacy and appropriateness of inferences and actions based on test scores or other modes of assessment.*
>
> (Messick 1989)

The above assertion should be compared with the more limited requirements of content and predictive validity. In fact, one can imagine a sequence of increasingly elaborate design worlds induced by increasingly demanding validity models. One could argue that the broadened view of tests embraced by much of the public – in contrast to the more limited view held by the testers – goes to the heart of many criticisms of present-day tests. A comment that I vividly recall from a meeting several years ago to the effect that 'multiple choice tests are psychometrically immaculate but educationally bankrupt' illustrates the point.

Lest we feel alone in the opprobrium we endure, here is a comment from a critic of another design artifact, a zoning code.

> *America's zoning laws ... have mutated ... into a system that corrodes civic life, outlaws the human scale, defeats tradition and authenticity, and confounds our yearning for an everyday environment worthy of our affection.*
>
> (Kunstler 1996)

His point, made throughout the article, is that architects and planners must look beyond building design to consider the functionality of the built environment. The point is the same – the need to take account of a broader set of criteria in evaluating the success (validity) of a design.

Indeed, the practice of test design and construction has become much more difficult. In the first place, purpose has become more ambitious and multifaceted. In school assessments, for example, sponsors seek tests that can both provide useful instructional information for the individual student while also serving accountability roles. Secondly, cognitive psychology and related disciplines have led to a deeper understanding of the nature of competence and more sophisticated models of particular domains. Designers must take account of these new understandings in their work. Advances in technology, particularly the rapid evolution of computers and communication networks, are leading to seismic changes in the infrastructure that supports testing. Finally, as has been mentioned above, validity models have become more comprehensive and the standards the testing profession is being held to have become more demanding and rigorous.

Test designers must cope with the complex and dynamic interactions among these various aspects of the process, in addition to trying to anticipate future directions. Hampered by reliance on old paradigms and the lack of tools to fully exploit scientific and technical advances, they tend to produce tests that are often very much like the tests of the past.

In the case of 'high stakes' assessment for selection, purpose is shifting from providing an assessment of overall proficiency along a unidimensional scale to providing an interpretable score profile that informs educational decision making. Modern requires us to consider what kind of data would support the adequacy and appropriateness of inferences and actions based on test results. For designers, the first question is what types of items or probes, what kind of test structures, and which inferential models would generate the sort of evidence required by the different decision makers.

I believe that we have to understand differences in performance among test takers in terms of various developmental trajectories and their implications for further learning. Thus, the 'static' structural perspective of a domain must be joined with a 'dynamic' developmental perspective of performance in the domain. This will have profound implications for the next generation of psychometric models, an issue that is treated very well by Mislevy (1996).

These ideas are by no means new ones, as the following quotations illustrate:

... modern cognitive psychology conceptualizes the acquisition of cognitive skills in developmental terms. Hence, modern educational and psychological measurement, to enhance its educational usefulness, should be sensitive to developmental differences in subject-matter learning and performance. (Messick 1984)

... learning theory is taking on the characteristics of a developmental psychology of performance changes. ...
... measurement must be designed to assess these performance changes ...
Coherence of instruction and assessment is the ultimate goal.
(Glaser, Lesgold and Lajoie 1987)

Until recently, though, these notions have been treated by practitioners as pointing toward idealized goals rather than realistic objectives. However, the development of measures of literacy skills both in large-scale assessments and in remedial programs (Kirsch, Jungeblut and Mosenthal, in press), and the work of Tatsuoka and her associates on Rule Space Methodology (1997) are important first steps. In the case of adult literacy, a strong theory of competence led to a test design process in which items could be generated to meet specific difficulty targets and different score levels could be given firmly grounded functional interpretations. Rule space methods, when successfully applied, allow cognitively based interpretations of test performance that meaningfully differentiate among individuals at different score levels and even among individuals at similar score levels but with qualitatively different response patterns.

Contemporaneous work by Gitomer *et al.* (1991) and Mislevy (1996) have shown that we are at the threshold of developing technology-based integrated modular assessment systems that can be tuned to support a range of purposes from instructional assessment to high-stakes assessment. These systems are characterized by domain models derived through cognitive task analysis, student models that are informed by the understanding of the nature of expertise and its acquisition, as well as statistical models employing Bayes inference networks that support dynamic assessment and the continuous updating of student models as additional evidence accumulates. These are exciting developments and promise to revolutionize the practice of assessment. They also imply a need for a radical revision in the test design process.

Until this point, I have focused on the impact of on test design. In contrast, attention typically tends to be directed toward the impact of technology. Indeed, there is no question that technology advances will influence the design world in many ways, as illustrated in the table below.

Table 16.3

Impact of technology

Items/Probes utilizing multimedia
Psychometric models relying on rapid realtime compulation
Automated scoring of complex constructed responses
Dynamic (adaptive) tests designs
Multiple delivery options (test centres, worldwide web)
Cost structures dominated by "seat time"

It is also important to recognize areas that technology may influence only indirectly. For example, the demand for authentic performance assessment coupled with multimedia capabilities will lead to the need for automated scoring of complex student-produced responses. In another forum (Braun 1994), I have argued that the development and implementation of these expert systems will lead to more rigorously defined tests with improved measurement properties. In particular, in order for an automated scoring system to operate accurately for a wide variety of instances of a particular problem type, developers are forced both to craft tighter problem specifications and to clarify the rules of evidence for scoring. This leads to greater comparability over time which is particularly important in an 'on-demand' testing environment with the concomitant requirement for large item pools to maintain test security. This has certainly been the case in the architectural licensing effort. See also Bejar (1995).

As the design process becomes more clearly delineated, technology will also facilitate a more experimental approach to the practice of test construction; that is, it will be possible to take a more generative approach, in which multiple candidate designs can be produced and then examined, leading to new cycles of generation and evaluation until a satisfactory design is found. This technique of automated design generation is being practised in such disparate areas as architecture and biology with interesting results.

In fact, it is already serving us well at ETS in various investigations. We are employing Automated Item Selection (AIS), a tool developed originally by Swanson and Stocking (1993) to provide near final form linear tests; and now, also, to produce computer-adaptive tests operationally in real time. At the heart of the system is a clever dynamic optimization algorithm that sequentially selects items from a pool so that the final result is a test that meets the varied constraints and requirements that embody the target construct. It is now used to generate multiple instances of a test under a particular set of conditions, permitting developers to experimentally determine the effects of different combinations of constraints or different item pool compositions on the properties of the resulting tests. Such a program of research would never have been feasible in the past when the assembly of a test could require as much as four days and not four minutes!

One model of a revamped test design process is presented in Figure 16.1 on the next page.

In this scenario, consultations with various constituencies provide test developers with three essential building blocks:
1 the constructs or underlying targets of the measurement process;
2 the communication goals or the kinds of information that are to be conveyed on the basis of the test results; and
3 the constraints or the relatively unchanging features of the setting in which the test will be designed, developed and delivered.

Together, the three 'Cs' determine the design space, the universe of feasible test designs that conform to the three Cs. Various candidate designs can then be generated by different means, with the goal of exploring different regions of the design space. These designs are evaluated using appropriate criteria. On the basis of these evaluations, one or more of the designs can be modified or entirely different designs can be generated. After some number of cycles, a satisfactory design is attained and operational implementation commences.

Of course, this is a highly simplified view of the test development process. None the less, there is a key notion of a generative phase in which an explicit effort is made to examine the attractiveness of a variety of very different designs. This is not standard practice and the usual result is a lack of innovation in the design process.

Figure 16.1

Model of a revamped test design process

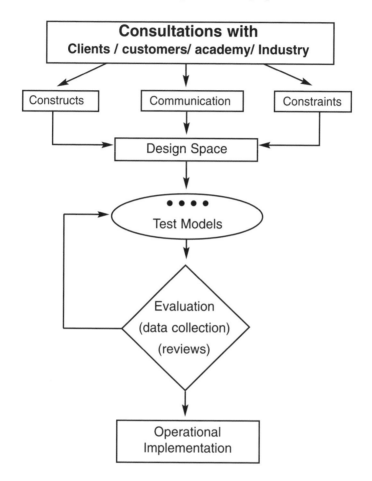

With all the excitement attendant on the role of technology, it is important to note that technology changes neither the purpose of measurement nor the criteria by which we judge the adequacy of an instrument with respect to the demands of contemporary psychometric practice and test theory. In my view, if the design profession takes the modern conception of seriously, the consequences for assessment will be as great as the more visible effects of technology.

Validity theory compels us to adopt a more ecological approach to test construction by fundamentally broadening the scope of the design world.

Indeed, elaborating the theoretical and practical implications of theory is essential to forestalling the ascendancy of an impoverished techno-centric approach to test design. It is only by respecting the emerging standards and employing technology thoughtfully that we will, over time, produce better tests – tests that are generated through a craft of test design that is at once more principled, more disciplined and more innovative.

These ideas are particularly germane to the area of language testing. For millions around the world, English language competence is the key to information, educational opportunity and employment. In ESL testing our purpose should be to help people realize their educational and career goals, while assisting institutions in making the resource allocation decisions they must. A successful and valid assessment will have to take into account such factors as: the multiplicity of purposes, the heterogeneity of language backgrounds, differential instructional strategies, as well as the role of psychological and social psychological factors in performance.

This is a complex and challenging undertaking. Indeed, I believe that serious consideration of the ecological approach to test design in this area will lead us to the construction of assessment systems that will support both extended instruction and relatively short certification episodes. This will lead to fundamental changes in the practice of assessment and promises an exciting future for all of us.

Notes

I would like to thank the LTRC for inviting me to deliver a keynote address at their meeting and, especially, to Professor Antony John Kunnan for providing assistance in making the necessary arrangements.

References

Bejar, I. I. (1995) From adaptive testing to automated scoring of architectural simulations. In Mancall, E. L. and Bashook, P. G. (Eds.) *Assessing Clinical Reasoning: The Oral Examination and Alternative Simulations.* Evanston, IL: American Board of Medical Specialties.

Braun, H. I. (1994) Assessing technology in assessment. In Baker, E. L. and O'Neill, H. F. (Eds.) *Technology Assessment in Education and Training.* Hillsdale, NJ: Lawrence Erlbaum Associates, Publishers.

Gitomer, D. H., Cohen, W., Gallagher, A., Kaplan, R., Steinberg, L. S., Swinton, S. and Trenholm, H. (1991) *Design Rationale and Data Analysis for Hydrive Content and Structure.* Princeton, NJ: Educational Testing Service.

Glaser, R., Lesgold, A. and Lajoie, S. (1987) Toward a cognitive theory for the measurement of achievement. In Ronning, R. R., Glover, J. A., Conoley, J. C. and Witt, J. C. (Eds.) *The Influence of Cognitive Psychology*. Hillsdale, NJ: Lawrence Erlbaum Associates, Publishers.

Kegan, R. (1994) *In Over Our Heads: The Mental Demands of Modern Life*. Cambridge, MA: Harvard University Press.

Kirsch, I., Jungeblut, A. and Mostenthal, P. B. (In press) Interpreting the adult literacy skills and literacy levels. *Technical Report for the National Adult Literacy Survey*. Washington, DC: National Centre for Education Statistics, U.S. Government Printing Office.

Kunstler, J. H. (1996) Home from nowhere. *The Atlantic Monthly*: 43–66.

Messick, S. (1984) The psychology of educational measurement. *Journal of Educational Measurement* 21 (3): 215–37. [Invited Address, National Council on Measurement in Education and American Educational Research Association.]

Messick, S. (1989) . In Linn, R. L. (Ed.) *Educational Measurement* (3rd ed.) New York NY: American Council on Education/MacMillan Series on Higher Education: 13–104.

Mislevy, R. J. (1996) Test theory reconceived. *Journal of Educational Measurement* 33 (4): 379–416.

Swanson, L. C. and Stocking, M. L. (1993) A model and heuristic for solving very large item selection problems. *Applied Psychological Measurement* 17: 151–66.

Tatsuoka, K. (1997) Computerized cognitive diagnostic adaptive testing: Effect on remedial instruction as empirical validation. *Journal of Educational Measurement* 34 (1): 1–20.

About the authors

Lyle F. Bachman is Professor of Applied Linguistics and TESL at the University of California, Los Angeles. His current professional interests include the development and validation of tests of language ability, the technology of test design and development, and the interfaces between language testing research and second language acquisition research. His publications include *Fundamental Considerations in Language Testing, Language Testing in Practice* (with Adrian S. Palmer), and *Interfaces between Second Language Acquisition and Language Testing Research* (co-edited with Andrew D. Cohen.) He has also published numerous articles in the area of language testing and evaluation. He is currently editor of the journal *Language Testing,* and co-editor of the Cambridge Language Assessment Series.

Henry Braun holds a doctoral degree in mathematical statistics from Stanford University. After teaching at Princeton University, he came to ETS in 1979 as a research scientist and is now the Vice President for Research Management. At ETS, Dr Braun has concerned himself with the development of statistical methodology and stochastic modelling. In 1986, Dr Braun received the Palmer O. Johnson Award of the American Educational Research Association and in 1991 he was elected a Fellow of the American Statistical Association. He is a co-recipient of the National Council for Measurement in Education's 1999 Award for Outstanding Technical Contribution to the Field of Educational Measurement.

Dan Douglas is a professor in the TESL/Applied Linguistics program at Iowa State University, where he teaches graduate and undergraduate courses inlanguage testing, second language acquisition, ESP, and introduction to linguistics. His research interests are in specific purpose language testing and second language acquisition in academic, professional, and vocational contexts. He has taught and conducted research in the US, England, Scotland, Japan, Sudan, and Botswana. His book, *Assessing Languages for Specific Purposes*, was published by Cambridge University Press in 2000.

Catherine Elder lectures on the specialist Masters program in Applied Linguistics (Language Testing and Language Program Evaluation) in the Department of Linguistics and Applied Linguistics at the University of Melbourne and has been a Research Fellow of Language Australia's Language Testing Research Centre since its inception in 1990. Her research interests are in sociolinguistics, language testing and language program evaluation with particular reference to speakers of minority languages in Australia.

William Grabe is a professor of English in the English Department at Northern Arizona University. His research interests include the development of reading and writing abilities in both first and second languages. More generally, he is also interested in literacy, written discourse analysis, cognitive processing and curricular efforts to move from theory to instruction in literacy. He has published a number of articles and chapters on reading and writing issues, and his most recent book, co-authored with R. B. Kaplan, is *The Theory and Practice of Writing* (Longman, 1996) He is also editor of the *Annual Review of Applied Lingustics* (Cambridge University Press)

Liz Hamp-Lyons is Chair Professor of English and Head of the English Department at the Hong Kong Polytechnic University. Her research interests include writing assessment, especially 'new methods' such as portfolio assessment, writing pedagogy, ethics in language testing, teacher professional development, and learner autonomy (including self-assessment). She has published numerous articles in journals including *Language Testing, TESOL Quarterly*, and the *Journal of Second Language Writing*. Among her book publications are *Assessing Second Language Writing in Academic Contexts* (Ablex 1991), and *Assessing College Writing Portfolios: Principles for Practice, Theory, Research* (Hampton Press 1999) with Bill Condon.

Marijke van der Heide has an MAT in Teaching Foreign Languages from Southwest Texas State University, in San Marcos, Texas. She has been a translator of French, German and Dutch, and for the past 13 years has served as Program Manager for Foreign Language Education and Measurement at FBI Headquarters in Washington, DC. She is frequently a presenter at government and academic conferences on language teaching. Her recent publications include Spanish for law enforcement (1998), in T. B. Fryer and G. Gunterman (Eds.) *Spanish and Portuguese for Business and the Professions*, Lincolnwood, Ill: National Textbook Co.

Michael Herriman is a professor of English at Nagoya University of Commerce and Business, Nagoya, Japan. He received his PhD from Cornell University. Until 1997 he was Director of the Centre for English as a Second Language and Senior Lecturer in Education at the University of Western Australia. He has had fellowships in Russia, USA, Canada, UK and Holland and has published widely including the areas of literacy, language awareness, academic writing and English language testing. He was involved in the development of test of English language used to test non-English language speaking university entrants in Western Australia.

Ebrahim Khodadady is an assistant professor of Applied Linguistics at Kurdistan University, Sanandaj, Iran. He received his PhD from the University of Western Australia. He has been the Director General of Research at Kurdistan University since 1998. His book entitled *Multiple Choice Items in Testing: Practice and Theory* is used as a textbook at the graduate level in Applied Linguistics.

Antony John Kunnan is associate professor in the TESOL program at California State University, Los Angeles. His interests include language test fairness and validation, test qualities and test reform movements. His publications include *Test Taker Characteristics and Test Performance* (Cambridge, 1995), an edited volume titled *Validation in Language Assessment* (Lawrence Erlbaum, 1998), an edited issue of *Language Testing* (Volume 15, 3) on structural equation modeling and language assessment research, and the article "Fundamentals" (in language testing) in the *Encylcopedia of Educational Linguistics* (Elsevier Science, 2000). He received the Outstanding Doctoral Dissertation Research Award from the TOEFL Program in 1994 and he is currently the Test Reviews Editor of *Language Testing.*

Yong-Won Lee is currently working as an associate measurement statistician for the TOEFL Program in the Assessment Division at Educational Testing Service (ETS). He has obtained his PhD in Speech Communication with an emphasis on Teaching English as a Second Language (TESL) and with a minor focus in Educational Psychology at The Pennsylvania State University (PSU). He also received his Bachelor's and Master's degrees in English Education at Korea National University of Education. His areas of interest include application of IRT-based testlet approaches and multidimensional IRT models in language testing, computerized-adaptive language testing, and computer-assisted language learning.

Peter Lowenberg is an associate professor of Linguistics and Language Development at San Jose State University. He has served on the Committee of Examiners for the TOEFL and on the Technical Research panel of the TOEIC. He has lectured on English as a world language and on language testing for the United States Information Agency in Mexico, Brazil, the Philippines, Belgium and Uzbekistan, and for two years he directed the Language teaching programs at the United States Binational Centre in Surabaya, Indonesia. He has published on the spread of English as a world language, language policy and planning, and second language acquisition and testing, and has been review editor and associate edotor of the journal *World Englishes*.

Beryl E. Meiron is the United States and Canada Manager of English as a Foreign Language for University of Cambridge Examinations and IELTS International. She received her MA in TESOL from California State University, Los Angeles and taught ESL in the Division of Humanities and Social Science at the California Institute of Technology and in the American Culture and Language Program at California State University, Los Angeles. Her research interests include language assessment, pronunciation and oral skills, and rater cognition.

Ron Myers is a veterinarian and professor of Veterinary Pathology in the College of Veterinary Medicine at Iowa State University. In addition to his duties as a postmortem and surgical pathologist, he teaches or has taught veterinary students from basic pathology for entering DVM students to advanced pathology for graduate students. He was instrumental in developing a parallel curriculum for a subset of veterinary students utilizing predominantly problem-based learning, authentic assessment, and other innovations such as extended and early preceptorships, structured clinical exams, and simulated clients and patients.

Bonny Norton is Assistant Professor in the Department of Language Education at the University of British Columbia, Canada. She has been active in the field of language testing for over ten years, working on the development of Canadian Language Benchmarks Assessment, the TOEFL, and the Test of Written English. Her research on language, equity, and assessment has been published in the *Encyclopedia of Language and Education,* the *Harvard Educational Review, Language Testing,* and the *TESOL Quarterly.* Her article, 'Demystifying the TOEFL reading test' (*TESOL Quarterly*, 1992) was awarded 'Best Article' by the International Language Testing Association.

Alfred Appiah Sakyi is a doctoral candidate at The Ontario Institute for Studies in Education/University of Toronto. He is currently working at the Student Evaluation Branch of Education, Alberta, Canada.

Laurie S. Schick is a doctoral student in Applied Linguistics at the University of California, Los Angeles concentrating on discourse analysis. She received her MA in TESOL from California State University, Los Angeles and has taught ESL for six years. Her doctoral research is on the co-construction of affect, values and epistemic stance in Japanese television dramas.

Elana Shohamy is a professor and chair of the language education program at the school of education at Tel Aviv univeristy. Her main areas of research are language testing and language policy. Her research in language testing focuses on oral testing, method effect, alternative assessment washback effects and the use of language tests for power and control in educational and political context. She is the author of numerous articles. Her latest book entitled *The Power of Tests: Critical Perspective of the Use and Consequences of Language Tests,* will be published by Longman in early 2000.

Mary Spaan is a Research Assistant in Testing at the English Language Institute of the University of Michigan, Ann Arbor, where she has been engaged for over thirty years in the development and production of ESL and EFL examination. She has also been involved in the administration of ELI-UM's large-scale testing programs, and has taught advance level assessment of literacy skills of reading and writing, and more recently she has become concerned with accomodating examinees with disabilities. With Antony Kunnan, she was Co-Chair of the 1997 LTRC.

Charles W. Stansfield is President of Second Language Testing, Inc. (SLTI). Prior to forming his own company in 1994, he was Director of the Division of Foreign Language Education and Testing and Director of the ERIC Clearinghouse on Languages and Linguistics at the Centre for Applied Linguistics in Washington DC. He is the author of numerous language tests and research articles on language testing. The test reported on here is the first test development project completed by SLTI.

About the authors

Weiping Wu is Senior Associate at Second Language Testing, Inc. (SLTI) and Research Associate at the Centre for Applied Linguistics (CAL). In addition to teaching (English, Chinese and courses in Linguistics) at universities in China and the United States, he has been providing linguistic services to the legal field for the past years. He is also a master court interpreter (NJ) in Chinese (including Mandarin, Cantonese and Minnan). He presents frequently and publishes occasionally in issues related to language and law, testing, interpretation and translation. He was the project manager for the test reported on here.

Authors Index

G

Gallagher, A.   271
Galloway, V.   155, 169, 172
Gamas, W.   256
Garcia, G.   6, 9, 12, 259
Gardner, D.   256
Gardner, H.   252, 255
Garnham, A.   233, 235, 255, 259
Gathercole, S.   238, 255
Garnaut, R.   83, 101
Gernsbacher, M. A.   228, 230, 132, 233, 234, 236, 237, 241, 252, 253, 255, 258, 259
Gee, J. B.   204, 220
Geva, E.   241, 245, 244, 245, 255
Gibbons, J.   84, 100
Gillet, J. W.   208, 220
Ginther, A.   6, 12
Gitomer, D. H.   268, 271
Givon, T.   236, 255, 257
Glover, J. A.   272
Goetz, E.   260
Golding, J.   258
Goulden, R.   232, 233, 255
Gordon, C. M.   155, 173, 257
Goodman, I.   261
Goodman, K. S.   205, 220
Goodman, Y. M.   205, 220
Goodwin, C.   165, 173
Gough, P.   228, 230, 231, 233, 240, 241, 254, 255, 256, 258, 259, 261
Glass, G.   256
Glaser, R.   268, 271
Grabe, W.   225, 226, 227, 229, 231, 233, 235, 237, 240, 241, 221, 245, 247, 249, 251, 253, 254, 255, 256, 257, 258, 259, 261
Graesser, A.   233, 253, 255, 258
Graves, M.   259
Greenberg, K. L.   20, 26
Greene, A.   10
Griffith, P.   241, 255
Grobe, C. H.   142, 148, 150
de Groot, A.   242, 254, 257, 258, 260, 261
Grosjean, F.   242, 256
Gupta, A. F.   45, 59
Guthrie, J.   229, 256
Guzzetti, B.   235, 256, 278

H

Hadden, B.   156, 169, 171

Haenszel, W.   86, 87, 88, 99, 101, 102, 106, 124, 125

Haladyna, T. M.   106, 110, 124, 202, 220

Hale, G. A.   6, 12, 105, 124, 208, 220, 239, 256

Hales, L. W.   145, 148

Hall, J.   59, 260, 261, 262

Hare, V.   251, 278

Harris, A. J.   113, 124, 204, 220

Harris, L. A.   222

Harrington, M.   232, 256

Hamayan, E.   6, 12

Hambelton, R.   106, 109

Hamp-Lyons, L.   6, 13, 20, 30, 32, 34, 129, 131, 133, 148, 150, 151, 174, 274

Hannah, J.   47, 59

Harris, D. P.   113, 124, 204, 220, 222

Hayes, D.   259

Haynes, M.   232

Hazenberg, S.   245, 246, 232, 242, 256

Heath, S. B.   229, 256

Henderson, J.   233, 256

van der Heide, M.   129 177, 179, 181, 183, 185, 187, 189, 191, 193, 195, 197, 199, 201, 274

Herriman, M.   129, 201, 203, 205, 207, 208, 209, 211, 213, 215, 217, 219, 220, 221, 223, 275

Hemphill, L.   261

Henning, G. H.   6, 11, 105, 106, 107, 108, 121, 123, 124

Hewison, J.   229, 254

Hicks, M. M.   220

Hidi, S.   260, 262

Hilliard, A. G.   6, 12

Ho, M. L.   45, 49, 55

Hoien, T.   252

Holland, P.   6, 11, 12, 13, 86, 99, 101, 106, 122, 123, 124, 126, 155

Homburg, T.   129, 136, 144, 149

Hood, S.   8, 12

Hoover, M.   6, 12, 228, 240, 241, 255, 256, 261

Hughes, D. C.   121, 145, 149

Hulstijn, J.   232, 242, 256, 260

Hymes, D.   45, 57, 168, 171, 173

I

Idol, B. 253
Idol, L. 253
Ijzendoorn, M. 253
Inbar, O. 6, 13
ILTA Code of Practice 36, 37

J

Jacobs, G. 244, 256
Jacoby, S. 61, 68, 75, 77, 78
Jaffarpur, A. 211, 220
Janopoulos, M. 147
Jefferson, G. 173
Jensen, A. R. 5, 101
Johnson, D. D. 108, 125, 149
Johnston, P. 108, 110, 124
Jones, R. J. 130, 148
Jonides, J. 132, 137, 257
Juel, M. 228, 231, 241, 255, 257
Jungeblut, A. 267, 271
Just, M. 10, 46, 52, 250, 253, 255

K

Kachru, B. B. 44, 54, 55
Kachru, Y. 54, 56, 57, 58
Kaplan, R. 126, 271
Kamil, M. L. 205, 221, 243, 255
Katz, L. 243, 258, 259
Keeling, B. 145, 149
Kegan, R. 54, 57, 263, 272
Kellerman, E. 244, 257
Kern, R. 244, 257
Kenyon, D. M. 199, 200
Khodadady, E. 129, 201, 203, 205, 207, 208, 209, 211, 213, 215, 217, 219, 220, 221, 223, 275
Kiely, G. 108, 110
Kintsch, W. 228, 230, 231, 232, 233, 234, 235, 236, 237, 240, 254, 257, 260
Kinzer, C. 262
Kirsch, I. 13, 267, 272
Kipp, S. 84, 98, 101

Knight, S. 257
Kobayashi, M. 208, 221
Koda, K. 243, 244, 257
Koster, W. G. 222
Kroll, J. 242, 254, 256, 257, 258, 260, 261
Kujore, O. 54
Kulick, E. 106
Kunnan, A. J. 5, 6, 10. 12, 13, 121, 170, 271, 275, 278

L

Lacelle-Peterson, M. 7, 13
Lajoie, S. 267, 271
Laufer, B. 242, 258
Land, R. 144, 149
Landauer, T. 229, 257
Lantolf, J. 229, 258
Lazaraton, A. 154, 173
Lee, Y -W 42, 105, 107, 109, 111, 113, 115, 117, 119, 121, 123, 125,
Lehman, I. J. 201, 221
Leseman, P. 229, 258
Lesgold, A. 267, 272
Leu, L. 262
Leung, C. 37, 38
Levy, B. 230, 253, 256
Lewis, C. 107, 109, 110, 116
Liberman, A. 228, 258
Liberman, I. 228, 258
van Lier, L. 153, 154, 172, 173
Linn, R. 13, 100, 101, 106, 125, 272
Lippi-Green, R. 9, 13
Liu, C. C. 199, 200
Long, D. 238, 258
Long, M. H. 58, 222
Lorch, J. 233, 236, 258
Lord, F. M. 106, 125, 159
Lotherington-Wolozyn, H. 58
Lowenberg, P. 6, 13, 42, 43, 46, 48, 50, 52, 54, 58
Loxterman, J. 252
Lukmani, Y. 108, 123, 136, 151
Lundberg, I. 252
Lupant, J. 254, 258
Lysynchuk, P. 237, 258

M

MacLean, S. 100
MacWhinney, B. 232, 244, 258
Maduas, G. 6
Mancall, E. L. 271
Mannes, S. 235, 258, 259
Mantel, N. 86, 87, 88, 89, 101, 102, 103, 106, 124, 125
Marini, A. 254, 258, 260
Marston, D. B. 202, 222
Mason, J. 229, 254, 258
Mathewson, G. 229, 239, 258
McCallen, B. 54, 56
McCann, A. 229, 256
McColly, W. 129, 149
McClelland, J. 231, 260, 261
McClintock, A. 252
McDaniel, B. A. 130, 144, 149
McDonough, M. 8, 13
McGilly, K. 229, 258
McGirt, D. 130, 144, 149
McKay, S. 246, 258
McKeough, A. 254, 258, 260
McKeown, M. 252
McLeod, W. T. 211, 221
McNamara, T. 60, 61, 75, 76, 77, 78, 235, 259
Meiron, B. 128, 153, 155, 157, 159, 161, 163, 165, 167, 169, 171, 173, 175
Mehrens, W. A. 201, 221
Mendelsohn, D. 130, 149
Messick, S. 13, 40, 41, 97, 99, 100, 101, 265, 266, 267, 272
van Meter, P. 253
Michaels, S. 220
Mikulecky, L. 229, 259
Milanovic, M. 154, 169, 172, 173
Millroy, W. L. 220
Millsap, R. E. 106, 107, 125
Mislevy, R. J. 202, 221, 227, 228, 272
Miyake. A. 253
Molloy, J. 105, 124
Mosenthal, P. 147, 148, 205, 221, 252, 267
Mullen, K. 130, 144, 149
Moy, R. H. 202, 221
Myers, R. 40, 60, 62, 63, 64, 66, 68, 70, 72, 74, 76, 78, 79, 80

Porter, D.   48, 58, 123
Potenza, M. T.   106, 125
Preissle, J.   220
Pressley, M.   228, 229, 230, 238, 237, 253, 258, 260
Pullin, D.   8, 13
Purves, A.   150, 221

Q
Quillian, M. R.   203

R
Rafoth, B. A.   129, 142, 144, 150
Raimes, A.   20, 26, 150
Ramsey, P.   6, 13
Rawls, J.   10, 13
Rayner, K.   230, 231, 232, 233, 238, 240, 260
Read, J.   255
Reed, L.   220
Rellinger, E.   253
Resnick, D. P.   202, 221
Resnick, L. B.   202, 220, 221, 259
Reynolds, T.   93, 101, 211, 221
Rifkin, B.   144, 150
Rivera, C.   7, 13
Roberts, F.   48, 58
Roberts, J.   144, 150
Rock, D. A.   220
Ronning, W.   272
Rosen. D.   149
Rosenbaum, P. R.   107, 108
Ross, J.   20, 26
Ross, S.   154, 174, 223
Roussos, L.   106, 107, 111, 115, 119, 122, 124, 125, 126
Rowe, K.   229, 260
Rubin, D. L.   230, 242, 244, 250
Rubino, A.   83, 101
Rumelhart, D. E.   110, 125, 202, 221
Rupley, W.   238, 239, 262
Ryan, K.   6, 13

Subject Index

A

accountability   24, 265

assessment   265, 267, 266, 270, 271, 262, 264, 273, 275

assessment criteria   56, 58, 59, 61, 66, 71, 73,74, 75

attitude   77, 85, 137, 228, 229, 239, 258

B

background knowlegde   259

C

Canada   274, 276, 277

Canadian Language

Benchmark Assessment   18, 19, 24, 276

checklist   179, 184, 191, 192, 193

Chinese   94, 99, 100, 194, 198, 208, 243, 254, 256, 262, 278

CLBA   19, 22, 23, 27

code of practice   34, 35, 36, 37

collection   50

communicative

competance   55, 75, 96, 149, 172

communicative

language ability   58, 61

conditional coveriance   115

contex-dependant

item set   106

criteria   11, 28, 29, 33, 35, 40, 58, 59, 60, 61, 62, 65, 66, 69, 70, 71, 72, 73, 74, 75, 93, 125, 128, 129, 130, 131, 132, 133, 134, 138, 140, 146, 147, 148, 162, 248, 264, 265, 266, 269, 270

D

E

F

H

I

J

W